"Do you know what it is like sleeping with one eye open? I have been the target of assassination by your country for many years. I keep moving, but I worry about my family and my children."

Colonel Muammar Qadhafi
To William Chasey,
Tripoli, Libya, November 9, 1992

"Why do you think you can help me, Chazzy? We have been paying money to your officials for a long time, and what do we have to show for it? Nothing!

"My leader (Qadhafi) is tired of no action. It makes me crazy, Chazzy. He wants something to happen now. He can't wait."

Youssef Debri
Chief, Libyan Intelligence

"Certainly if we had to pick our demons, we would rather have Qadhafi than someone who might play a peace making role in the future." (In other words, it was much more politically expedient to sacrifice a Qadhafi than an Assad.)

Judge William Webster,
Former Director, CIA and FBI

When told of the vindication of Syria and Iran a London newspaper said that, "Without it, Mr. Waite would still be languishing in a Beirut cellar."

The Daily Telegraph,
November 1991,

"Fresh Clues Point to Lockerbie Cover-Up."

London Sunday Telegraph
November 13, 1994

"Our joy at their freedom (Waite and Sutherland) should be tempered by the shame of the cost: the relatives of the victims of the Lockerbie bomb must now come to terms with the fact that most of those behind the murder of their loved ones are going to get away with it. The cause of justice is being sacrificed on the altar of diplomatic convenience. We will live to regret it."

The Sunday Times
November 24, 1991

"It does seem strange to us that while all of the evidence was pointing towards the Syrian based terrorist group, financed from Iran, all of a sudden it was all worth nothing, and there was a switch. That has disturbed us a great deal. I think needing the help of Syria and Iran in the Middle East, and the war that was coming against Saddam Hussein, it could well be that attention was switched. We needed those people, but who needed Qadhafi?"

The Reverend John Mosey,
Lockerbie relative

"The bomb was put on board Pan Am 103 in Frankfurt with the unwitting compliance of CIA agents who were running a drugs-for-hostage operation."

A Pan Am report leaked to
Congressman James Traficant, Jr.

In a very thick Arab accent he warned Dr. Chasey not to pursue the Libya case further. That is, if he wanted to "stay healthy."

Anonymous telephone caller

FOREIGN AGENT 4221

"The Lockerbie Cover-up"

BY

WILLIAM C. CHASEY

FOREIGN AGENT 4221

"The Lockerbie Cover-up"

© *WILLIAM C. CHASEY 1995*

Published by:

ProMotion Publishing
3368 F Governor Drive
Suite 144
San Diego, CA 92122

(800) 231-1776

ISBN 1-887314-01-6

DEDICATION

To my beloved Virginia and Katie, for your faith in God, your courage under pressure and your unflagging devotion to me. It is through your love that God's blessings abound.

Government is not eloquence. It is not reason. It is a force.
Like fire, a dangerous servant and a fearful master.

George Washington

I love my country, but I fear my government.

William C. Chasey
1995

ABOUT THE AUTHOR

Dr. William C. Chasey received his B.S. degree in 1962 from Springfield College, a Master of Arts degree in 1965 from East Carolina University, and a Doctor of Philosophy (Ph.D..) degree from the University of Maryland in 1969. He served with distinction as a United States Marine Corps Infantry Officer with the 2nd Marine Corps Division, Camp LeJeune, North Carolina from 1962-1965.

He completed a distinguished academic career at a very young age, having served on the faculties of six major universities. He started his academic career as an Instructor at the University of Maryland, served as an Assistant Professor at Delta State University and the University of Texas at Austin, and was awarded the only Named Professorship in his field, The John F. Kennedy Professorship at Peabody College and Vanderbilt University. He served as an Adjunct Professor at The George Washington University and at The Ohio State University. He is the author of over 100 research investigations and publications.

Dr. Chasey, President of the William Chasey Organization, is a Registered Lobbyist with both the Clerk of the United States House of Representatives and the Secretary of the United States Senate. He is a Registered Foreign Agent with the United States Department of Justice (RFA Number 4221). For the past 21 years, he has represented some of the world's most prestigious business clients, and 23 foreign governments and businesses before the United States Congress. Issues represented have included health care, banking, taxation, biotechnology, telecommunications, defense, trade, education, and all aspects of foreign relations.

i

Dr. Chasey's successful lobbying career is based on his direct, personal relationships with, and access to Members of the United States Congress. Known for his insightful political knowledge and his command of legislative tactics, he is uniquely qualified to guide his clients through the bureaucratic maze of Capitol Hill.

He has received numerous national and international awards, including an Honorary Doctor of Humane Letters (DHL) for his lobbying efforts for the Central American Peace Plan on behalf of Nobel Peace Laureate, President Oscar Arias of Costa Rica, author of the plan. He was honored by President Cristiani of El Salvador for his work on behalf of the war-torn country's amputee population of soldiers and children. He was the head lobbyist for one of America's largest lobbying efforts, the Caribbean Basin Initiative (CBI), in which he represented 18 Latin Countries and 164 U.S. Corporations.

Dr. Chasey was recently featured on NBC's new prime-time magazine program, TV Nation. This program, a joint-venture between NBC and the British Broadcasting Corporation (BBC), played to over 40 million viewers. It depicted a day on Capitol Hill with Dr. Chasey, as he lobbied a Congressional Resolution on behalf of NBC.

He chaired the Ethics and Conduct Committee of the American League of Lobbyists and authored the League's Code of Ethics. Congressional Quarterly selected Dr. Chasey as one of Washington's "Insider Lobbyists."

Dr. Chasey is married to his wife of 15 years, Virginia, and has three daughters, Katie, Christie and Cherie. He lives in Rancho Santa Fe, California.

INTRODUCTION

This book could easily be mistaken for a carefully crafted international thriller drawn from the mind of a creative Hollywood screen writer. Albeit, this story is a thriller, it is not the product of imagination. This is a true story of a segment of my life as a Foreign Agent, Registered with the United States Department of Justice as RFA #4221.

This story is replete with political intrigue, clandestine meetings, life and death situations, limos speeding through the Libyan desert, political figures, notorious terrorists, government harassment and threats, and an international cover-up conspiracy. The underlying theme, however, is the emergence of previously unknown and suppressed information, which brings into serious question the accepted theory of who was responsible for the bomb that exploded in the forward cargo hold of Pan Am 103, on December 21, 1988, 31,000 feet above Lockerbie, Scotland, killing 270 people.

In 1992, I became a Registered Foreign Agent with the Criminal Division of the United States Department of Justice on behalf of the Government of Libya. I was employed to help normalize relations between the United States Government and the Government of Libya over the Lockerbie incident.

The real likelihood of a Lockerbie cover-up had never entered my mind, until I went to Libya. There I met with Colonel Muammar al-Qadhafi and the two suspected Libyan terrorists who had been indicted in the United States and Scotland for blowing up Pan Am 103.

I had approached this Libyan assignment with little emotional attachment. Up to that point Libya had been just

iii

another client. Although I was concerned about the families of the victims and resolving the situation, I equally enjoyed the challenge of getting a sitting Congressman to meet with the Libyans. I would be responsible for taking the first elected U.S. official to Libya in the past thirty years. If nothing else came out of my trip, I had at least made history as a foreign agent.

The Arab World was far from being my specialty. This was my first trip to Africa. I had always accepted the Western account of what happened to Pan Am 103. I, like so many other patriotic Americans, never questioned whether our government was being completely truthful with us in relation to our foreign policy positions. As a former Marine Corps Officer, and a faculty representative to the ROTC Committee at the University of Texas in the early 70's, I learned to despise the Vietnam War protesters. Who were they to second guess my country? They were a dirty lot of Communists hell bent on bringing down the United States Government. I felt the same way in 1992. My country could never be party to a plot to cover-up what turned out to be the world's greatest terrorist attack.

But, was it beyond the realm of reason? On April 9, 1986 President Reagan had called Qadhafi "The Mad Man of the Middle East," and Secretary of State George Schultz said, "Why don't we give him (Qadhafi) AIDS?" These were hardly words right out of the "Professional Foreign Service Officer's Manual of International Diplomacy."

As I dug deeper into the Lockerbie case, I began to consider Washington's track record of honesty with the American people. Government officials have withheld and misrepresented information about the bombing of Cambodia, Operation Phoenix (mass assassinations in Vietnam), Watergate, BCCI, Irangate and now Whitewater. What about the cast of characters who have lied to Congress and the American people while serving in responsible governmental positions: Oliver North, Elliott Abrams, William

Casey, Joe Fernandez, John Poindexter, Clair George, Alan Fiers, and Robert (Bud) McFarland?

Some of these Reagan/Bush people were in positions of authority when the U.S. bombed Libya in 1986. They were also some of the same people in power when the blame for Lockerbie conveniently shifted from Syria and Iran to Libya. What made me think that they hadn't orchestrated a very successful U.S. disinformation program aimed at Libya? Was it beyond them, or others like them in the White House, to lie to the world about Libya, Qadhafi and Lockerbie?

White House and Congressional staff members have become increasingly powerful in Washington, and often execute their own agendas without the benefit of any form of administrative, legislative or judicial oversight required of elected representatives.

Whitewater has recently provided a new list of questionable players appearing daily on our television screens. The following people raised their right hands and swore to tell the truth, the whole truth and nothing but the truth, only to be caught in major acts of deception: Deputy Treasury Secretary Roger Altman, Treasury General Counsel Jean Hanson and Treasury Chief of Staff, 28 year old Joshua Steiner.

Time Magazine in an article entitled, *Culture of Deception*, August 15, 1994, described the testimonies of some White House Staff members before the U.S. Congress like this:

> In fact, the tangled web was spun by the Administration itself. What emerged from more than 100 hours of complex testimony about the Whitewater scandal was evidence of a persistent pattern of deception among White House staff members.

The parade of failed memories, studied evasions and half-truths by White House aides goes a long way toward explaining why Clinton's presidency has stalled and why so many voters - as well as the lawmakers on Capitol Hill who control the fate of his agenda - don't trust the President or his men.

This book tells how I went to Libya and met with Col. Muammar al-Qadhafi. It tells about my personal relationship with Col. Qadhafi, the man *Newsweek* Magazine called *"The Most Dangerous Man in the World,"* and the man President Reagan ordered killed in his sleep.

I relate stories Qadhafi told me about Libya's relationship with the PLO, the IRA, the Sandinistas, and Qadhafi's feelings toward Presidents Carter, Reagan, Bush and Clinton. I tell of my very personal discussions with Col. Qadhafi, about his life, including the loss of his 16 month old daughter in the 1986 bombing of his home by United States warplanes. I also relate my discussions with the two Libyans indicted by the United States and Scotland for the 1988 Lockerbie bombing, and who, for the first time, revealed their side of the story.

Most importantly, I disclose information which has been previously covered-up by the United States, Great Britain and France, information which points the finger of guilt for the 1988 bombing at Syria and Iran, and by reasonable doubt, clears the Libyans of sole responsibility for the attack. I name the terrorists actually responsible for Lockerbie, the biggest crime against Western civilians since 1945.

There are those who, at long last, will be relieved to hear the truth of what happened to their loved ones and friends that winter's night over Lockerbie, Scotland. There are others, like the Government of the United States, who have tried their best to stop me from telling my story.

I have been the recipient of late night death threats. The Office of Foreign Assets Control of the United States Department of the Treasury has frozen my assets and fined me. The FBI and the CIA have followed me, tapped my phones, used a former U.S. Congressman and undercover agents wearing hidden "wires" to record my conversations, and set up an elaborate scheme to entrap me into performing an illegal business transaction with Col. Qadhafi.

There will also be those who will say that Chasey sold out to the Libyans. One does not have to agree with any or all of the policies of the Libyan government to question the amorality and political cynicism thrust upon Libya by Washington and Great Britain. My hope is that my potential critics will read my book before making such a definitive judgment.

I have thought long and hard how best to tell this story—or for that matter, if I should risk telling it at all. Col. Qadhafi told me that I would never know what it is like to experience the wrath of the United States Government. He was wrong...I now know, and the story needs to be told.

William C. Chasey, Ph.D.

ACKNOWLEDGMENTS

This book could not have been written without the creative talents and invaluable contributions of my wife, Virginia. She was my editor, proofreader, confidant and inspiration. Most importantly, she and our daughter Katie have courageously lived through this compelling, but fascinating drama with me.

I extend my special appreciation and love to my family and friends who were there to help these past two years when my plight seemed the most bleak. I especially want to thank my parents, William and Hazel Chasey for their continued love and support. I owe my deepest gratitude to Mary Borys, Don and Marie Coro, Hank and Delores Borys and Frank and Betty Ruth Hagan who helped in ways only we will know.

I want to thank my friend Bob White for all the long hours and late nights preparing my manuscript for publication.

To the victims, relatives and friends of Lockerbie, I pray that through this book the truth will at last be known.

ix

TABLE OF CONTENTS

Chapter One

December 21, 1988
Peaceful Lives Shattered

The snow couldn't have been better that Christmas week in Vail. Few could judge better than I, having skied it almost every Christmas vacation for the past 20 years. The clean brisk air of the Rockies was filled with excitement and anticipation of the joyous Christmas holiday now just four days away. It was December 21, 1988, a day that will have a special place in history and, unknown to me, would change my life forever.

I especially remember the warm sensation I felt as I sipped a glass of mellow California Merlot, so welcome after a vigorous day of skiing the groomed trails of North America's finest ski resort. It is hard to imagine a more perfect place to be at Christmas. The tiny Swiss-like village, engrossed in sunshine during the day, and snow flakes at night, provided an ideal background for a storybook Christmas holiday.

One of the most welcome rewards after a hard day of skiing is the traditional ski boot removal ritual, experienced in ski resorts all over the world. Proper fitting ski boots are something to be cherished by the avid skier, but even with such a pair, their removal is a most pleasurable experience. The ritual completed, we comfortably settled into our small, cozy condo in The Willows, just steps from the main chair lift of Vail.

This was a time reserved for my ski buddy, and wife, Virginia and I to relax and reflect on the day's skiing. As we talked and sipped our wine, I unconsciously clicked back and forth between TV stations with the remote control, a most annoying habit, finally alternating between

CNN and the Vail Ski Report. I don't think I could have been happier than I was at that very moment. I was sharing a special time with the woman I loved, while admiring our 6 year old daughter Katie, as she played with her Barbies on the floor in front of the fireplace, still wearing her ski pants, boots and long johns.

Why are these details so vivid in my memory six years later? The events of that day are permanently etched in my mind, which is not unusual when something of major magnitude in history occurs. We all remember what we were doing when President Kennedy was shot in Dallas, or where we were when Neil Armstrong first stepped on the moon's surface. These events are often imbedded in our minds forever. Their memory can trigger an emotional or physical sensation, such as a smell or even a tear, many years in the future.

Our small, Katie decorated Christmas tree, with all of our Christmas gifts neatly stacked beneath, was in the corner of the living room next to the fireplace. This was our third Christmas tree of the holiday season. We left the other two, large and meticulously decorated with special family ornaments, standing solitary in our La Jolla, California home two days before. One cut tree was in the large upstairs entry hall, and the other, a live tree for Katie and her friends, was in the downstairs family room.

These trees were decorated early in December for our first Christmas celebration of the year, which had taken place the previous Sunday afternoon. Our personal, business and political friends converged on the Chasey home for our traditional holiday open house. While the adults enjoyed the holiday festivities upstairs, Katie and her friends were being entertained downstairs by a Rent-a-Christmas Elf, performing magic tricks. We had been hosting this annual event since we first moved our permanent residence from Washington, D.C. to La Jolla five years before.

We were completely unaware that events taking place that day in a little Scottish town we had never heard of would put an end to this festive traditional celebration six years in the future.

Christmas in Vail is one of the highlights of our year. As is the case in all of our social activities, it is difficult to distinguish between what is work and what is play.

Our day of skiing had been no exception for the Chasey family. We skied with Rudy Boschwitz, Senior United States Senator of Minnesota. Actually we started skiing with Rudy and his wife, Ruth, but she soon fell behind the famous Boschwitz pace, and as a repeat of the past, she eventually disappeared for the balance of the afternoon.

To ski with Rudy, as we often do, is a great challenge even for good skiers like ourselves. Style for Rudy Boschwitz is secondary to speed. The word fear is not in his vocabulary and safety is of no consequence. His skiing style closely approximates his political style. To use a ski analogy, one might say he is fast, but a bit rough on the edges. Rudy vigorously skis Avanti Trail with friends in tow, just as he walks the U.S. Capitol, with staff and/or constituents in tow. He is well known in Vail, not only for his reckless speed, but for his black stove top hat that has become his trademark on the slopes.

Virginia and I really like Rudy Boschwitz. Since his defeat in 1990, his enthusiastic spirit is missed in the Halls of Congress. We did our best to get him reelected to the U.S. Senate by organizing a Washington, D.C. fund-raiser for him at the home of one of my clients, Dr. Ellen Segal.

Vail is a political town at Christmas. While Aspen attracts the Hollywood set this time of year, Vail has become the Christmas vacation of choice for politicians. It probably started with Gerald Ford. Many of his former staff and cabinet members who now frequent Vail were first exposed to the splendor of the Rockies during his well

3

publicized Christmas ski vacations. Ford remains the un-official mayor of Vail and Christmas wouldn't be complete without him lighting the community Christmas trees at Beaver Creek, Lions Head and Vail Village.

Many political names and faces of the past are often seen mingling with the politicos of the present in the quiet little haunts of this pristine village during the holidays. Of particular interest to me is the large number of Members of Congress who now frequent Vail. As a Registered Lob-byist and Foreign Agent, these are the people I must know and influence in the course of my daily business life.

Sometime during the Christmas week, I could count on exchanging pleasantries and some political talk with the Senior Senator from Ohio and former astronaut John Glenn. John skied most days with his good friend Henry Mancini, whom I had gotten to know through his gracious wife Ginny Mancini. I had given Ginny and her Society of Singers Group some political advice a few years back, and I enthusiastically accepted their invitations to visit Henry and Ginny's Oscar/Emmy/Grammy laden Beverly Hills home twice.

Virginia and I also attended a memorable Hollywood dinner party in the Mancini home, honoring the 100th birth-day of Irving Berlin. After dinner we sat around the fa-mous Mancini piano with various titans of industry and the entertainment world, singing Berlin tunes with the likes of Andy Williams, Jack Jones and Dionne Warwick. We were, as John Glenn was, saddened at the recent death of Henry Mancini at the age of 70.

I wouldn't have very much time this year with Senator Dan Quayle of Indiana, whom I had known since his days in the House of Representatives. His circumstances had changed drastically. He returned to Vail with a new title, Vice-President-Elect of the United States of America, and a large contingent of staff and Secret Service Agents close

4

by his side. We only had a few minutes to talk, but I did have the opportunity to introduce Quayle to our good friends, Ken and Noreen Willig, as he skied off the mountain with his newly acquired political status and entourage.

Whenever necessary, I have a unique opportunity of visiting with the Vice-President back in Washington. It is traditional for the Vice-President to attend the Republican Senators' Policy Luncheon in the Capitol each Tuesday at noon. He usually meets privately for about a half hour with individual Senators, in his small office just off the Senate floor. The Lead Secret Service Agent, and my good friend Jim Varey, usually gives me the "heads up" as the Vice-President prepares to leave his office for the short walk to lunch across the Senate Reception Room and into S211, the LBJ Room. I make sure that I am well positioned so that he walks past me to reach his destination. He usually stops and we share a little small talk.

Our good friends Jack and Joanne Kemp also vacation in Vail at Christmas. This time together gives us an opportunity to relax and get caught up on our personal lives, outside of the political pressure cooker of Washington, D.C. Our times skiing with the Kemp family are very special to us. The Kemps are great athletes and skiers and we really enjoy their company.

Like us, Jack and Joanne are committed Christians, and over the years we have shared our Christian faith and friends. Joanne, for example, has for the past twenty years held a Friday morning Bible study for Christian wives of Members of Congress in her Maryland home. Virginia has a standing invitation from Joanne and attends these studies when she is in Washington.

That year, the Kemps and Chaseys were joined for a day of skiing by Frank Lautenberg, United States Senator from New Jersey. Frank is a very wealthy former com-

5

puter company executive who was first elected to the Senate in 1982. We knew little about his skill on skis when he first joined us at the top of Chair Lift 6. Frank's brown, military looking, one-piece ski outfit looked quite amateurish and proved to be rather deceptive. It led all of us to underestimate his skiing ability.

I was convinced that with Frank along, I wouldn't be the last in line on our sojourn down the mountain. Much to my surprise and embarrassment, I learned that Frank had been skiing since he was a child. Although 16 years my senior, he quickly took the lead, leaving all of us in a spray of snow.

The contrast was almost laughable that afternoon. Here was this liberal Democrat Senator enjoying a sunny ski afternoon with a Conservative Republican Congressman, who is often touted as a future President of the United States.

Frank Lautenberg was on our topic list that evening as the Kemps were our dinner guests at the Lodge at Vail. None of us could have known that evening how the events of December 21, 1988 would later effect the Chasey Family or Senator Frank Lautenberg. Little did we know that Frank was soon to become a member of the Presidential Commission investigating the Pan Am 103 disaster.

I had an empty feeling in my stomach as I heard the all too familiar announcement on the television news, "We interrupt our scheduled programming to bring you this special news bulletin." This was nothing new for us this time of year. We had heard this same announcement before while Christmas vacationing in Vail.

We heard the familiar phrase the year President Reagan sent Troops into Grenada to rescue U.S. medical students studying in that country. We heard it again when the U.S. invaded Panama to capture strongman Manuel No-

6

riaga. As a matter of fact, we had wondered on our way out that very morning, just what crisis would be in store for us in 1988. Well, we were about to find out.

The first reports of the crash of Pan Am 103 were being broadcast in the United States. The thought of a major airline disaster just 4 days before Christmas was hard to fathom. Could it really be true? The report indicated that a 747 Jumbo Jet enroute from London's Heathrow Airport to John F. Kennedy Airport in New York, crashed in Lockerbie, Scotland just after 7 P.M.. It seemed at that point that all passengers had perished in the crash.

Later reports said that the plane contained a large number of American exchange students from Syracuse University who were returning to the United States for Christmas vacation. The news was especially troubling, since my own daughter, Christie, planned to participate in just such an exchange program while attending The University of Wisconsin. I immediately thought of Gina Nocera, the daughter of our close friends, Mickey and Brenda, who had participated in the exact program the previous year while a student at Syracuse University. It was highly likely that she was a passenger on the same flight only a year earlier.

One could only guess the fear and terror the passengers must have felt as the plane, for what ever reason, fell the 31,000 feet from the sky. The details were sketchy at this point as our CNN vigil began.

It is difficult to imagine a plane crashing in this day and age. Being an experienced pilot myself, with a commercial license and over 2000 hours as pilot in command, the prospects of a crash seem incomprehensible. The million, uneventful miles I log each year as a passenger on commercial airlines has hardened me to the realities of what the dangers of modern air transportation really are.

7

I am American Airline's most frequent traveler, and truly bi-coastal. My work week is divided evenly between my lobbying activities in the United States Capitol in Washington, D.C., and my home and family life in La Jolla, California. My Mondays find me in seat 3B, in the first class section of American Airlines Flight 76 in transit to The Dulles International Airport just outside the Nation's capital. This is my preferred flight because it gets me to Washington about 4:15 P.M.. There my faithful driver and personal assistant, Paul Williams, is waiting to chauffeur me the 30 minute drive to my Washington home at the Flourmill located between the Potomac River and the C&O Canal in Georgetown.

I have this half-hour to catch up on the mail and phone messages that Paul has neatly arranged on the back seat of my black Lincoln Town car. I usually try to intersperse a few phone calls in between Paul's new renderings of Washington Red Skins jokes and "what's hoppin mon" to his family back home in Spanishtown, Jamaica.

After a quick shower and change of clothes, I'm off to some Monday night political fund-raiser, dinner, or in the event the House or Senate should still be in session, a trip to the Capitol. Tuesday, Wednesday and Thursday are spent walking the halls of Congress espousing the issues I have been hired to lobby. After three days of walking some 36 miles in the Capitol building, I am back in seat 3B on Thursday nights on American Airlines Flight 75 enroute to San Diego. The best part of my week is the Thursday night, Friday, Saturday and Sunday I spend with Virginia and Katie in our La Jolla home. This schedule is repeated the following Monday morning.

The CNN reports became more exacting as the television drama played out before our eyes. Flight 103 had been lost from radar screens at three minutes past seven, shortly after crossing the Scottish border. The first reports indicated that there were 276 people on board. As time passed, the number of passengers on the plane was reduced to 259, when it was realized that Pan Am officials had mistakenly counted the crew twice. Early reports also stated that an unknown number of people in the path of falling debris were killed on the ground. It was clear that the doomed jet was New York bound from London's Heathrow Airport when it crashed on a small, quiet Scottish hamlet called Lockerbie.

Lockerbie was anything but a household word before that night. No one, including myself, could have ever guessed that the mere mention of this town, from that time forward, would foster terror in the minds of people the world over. Lockerbie would become synonymous with one of the deadliest air disasters of all time.

Lockerbie is an unlikely spot for a disaster. It is a tiny village tucked into the fertile Annandale Valley of southern Scotland, where winters are damp and drizzly, and summers are cool and mild.

In the late 1980's, Lockerbie was simply a peaceful farming village of 3,000 people. The Lockerbie residents lived quietly, their ways untouched by the hustle and bustle of city life. Few people hurried from shop to shop along the streets of Lockerbie that December 21, 1988. Colorful Christmas lights twinkled in store windows in Lockerbie as they did throughout the world.

Chapter Two

The Crash of Pan Am 103

In London, Pan Am Flight 103 had just lifted off the ground, twenty-five minutes past its scheduled 6:00 P.M. departure time. This was the second leg of a long journey. The flight began earlier in the day in Frankfurt, West Germany, on a Boeing 727.

At Heathrow Airport, passengers and baggage from the 727 had been transferred to a bigger Boeing 747, named *Maid of the Seas*, for the trip over the Atlantic Ocean. The plane was the fifteenth 747 to be built by Boeing and, at the time of the crash, one of the oldest jumbo jets flying. Since 1970, the plane had flown seventy-two thousand hours and taken off and landed 16,500 times. This was well below the number of takeoff and landings considered high for this type of aircraft, which is normally 50,000.

A number of new passengers boarded the plane at Heathrow. Flight 103 was scheduled to stop at JFK Airport in New York, then continue on to its final destination, Detroit Metropolitan Airport.

On board were 259 people, including a sixteen-member flight crew. Fifty-five-year-old Captain Jim MacQuarrie was an experienced pilot who had flown the intended route frequently. MacQuarrie's copilot was Ray Wagner. Both men were fathers of two children. The flight attendants on board Flight 103 represented many countries, including Sweden, Spain, the Philippines and the United States.

The passengers were a diverse lot, including university students, business people, and military personnel from U.S. bases in West Germany. It was a very young passenger list with an average age of 27 years. Most were going home for the holidays, and the overhead compartments bulged with handsomely wrapped presents. The air was charged with festivity and anticipation as the plane climbed toward its designated altitude of 31,000 feet.

Thirty-five students from Syracuse University were returning home that evening, having completed a fast-paced overseas study program in London. Many of the flight's business passengers had wrapped up meetings and projects in time to travel for the holidays. Flight attendants served drinks and handed out headphones for the in-flight movie. At the same time, in the tranquil town of Lockerbie, people were taking care of last minute preparations for the holidays.

As the 740,000-pound jumbo jet lifted off runway 27 Left and climbed higher into the slate-gray skies, reunions with family and friends undoubtedly filled the thoughts of the unsuspecting passengers. The weather was favorable for flying, although not great. There was a slight drizzle falling at Heathrow Airport when the *Maid of the Seas* pushed back from the newly remodeled Terminal 3 building. The winds aloft report predicted that 103 would encounter headwinds of nearly 100 miles per hour when it reached cruising altitude. Because of the huge size of the Boeing 747, the strong winds that buffeted the plane would go unnoticed by the passengers and crew. Nothing indicated that this flight might be anything but routine.

I owe some details of the crash to Emerson and Duffy, *The Fall of Pan Am 103,* 1990, to David Johnston, *Lockerbie,* 1989, and Madelyn Horton, *The Lockerbie Airline Crash,* 1991.

"Clipper One-Zero-Three," MacQuarrie radioed from the darkened flight deck. "We are level at three-one-zero." Pan Am 103 had reached its cruising altitude of thirty-one thousand feet above sea level.

Alan Topp, air traffic controller at the Scottish Air Traffic Control Center in Prestwick on the southwest coast of Scotland was tracking the plane's progress. He requested that 103 identify its position by squawking identification code zero three five seven on the jet's transponder. He checked the identification code on his radar screen and confirmed the plane's position and altitude. Topp directed Captain MacQuarrie to fly a route direct to way-point five-nine north, one-zero west. This routing would take the 103 directly over Lockerbie.

Topp, a 23 year veteran air traffic controller, watched carefully as the plane, a bright green box about 2 millimeters across on the radar screen, moved in the appropriate direction according to his instructions. The fifty-three year old Topp took his job very seriously.

He continued to watch the green box on the screen, and then, in a split-second, it was gone. In its place were five little blinking boxes that reminded Topp of a Christmas tree. Almost immediately, the green boxes disappeared from the screen altogether. An obvious mechanical problem, he thought.

"Clipper One-Zero-Three," Topp radioed. "Clipper One-Zero-Three." There was no response to his call. He knew now that something was very wrong as he screamed into his microphone, "Clipper One-Zero-Three."

In desperation Topp called across the room to his shift manager, Adrian Ford. Ford was busy listening to the pilot of a London-Glasgow shuttle reporting that, as he was descending to 24,000 feet, he had seen a fiery explosion on the ground ahead of him. "I've got a report of an explosion on the ground," Ford called out.

"You're kidding," Topp said. His stomach began to ache. "I've lost the Clipper, One-Zero-Three. That must be him." Topp knew there was no need to try to raise MacQuarrie on the radio again. There would be no answer.

13

The awful truth was that Pan Am 103 had just been blown out of the sky. Bodies, plane parts, baggage, and blazing debris were raining down on Lockerbie below.

At exactly 7:03 P.M., seismographers at the Earthquake Monitoring Center in Dumfriesshire, about 14 miles from Lockerbie, reported a 1.9 reading on the Richter scale. The reading was caused when a major portion of the Boeing 747 fuselage hit the earth in Sherwood Crescent in the southwest end of town. The impact gouged a deep crater in the earth and sent an exploding fireball three hundred feet in the air. A gas main ruptured as the debris landed and added fuel to the already roaring fires. The raging flames engulfed everything that could burn. Buildings, cars, trees and bushes were an inferno.

Rubble and airplane wreckage were strewn everywhere. What moments before had been a peaceful little hamlet, was now a panorama of death and destruction. Bodies of people still strapped into their airplane seats were found scattered about the town. Seventy-one bodies from the plane were found in one destroyed home alone.

Sherwood Crescent was the part of town most devastated by the crash. There the jumbo jet's huge engines and the wings, containing the fuel tanks with 200,000 pounds of jet fuel, crashed to earth.

The human carnage and damage to property was evident everywhere. Bodies were wretchedly dismembered. Feet were missing from some. Others had been horribly compressed by the impact of the fall from five miles above. At this altitude, the victims would have experienced a two and a half minute free fall, and would have reached speeds of nearly 120 miles per hour before impacting the earth. There was nothing anyone could do. The town was aflame within minutes.

According to pathologists who testified before a fatal accident inquiry in Dumfries, Scotland, it is very unlikely that any of the passengers could have survived Flight 103. Eight pathologists grouped the victims into three categories: the majority of passengers who most likely died immediately from injuries; a smaller number with less-severe injuries, but whose vital organs were extensively damaged, causing immediate death or unconsciousness; and two passengers with less-severe injuries. There was some speculation that, with immediate emergency care, the two passengers in this last category might have survived.

At the center of the explosion, where the heat was most intense, homes and the people in them had vaporized, disappearing without a trace. Several unsuspecting residents of Lockerbie died in their own homes. In the first hours after the crash, the extent of the destruction made it impossible to tell how many townspeople had lost their lives.

The Police attempted to account for those who lived in the most badly damaged areas of town. They went door to door, registering the names of residents still alive and those thought to be missing. At 10:00 P.M. they posted lists of the known survivors on the doors of the town hall, adding to the lists during the night. Anxious friends and relatives of the missing gathered outside the hall, scanning the lists for the names of their friends and loved ones.

The whereabouts of many of those missing were determined over the next few days. Some had been away on vacation or visiting friends in town. Some had fled their homes in panic. But others had not been so lucky. The final death count was 259 people killed in the air, and 11 killed on the ground, for a total of 270 deaths.

The plane had landed within yards of the A74 highway, the main road that runs through Lockerbie and connects Scotland to England. The fiery crash stopped traffic and ignited cars. Wreckage from the plane also reached to the outskirts of Lockerbie.

15

The now very familiar cockpit section of the plane, with *Maid of the Seas* inscribed on its side, was found in a farmer's field three miles from town. MacQuarrie's body had been ejected and lay outside the cockpit. Three more crew members' bodies remained inside. Despite all the damage, the cockpit lights glowed on, powered by an emergency generator. It was the only life remaining on Pan Am 103.

The *Maid of the Seas* had been devastated by a massive explosion right under the cockpit, in the most sensitive area of the plane. The force of the blast and resulting depressurization caused it to break up into thousands of pieces, throwing its human cargo into the blackness of the night. It was a secondary shock wave that was to cause the deaths of MacQuarrie, Wagner, the other crew members and the 243 passengers. This secondary shock wave burst a large jagged hole in the side of the aircraft, probably injuring some passengers and signalling to others that the plane was starting to disintegrate.

Fractures from the starburst hole spread rapidly in various directions, one fracture running for more than 40 feet along the fuselage. Within seconds the skin panels were peeling backwards and the entire nose section had fallen away. As the shattered aircraft plunged into a vertical dive, the Pratt & Whitney turbofan engines were torn off and baggage and passengers were disgorged into the freezing atmosphere. The wings, heavy with a full complement of aviation fuel, crashed at a speed of more than 200 miles per hour into Sherwood Crescent. The fireball that resulted was visible more than six miles away.

As the bodies fell, the force of the air rushing past them ripped the clothes away from the limbs and pieces of human anatomy were stripped of tissue by the friction. Most landed in the fields stretching out from Lockerbie, the force of the impact making them sink inches into the ground softened by the heavy rain of the previous few days. Fathers, mothers, sons, and daughters, whole families were wiped out in seconds and impacted into the face of the earth.

About an hour before the scheduled arrival time of 103, friends and relatives began arriving at JFK Airport in New York. They heard the terrible news of the fatal crash as they arrived. Word of the disaster began to spread quickly. Some rushed to the airport after seeing news of it on television. On the other side of the Atlantic, relatives began arriving at Heathrow Airport in London.

Social workers and chaplains offered comfort to the anguished families of the victims. Pan Am knew there had been no survivors from the plane, but before they could contact relatives, they needed to verify the names of Flight 103's passengers. Communications between Lockerbie and the airports made this difficult. It was 10:30 P.M. (EST) before Pan Am officials could confirm the fate of loved ones for anxious relatives.

The search for remains and clues to the cause of the disaster was enormous. Because the airplane had been traveling at 550 miles per hour when it broke apart, the wreckage spread far and wide. A ten foot high piece of fuselage was found sticking up in a field five miles from Lockerbie. A body still strapped to a plane seat was found ten miles from town.

Strong winds carried lighter items from inside the plane even farther. Mailbags from the flight were found thirty miles away in the town of Northumberland. Debris scattered in a wide arc across the border area between England and Scotland and as far as the North Sea, seventy miles away. A watch torn from a body that fell in a Lockerbie field was discovered in a village eighty miles away. In the early hours the search expanded to include locations over one hundred miles away. Later, it would have to extend much farther.

One more point seemed clear from the outset. Investigators immediately suspected that the crash of Flight 103 had not been an accident. Huge 747's did not just fall from the sky. The nature of the damage suggested that a bomb brought the plane down, but investigators would have to find solid evidence that could be tested at a crime lab to be absolutely sure. If it turned out the disaster had been the calculated work of a terrorist organization the authorities would have a criminal investigation on their hands.

For that reason, the search had to be absolutely thorough. Everybody had to be treated as a potential murder victim. Every piece of debris was a vital clue to be documented. Every body was invaluable evidence for a possible future trial. All those involved with the investigation felt the same way: If this was murder, it was murder on a massive scale. Those responsible must be brought to justice.

The holiday season passed and the 1989 New Year found people back to their usual routines. What actually occurred that December night became clearer over the next few months. News reports flooded the airways and what people had feared most had been confirmed. A terrorist bomb was the cause of the Lockerbie disaster. The world followed in horrified fascination as a tale of international terrorism, airline ineptitude and political gamesmanship unfolded. The biggest manhunt in the history of western civilization was now underway to find those responsible.

Chapter Three

Getting Involved

As the years passed, I, like so many others, felt a near total detachment from the events of that stormy night almost four years before. As current as I am about world affairs, I had failed to focus on the events of that awful tragedy for some time.

I knew the basics. There had been a major investigation that initially focused on Syria and Iran as the perpetrators.

I remembered in 1991 being surprised when, after a long, extensive investigation, the focus switched from Syria and Iran to Libya. Libya had now been singled out as the country responsible for the terrorist attack on Pan Am 103. This resulted from some new cryptic evidence, which I didn't remember, that led the United States and Scotland to indict two Libyan Intelligence Officers for the act. The West was frustrated in its attempts to extradite the two for trial in the United States by Libyan Leader Colonel Muammar al-Qadhafi. The United States and the United Nations responded by imposing sanctions on Libya for hiding the two terrorists.

I had flown the route of Flight 103 many times without a thought of what had occurred below. It wasn't until a dark, stormy, fall night of 1992, as I flew over Lockerbie, that I reconstructed in my mind the tragedy that had occurred in this sleepy little town 31,000 feet below. I had done some homework and reviewed the events surrounding Pan Am 103.

It was almost sunrise as I envisioned the now familiar landmarks that passed below: the Tundergarth church, the houses in Sherwood Crescent and the pristine streams into which so many of the victim's bodies and body parts had been discovered. It was at that moment that what had happened four years before, became a real part of my life.

I was about to meet some of the Libyan leaders accused of harboring the terrorists responsible for causing the death and devastation to the town below. This meeting would set in motion a series of bizarre and inexplicable events for me, in such glittering capitals of the world as New York, Washington, Geneva, Tunisia and Tripoli.

My Libyan saga began when I met a mysterious Dutchman by the name of Gerrit P. Van de Bovenkamp, President of a New York based, Delaware Corporation, International Communications Marketing, Inc., "ICM."

I was introduced to Bovenkamp on September 23, 1992, at a fund-raiser for my friend John McCain, Junior United States Senator from Arizona.

John McCain is well known in most circles for the more than five years he spent as a prisoner of war after being shot down over Vietnam. Few know that John has a home in La Jolla, just across the street from the La Jolla Beach and Tennis Club, one of our favorite places to relax, away from the hustle and bustle of Washington, D.C. We get to visit with John and his wife, Cindy, from time to time on the Club Beach.

The Senior United States Senator from Arizona, Dennis DeConcini, also has a residence in La Jolla that was easily visible from our home. Virginia and I hosted a fundraiser for Dennis and his wife Susie at our La Jolla home, and they have attended parties at our place in Georgetown. I helped Susie raise money, some time back, for an Indian School in Arizona that was sending a group of students to Costa Rica.

I didn't think the $1,000 per person McCain Washington Fund-raiser was any different than the hundreds I have attended over the past 21 years. These events are obligatory to my lobbying profession. It is not unusual for me to receive as many as 20 such invitations in one day. We, inside the beltway, call these events "drop bys."

I have to say that I personally prefer the more civilized Washington "drop bys" to the less pleasurable "must stays" that are the standard in California and other real American communities. I know for sure that in Washington, after some small talk, a glass of red wine and a Ritz cracker, I can be on my way to one or two more events of the evening, and be home by 8:00 P.M. Outside the beltway, an accepted invitation means a "must stay" for the balance of the evening, no matter how boring.

It had been a rather long day, starting with an 8:00 A.M. breakfast fund-raiser at the La Coline Restaurant for Congressman Norm Dicks, Democrat of Washington. Dicks was a key member of the Defense Appropriations Sub-Committee and was sponsoring some language for me in the Appropriations Conference Committee on behalf of my Client, Titan Corporation, a San Diego Defense Contractor. I had arranged to have $35 million added to two appropriation bills for Titan. Dr. Gene Ray, President and CEO of Titan, was in town for the fund-raiser, and I had arranged two days of meetings for him.

The meetings were focused on a new communications program Titan was about to launch as part of a corporate defense conversion strategy. The post-communist world of the defense contractor was getting smaller every day, and most of these defense giants were looking for a new way to sell their wares. During Ray's two day visit to Washington we met with Congressmen Duncan Hunter, Randy "Duke" Cunningham, Jim Cooper, Tom McMillian, Norm Dicks, and Tom Campbell. Additionally, we met with

21

Senators Bob Packwood, John Seymour, John McCain, Larry Pressler and Conrad Burns.

I also took Gene Ray to the Marine Corps Barracks at 8th and I Streets for a farewell parade and reception for three former Marines who were retiring from Congress at the conclusion of the 102nd Congress session in January, 1993: Senator Steve Symms, Congressman Larry Coughlin and Congressman Larry Hopkins. I had been active with the Congressional Marines for many years, and Gene enjoyed mingling with the Commandant of the Marine Corps and the various other Congressional and Military dignitaries in attendance.

John McCain thanked those assembled for their contributions, and began introducing his Senatorial colleagues who had dropped by to show their support for his reelection campaign. Will Rogers once said that he never lacked material for his humor column when Congress was in session. That night was no exception.

It has become a tradition among frequent attendees of these events to keep an eye on the oldest U.S. Senator, Strom Thurmond, Republican of South Carolina, as he negotiates his 92 year old body around the customary hors d'oeuvres table. He has been observed more than once, spreading some juicy dip on a cracker, wrapping it in a napkin, and sliding it in his suit coat pocket for later consumption. Its doesn't take long before the runny crab dip, or the like, oozes through the garment leaving an obvious grease stain for all to see. Strom is affectionately known on the hill as "Sperm" Thurmond for his special ability to father two of his children in his late 70's.

Thurmond served as Chairman of the Senate's powerful Judiciary Committee from 1981 to 1987. He withdrew from the Democratic Party in 1964 and became a

Republican. In 1948, he also left the Democratic Party to run as the States' Rights Democratic (Dixiecrat) candidate for President. Strom carried four states and received 39 electoral votes. Thurmond served as Governor of South Carolina from 1947 to 1951. He was elected to the U.S. Senate in 1954 as a write-in candidate. Thurmond holds the Senate record for a single-handed filibuster, 22 hours and 44 minutes. He has an aid who leads him around Capitol Hill and makes sure he doesn't get lost on the way to a vote or to a Committee meeting.

As I write this in 1995, just days after his 92nd birthday, Strom is poised to take over the chairmanship of the Armed Services Committee, responsible for the overall strength of the military. He is still very quick and alert. When Ted Kennedy reproved him for mispronouncing the name of an Hispanic witness, Thurmond shot back: "My, Senator, I didn't know you knew any Spanish" —a reference to Kennedy being caught cheating in a university language exam.

As I was about to leave the McCain event to make my next scheduled fund-raiser of the evening, I was approached by my long time friend Senator Larry Pressler, Republican of South Dakota. Larry expressed his delight in seeing me and indicated that he had been looking for me in the Capitol during the day. He was anxious for me to meet his "good friend," Gerrit P. Van de Bovenkamp, of New York City.

Larry had brought Gerrit along with him to the fund-raiser, which was held in the Powers Court of the Phoenix Park Hotel, directly across the street from Union Station. I was told that Gerrit would take the Metroliner back to New York later that evening but had been convinced by Larry to stop by this event in hopes of running into me.

After basic introductions and pleasantries, Larry told me that Gerrit was involved in an interesting cause and

23

needed my expert advice. He asked if I would consider helping Gerrit. Larry later reinforced his interest in Bovenkamp by whispering, out of ear shot, that Gerrit was a wealthy, New York Socialite who had helped him financially in his Senatorial campaigns. Pressler continued that Gerrit had stopped by his office earlier in the day and briefed Larry on his situation. Larry thought that the issue had merit, but was far too hot for him to handle in his public role, so he thought of me.

I have known Larry Pressler since he was first elected to the U.S. House of Representatives in 1974. Although Larry received an M.A. from Oxford University, where he was a Rhodes Scholar, and has a law degree from Harvard, he is often known as the "Space Cadet" on the Hill. He often seems forgetful, or completely introspective, as he moves around the Capitol. He often loses contact with on-going conversations and gives the impression that he is off in space.

Larry has been a frequent guest in our home in California. He often calls to say he will be on the West Coast and would like to play some tennis or golf with me. Virginia and I hosted a fund-raiser for him in our home, and he has even attended church with us at the La Jolla Presbyterian church. In spite of his standoffish demeanor, Larry has a big heart.

At dinner in our home one evening, Katie asked Senator Pressler if he would come to speak to her third grade class at The Evans School in La Jolla. Larry was more than pleased to do so and, after a quick phone call to the Headmistress Gayle Baer, the Senior United States Senator from South Dakota addressed the third grade class the next day. After a little lobbying of her own, Katie also convinced the Senator to repeat his presentation to the sixth grade class two doors down.

In his typical politician style, Larry followed-up by sending the school a flag that had flown over the U.S. Capitol. (The Capitol Flag Office runs hundreds of flags up and down special flag poles on the roof of the Capitol each day, so there is a sufficient supply of flags for Members of Congress to give to their constituents and special friends). Needless to say our morning golf game was delayed to the afternoon.

Senator Pressler has also attended a couple of parties at the Georgetown Condo that we purchased through his wife, and real estate broker, Harriet. As a matter of fact, ours was the first sale of Harriet's new real estate career. We almost ran afoul of another real estate friend, Anne Simpson, when we purchased the condo from Harriet. Anne and her husband, the Republican Whip, Senator Alan Simpson of Wyoming, have been friends of long standing. They have been guests in our La Jolla home and helped us raise funds for Senator Steve Symms, Republican of Idaho.

Larry and I have often escaped the crazy pace of the Capitol to play golf at Andrews Air Force Base and tennis on the campus of Mt. Vernon College in Georgetown. We have played a lot of early morning tennis at the "Senators Only" indoor tennis court well hidden away behind two steel doors on the third floor of the Dirksen Senate Office Building. The court was built by private funds and was an unknown entity until President George Bush got caught playing there a few years ago.

One of our most interesting matches was held at the U.S. Ambassador's residence in San Jose, Costa Rica. I had taken Larry Pressler to Costa Rica in 1984, to give the commencement address for one of my clients, National University. Larry was awarded an Honorary Doctor of Humane Letters Degree by the University at the ceremony. I had been hired by National University to help with

Washington recognition of its U.S. MBA Degree program in Costa Rica.

Our U.S. Ambassador, Curtin Windsor, invited us to stay at the ambassador's residence as his guest and Larry chose to do so. I stayed at the Irazú Hotel with Virginia and the National University President and members of his staff. Curt Windsor and his wife hosted a lovely dinner party for us at their residence.

Larry, Curt and I were engrossed in conversation when Curt received a call from the U.S. Department of State in Washington. He returned to our conversation a few minutes later very pale and visibly shaken. He quietly announced to us, out of ear shot of the other guests, that he was being recalled from his post and had two days to be back in Washington. It seemed that Secretary of State George Schultz, and Assistant Secretary of State of Inter-American Affairs, Tony Motley, had decided to fire Curt for what they considered his ultraconservative views on Central America.

Curt's last official duty as Ambassador was to join Senator Larry Pressler on the stage of the National Theatre in San Jose to welcome the attendees at the National University graduation ceremony the following morning. He returned to the U.S. the following day.

His wife Ann would be left behind with their two small children to pack up their personal belongings and be out of the country by the next weekend. This, of course, put a damper on the party and the rest of our time in Costa Rica.

The events of the next few years revealed the real motivation behind the firing. The State Department was orchestrating an effort to supply the Nicaraguan Contras from a secret air strip in Northern Costa Rica. They needed an Ambassador who would play along with their scheme. Louis Tambs, who was then U.S. Ambassador to Columbia, fit the bill perfectly and was appointed by President Reagan.

26

I have worked for three Costa Rican Presidents as a Registered Foreign Agent in Washington, and also represented the Coalition for the Promotion of Costa Rica Abroad for six years.

It was because of these experiences, and my reputation of working for 22 other foreign governments, that Larry felt secure in trusting me with his "good friend," Gerrit P. Van de Bovenkamp.

I had very little time for Gerrit that evening. I was expected at the Mayflower Hotel to attend a legal defense fund-raiser for former Defense Secretary Casper Weinberger. I was invited to the event by my dear friend, Frank Hagan. Frank and his wife Betty Ruth have been our closest personal friends since we first met some 14 years ago at a Christian function for Campus Crusade for Christ International. Frank is now Comptroller of the U.S. Merit Systems Protection Board, an agency stemming from the days of Jimmy Carter.

Weinberger was facing trial on corruption charges that were later dropped for lack of evidence. I was anxious to get there since it was billed as the political event of the year and a reunion of former Reagan/Bush officials. I hadn't seen Ed Meese or John Harrington since they left the Reagan Administration, and I was looking forward to seeing them again. I also expected that there would be a large number of Members of Congress in attendance. Larry Pressler told me that he had the event on his 3X5 card in his coat pocket for the evening also. I did see him arrive at the Mayflower some time later, although I didn't speak to him further that evening.

Bovenkamp was a six-footer with a good head of hair and a very captivating smile that became more pronounced as he spoke. He was wearing a navy blue blazer, white shirt and a rather average necktie.

27

We began our discussion in the reception room of the Phoenix Park Hotel where we were first introduced. However, when Gerrit whispered that the country of interest to him was Libya, I suggested that we move outside to a small, noisy area of the hotel lobby where we couldn't be heard.

Bovenkamp continuously reverted to the same question. "You know this country, Libya, eeh?" "Would you like to get involved in helping me in this country, eeh?" His Dutch accent wasn't at all offensive, but his secretive style and constant "eeh?" was about to drive me crazy. "I would like to talk to you about this country, you know the one I mean don't you, eeh?" "Will you come to New York and discuss this place with me, eeh?"

Being aware that time was slipping away, I suggested that he ride to the Mayflower with me in my car. Paul was waiting directly outside the front entrance, having made some special deal with the hotel doorman for the choice parking spot. Gerrit agreed and we made our way to the back seat of the car where I introduced Paul.

Gerrit was concerned about talking openly with Paul in the car. I assured him that Paul had heard just about everything one could hear in this town from his vantage point in the front seat.

Paul tried to ease Gerrit's mind by repeating one of his favorite stories of how we had to sneak Senator John Kerry, Democrat of Massachusetts, up the back steps of the Sheraton Grand Hotel in Washington to meet with President-elect Oscar Arias of Costa Rica in 1986.

After Arias was elected President of Costa Rica, I was asked to help him meet with key Democrats on the Hill. Oscar was determined to work out a peace plan for Central America but, because of the Reagan/Bush support for the Contras, he felt he needed backing from the Democrats who were more likely to push for a compromise solution.

28

In the Spring of 1986, President-elect Arias planned a visit to the U.N. in New York City and to Washington, D.C. The State Department made all of the arrangements for Washington. They did not, however, include a meeting with the Democratic Leadership in Congress. Arias was considered a "Latin Liberal" by the Reagan/Bush Administration because of his open approach to negotiations with Sandinista President, Daniel Ortega. The last thing the State Department wanted was this new President-elect meeting with "Bleeding-heart Liberals" in Congress.

The night before Arias arrived in Washington, the Costa Rican Ambassador-designee to the United States, Guido Fernandez, called from New York and asked if I could arrange for Arias to meet with Majority Leader, Senator Robert Bird of West Virginia, and other key Democrats in the Senate. Although I am known for having great relationships on both sides of the political aisle, I knew that my efforts on behalf of Arias would not put me in good standing with my Republican friends on the Hill, the State Department in general or with the U.S. Ambassador to Costa Rica, Louis Tambs, specifically. However, besides my respect for the new Costa Rican President, I had tremendous love for this wonderful country and my friends in Costa Rica. I promised to do my best and the next morning I headed for the Hill.

The task proved easier that expected. The Democratic Leadership was enthusiastic about meeting with Arias. A meeting was set up for 4:00 P.M. the following day in Room 211—the LBJ Room of the U.S. Capitol. Senator John Kerry would not be able to meet with us, but expressed a real interest in meeting with the President-elect personally and in private. After talking with Arias we agreed to a secret meeting between Arias and Kerry in Oscar's suite at the Sheraton Grand that evening.

Since security and State Department officials were crawling all over the hotel, Kerry and I surreptitiously

29

worked our way up the back stairway to Arias' room. There Kerry and I met with the President-elect and his Ambassador-designee to the U.S. for more than two hours. During this special time together, the three of us laid out the rudiments of what would later become the Central American Peace Plan.

The next morning Arias attended a State Department meeting with the House Minority Leader, Bob Michel, and a dozen other Republicans, in Michel's Conference Room in the Capitol. Although I was clearly included in Arias' party, I was snottily informed by Michel's secretary that I would not be welcome at this meeting.

After a rather nerve-wracking day, the 4:00 P.M. meeting with the Democrats finally took place. Senators Bird, Paul Simon of Illinois, Claiborne Pell, Chairman of the Senate Foreign Relations Committee and Frank Lautenberg of New Jersey were there. Other than personal staff members of the Senators and Costa Rican Ambassador-designee Fernandez, I was the only other person in the hour long meeting.

President-elect Arias proceeded to outline the preliminary plan for peace in Central America that we had designed the night before at the Sheraton Grand Hotel. The assembled Senators were transfixed by the discussion. Oscar stated that the Reagan Administration was doing all it could to keep him away from meeting with the Democrats of Congress and he thanked me in front of the group for arranging the meeting.

A very anxious U.S. Ambassador Louis Tambs, and a dozen State Department people assigned to Arias, waited anxiously outside the room wondering just what we were plotting. The Capitol Police had strict instructions from Senator Bird that no one else should be admitted to the meeting. I felt exceptionally proud to have collected this roomful of such powerful Senators for the President-elect of this tiny Central American country

Little did any of us know that in 1987, Oscar would be standing in Oslo, Norway, receiving the Nobel Peace Prize for designing the Central American Peace Plan that Senator John Kerry and I helped him create.

Kerry and I often joked that we should have shared in the prize, but we were most willing to let Oscar take all the accolades. National University did recognize my efforts on the plan by awarding me an Honorary Doctor of Humane Letters.

Paul's retelling of the Kerry-Arias story caused me to reflect on another key player in the American debacle in Central America—Mr. Louis Tambs—Reagan's replacement for Curt Windsor as U.S. Ambassador to Costa Rica.

Lewis Tambs was a big Reagan supporter while on the faculty of Arizona State University. He had lived in a virtual bunker while serving as U.S. Ambassador to Columbia. His life had been threatened by the Colombian drug cartel and he went underground. We overlapped in Costa Rica many times and he developed a hate for me early on. However the tables turned when it was Tambs who quickly became the most hated U.S. Ambassador in Costa Rican History.

He went nowhere without his own personal army of bodyguards plus a dozen Costa Rican bodyguards in tow. Upon his arrival in San Jose, Tambs turned the Ambassador's residence into an armed camp, including a ten foot wall and a guard shack at the entrance. The outdoor security lights he installed lighted up, and blighted, most of the quiet Escazu section of San Jose, Costa Rica.

Tambs was a diminutive man, with a small man's complex. He was truly an ugly person with a personality to match. He felt so important in his armor-plated van as his caravan sped through the early morning Costa Rican

31

*traffic. An advance car would stop the sleepy eyed resi-
dents of the Escazu section of San Jose as the Tambs motorcade sped by, taking him to his office in downtown San
Jose. The "Ticos"—as Costa Ricans are affectionately
called— were outraged. Theirs is a peaceful country, referred to as "The Switzerland of Central America." In the
1940's its army was dismantled and guns are a rare sight.
Even the President of Costa Rica had no security force
during those years.*

*One evening, Augustin Penon, Arias' Brother-in-law,
and I were visiting with Arias in his home. The President
asked if we would drop him off at the El Pueblo Shopping
Center, just a short distance across town, where he was to
give a speech. We did so obligingly. As he was leaving the
car, I asked if he needed a ride home. He said, " I'm sure
someone will drop me home after the speech is over."*

*And here we Americans had an Ambassador with
enough armament to invade Cuba. What an embarrassment for me and the United States.*

*The rumor was, and I later personally verified it,
Tambs had a picture on the wall behind his desk of him
wearing a flack jacket and holding an Uzi machine gun
with the caption, "When Diplomacy Fails."*

*My relationship with Tambs started off fairly well. He
hosted a number of Congressmen that I brought to Costa
Rica at various times to help my client, National University. Congressman and Mrs. Julian Dixon of Los Angeles
were such guests of Ambassador Tambs. On another occasion, Tambs provided a reception at his residence for
Congressmen Jerry Lewis, Bill Lowery, Mickey Edwards
and their wives. He also provided secret briefings for the
Congressmen during their visits.*

*Ambassador Tambs and I parted ways during prepa-
rations for the inauguration of Oscar Arias as President
of Costa Rica. I had been asked by the President-elect to*

get Vice-President George Bush to represent the United States at his inauguration. This proved to be no easy task.

My good friend and business associate, Humberto "Vico" Pacheco, one of Costa Rica's most prominent attorneys and Chairman of the Coalition for the Promotion of Costa Rica Abroad, came to Washington two times in March-April 1986 to help me lobby Bush to attend Arias' inauguration. I arranged for Pacheco to meet with Bush in the Vice-President's office in the Capitol. This meeting lasted 30 minutes and Bush expressed his interest in attending the ceremonies. He checked his pocket calendar and indicated that he was scheduled to address a Republican Fund-raiser that date in New York City. He said he would do all he could to attend. I followed up with the Vice-President in two separate conversations with him in the Capitol.

The second trip for Pacheco took place a month later when he and Arias' brother-in-law, Augustin Penon, came to Washington with a personal letter to Bush from Oscar. The letter outlined his continued support for the United States and how important it was for the Vice-President to attend the inauguration.

I was unable to get another meeting for this delegation with the Vice-President, but did arrange for the emissaries to meet with members of the Foreign Relations Committee, Committee Chairman Claiborne Pell and Senator Richard Lugar. We also met with Congressmen Jack Kemp, Bob Dornan, Jerry Lewis and Mickey Edwards.

I made arrangements for me to drop Arias' personal letter to Bush by the White House the following day. I gave the letter personally to Bush Military Aide, Col. Sam Watson, who promised to give the letter to the Vice-President. After a few weeks of hard lobbying, Watson called me to say that Bush would lead the U.S. Delegation to the inauguration.

*I received a call from Congressman (B-1 Bob) Dor-
nan the following day asking if I could arrange for him to
be a part of the delegation. I worked with the White House
staff and won approval for his trip. Dornan and Senator
Richard Lugar would be members of Bush's official delegation. It is interesting to note that it was on that trip that
Bob Dornan and George Bush became good friends. Dornan was the first Member of the House to endorse Bush's
Presidential Candidacy in 1989.*

*Right after Bush's Presidential inauguration, I was
having lunch in the Senate Dinning Room when the new
President came in with Bob Dornan. As they passed by
my table, I made the comment heard by many in the dinning room, "who's the guy with Dornan?" Both Bush and
Dornan got a laugh out of the comment.*

*For weeks in advance of the May event, I was con-
tacted by the White House concerning arrangements for a
possible Vice-Presidential representation at the Costa
Rican inauguration. Two White House Military Staff Members were in charge; Marine Corps Lt. Col. Oliver North,
and Air Force Col. Sam Watson. Although these two maverick officers would eventually become famous, they were
total unknowns to me at the time.*

*It seemed that all of my efforts to secure a commit-
ment from Bush were being thwarted by elements within
the Reagan Administration. It became more and more obvious as the weeks went by that I had powerful enemies
inside the White House, including North and Watson and,
in Costa Rica, Ambassador Tambs.*

*It was reported later during the Iran-Contra investi-
gation that my office and home phones had been tapped
during this period by Oliver North and his merry band of
arcane operatives. I should have been suspicious when,*

one day in early May, 1986, I received a phone call from Sam Watson asking me if the Juan Santamaria Airport in San Jose was closed daily between 2:00 P.M. and 4:00 P.M. Anyone could have obtained this information from an airport guide or travel agency. There certainly was no reason for the White House to call me in California to check on a Central American airport other than to check if a wire tap had been properly placed.

It wasn't until the revelations of the Iran-Contra investigation were disclosed that I found out why the Reagan/Bush handlers didn't want the Vice-President in Costa Rica during the time of the inauguration.

The Administration had taken a rather restrained position toward Arias' liberal desire to open talks with Nicaraguan President Daniel Ortega. Arias' peace platform didn't coincide with the U.S. strategy to overthrow the Ortega regime by force.

Unknown to Bush, Arias or myself an airport was being built in Northern Costa Rica, close to the Nicaraguan Border. This Santa Elena airport was to serve as a supply station for the arms that Lt. Col. Oliver North and his associates were supplying to the Nicaraguan Contras. This was in violation of the Boland Amendment (named after Congressman Richard Boland of Massachusetts). This amendment severely restricted support for the Nicaraguan resistance and made these arms shipments illegal without Congressional approval.

Ambassador Tambs had told President Monge, Arias' predecessor, about the air strip. With just months left in his Presidential term, Monge went along with the program. Tambs briefed Arias on the Northern Costa Rican Airstrip immediately after he was sworn in as the new President. Arias went ballistic and his dislike for Tambs grew from that day forward. Arias once confided in me that he was surprised that a great country like the U.S. couldn't come up with a better representative.

35

It so happened that Bush was addressing a Chamber of Commerce Luncheon in San Diego just prior to his trip to Costa Rica for the inauguration. Once again I briefed the Vice-President on my interest in Costa Rica at a reception prior to his speech. I told him I would be waiting for him at the airport in San Jose, and I was!

On the morning of the Costa Rican Presidential Inauguration, May 8, 1986, I arrived at the Juan Santamaria International Airport with Vico Pacheco and Augustin Penon. There was a rather large reception held for Bush at the VIP Lounge on the ground floor of the airport. The guests had been invited by Ambassador Tambs. I was not on the guest list. However, I had no difficulty gaining entrance to the event with Augustin's family pass. Most of the security was provided by the Costa Rican Police Force, which was more than anxious to accommodate the new President's family.

I welcomed Vice-President Bush to Costa Rica, and he loudly commented, "You sure get around, Washington, California and now Costa Rica." I also reintroduced Penon and Pacheco to Senator Lugar and Congressman Dornan to whom I had introduced them in Washington when they came to help me lobby Bush. Dornan said how hard it was to pick up a morning coat (the uniform of the day for the inauguration) in time to catch Air Force Two for the trip.

Before leaving for the actual swearing in, we also exchanged pleasantries with staff assistant Jennifer Fitzgerald, Special Envoy for Latin America, Phillip Habib, and Assistant Secretary of State for Latin America, Elliott Abrams. Tambs had left before our arrival to prepare for the Vice-President's reception he was hosting at the Ambassador's Residence.

The inaugural ceremonies were held in the San Jose Stadium before tens of thousands of Costa Ricans. It was very colorful and festive. Immediately following the

36

ceremony Bob Dornan rushed up to me before he got into Bush's limousine and shouted, "I feel like I have been at the Olympics and Democracy won."

Later in the evening I stood with a variety of dignitaries on the tarmac of the airport as we bid farewell to Vice-President Bush. As the lights of Air Force Two grew dim in the fading light of that May evening, Ambassador Tambs confronted me in a most hostile fashion. It was obvious that he had been waiting all day for this opportunity. In his crude, undiplomatic way he verbally attacked me through his yellow, cigar stained teeth. "What in the hell were you doing talking to Bush this morning? Was your name on the invitation list for the reception?"

By this time all of the Costa Rican dignitaries had stopped their conversations. They watched and listened as Tambs made a complete fool of himself. He began to slobber from the corner of his mouth. His cigar breath was more than I could stand. Tambs threatened to have me expelled from the country. He said he was going to confiscate my passport and have me arrested. The dumbfounded Costa Rican security guards didn't know what to do. Not wishing to create a scene, I quietly stated that I was a foreign agent of the new President, Oscar Arias, and that I had been a guest of Mr. Penon at the morning arrival reception at the airport.

I think Tambs realized by this time that he was making a complete ass of himself. He began to back off. I remember saying to Tambs, "Let's get things straight, Mr. Ambassador, you are here to work for me and all of the other American taxpayers. You are not a cop."

His final words were that he would see that I would regret crashing "his party." As he left the tarmac in his armored car, the crowd of local officials shook my hand and patted me on the back. President Arias was briefed on the behavior of Tambs the following day by Augustin Penon.

That altercation was clear in my mind a few months later when Arias once again visited the U.S. Capitol. Tambs trailed far behind as I escorted the Costa Rican President from meeting to meeting.

As we left a meeting with Speaker Jim Wright, I couldn't resist one of my Marine Corps expressions used when an officer candidate arrives from college for boot camp. I quietly whispered to Tambs, "You are on my campus now, Boy!"

I remember now with delight, the occasion of Mr. Tambs' Congressional hearing on his role in the Iran-Contra scandal. He didn't change his demeanor one bit in front of the Senate Committee, and his arrogance was overwhelming. The whole world got to know, what I and the people of Costa Rica already knew. Our Ambassador was a complete fool, a pawn for Assistant Secretary of State Elliot Abrams, and Marine Lt. Col. Oliver North. To the best of my knowledge, Tambs is still running around Arizona State University, where he now teaches, with a 9mm pistol in his book bag looking behind trees for Colombian Drug dealers.

Now, as we approached the Mayflower Hotel Gerrit asked if I would be interested in discussing the project further and if I could come to New York to meet his partner at ICM, Brendan Kelly. I only agreed to think about it and said that I would get back to him later in the week. Gerrit assured me that he was for real and that Senator Pressler would be pleased if we could work together on this project.

After leaving me off at the door of the Mayflower, Paul drove Gerrit back to Union Station to catch the 10:00 P.M. Metroliner to New York. I didn't know if I would ever hear from Gerrit again. In my business, I run into all types of people with a cause but very few with substance.

38

The ringing of the telephone startled me from a sound sleep early the next morning. Much to my surprise, it was Gerrit P. Van de Bovenkamp. I recognized his distinctive Dutch accent immediately. "Have you had a chance to think about our discussion last night, eeh? I think you are the man who can help us do the job we discussed in the "Home Country" (this was to become the code word for Libya). Before I could answer, he asked if I could come to New York the following day. "I will get you a plane ticket and a hotel. We need to get moving on this project right away, eeh."

I explained that I had the President of Titan Corporation in town that morning, and that I would be leaving for California later in the day. He insisted, "How about next week? I will send you a plane ticket. We will only need one day to complete our business."

I told Gerrit that I would be back in Washington the following week but that I had a Board Meeting in Richmond, Virginia, which would keep me out of town until late Wednesday evening. I would then be returning to California on Thursday to attend a NAFTA meeting with my client Cal State Lumber Sales. Carla Hills, the U.S. Trade Representative, would be in San Diego generating support for the NAFTA initiative and I was committed.

We agreed that I would fly to New York in two weeks on October 6th to discuss the prospects of a business relationship. Gerrit said that he would wire transfer the money for my ticket and make hotel arrangements for me at a hotel close to the ICM offices. He did do this and I put the date on my calendar.

Gerrit, Brendan and I met in the coffee shop of the New York Hilton Hotel, Wednesday October 7th. Brendan Kelly was a delightful, slow-talking Irishman who had traveled to Geneva with Gerrit from September 30, 1992 to October 2, 1992 to meet with the Libyans. They had been invited to Switzerland by an Egyptian named Abduhl Salih Rachman.

I never did understand who Rachman was, other than he was supposedly married to the daughter of former CIA Director, William Colby. Although I had never met the man, he apparently had a specific interest in me. I received various reports over the next couple of months that he was trying his best to discredit me with the Libyans and the Americans. Looking back now, Gerrit believes that Rachman was an agent of the CIA and that the entire incident that was about to unfold was a carefully orchestrated entrapment plot by the CIA with Rachman as a key player.

I was told by Gerrit and Brendan that ICM had been hired by the Government of Libya to help normalize relations between the United States and Libya. Apparently, this had all happened during their one trip to Geneva. Both gentlemen expressed a great interest in having me on their team.

After a $15.00 cup of coffee and a bagel, the three of us walked the two blocks to the ICM Offices at 666 5th Avenue.

I am very much aware of the trappings of a potential client. This is part of how I do my due diligence. I can tell so much by observing the way a person dresses, talks, eats and the kind of offices out of which they work. These are my litmus tests to judge the probability of collecting my fees.

The total extent of the ICM operation turned out to be one small office housed in an office-sharing complex in the "Top of the 6's" Building. Gerrit had arranged for us to meet in the conference room, since there was no way the three of us could have possibly fit in their tiny office space. There was no question in my mind that if Senator Pressler hadn't given Gerrit such a good recommendation, I probably would not have proceeded further with ICM after seeing their office operation!

Gerrit and Brendan explained that they had recently met in Geneva with Youssef El Debri, Chief of Libyan Intelligence, and Dr. Omar Mustafa al-Muntassir, Minister of Economy and Finance, soon to be named Foreign Minister of Libya. The mysterious Abduhl Salih Rachman was also at the meetings.

By all reports their meetings had been a combination of work and play. The little twinkle in Gerrit's eyes as he discussed his time in Geneva indicated that there had been more play than work. They related the late night dinner meetings and referred often to the large amounts of alcohol consumed by all participants. In any event, Brendan reported that a warm relationship had developed between ICM and the Libyans and that they had been hired on the spot.

The ICM/Libyan contract called for ICM to perform two major objectives. The first was to develop a positive public image in the United States for the government of Muammar al-Qadhafi, through a series of press and media events. The second objective, which required my services, was to develop a pro-active, Libyan public relations campaign on Capitol Hill. Gerrit admitted that the only person he knew in Washington was Senator Pressler and that wouldn't take them very far.

They needed me to provide them with access to key Members on the Hill before they could tell their story. The emphasis of my involvement would be to get Members of Congress to listen to the Libyan side of the Pan Am 103 issue. Gerrit said that he had seen correspondence in which Col. Qadhafi had been trying to open a dialogue with the United States over Lockerbie but had been rebuffed by Washington in every instance. He also said that he had been told that there were many people in Washington, and some actually in the Bush administration, who had taken large fees from the Libyans under the pretense of helping to normalize relationships between the two governments.

He pointed out that the Libyans had been rather skeptical of ICM at first but that there now was a strong trust factor between ICM and the Libyans. Brendan was described as the ICM expert in press/media relations and Gerrit was to be in charge of the Washington side of the deal.

Both Gerrit and Brendan were convinced that the United States was part of an international conspiracy to blame Libya for the Pan Am disaster. Gerrit said, "The Libyans will spend whatever they need to resolve the Lockerbie standoff, so why not make some big money while we help them?" They wouldn't tell me what they were being paid for their efforts, nor would they let me see their contract with Libya.

I agreed to represent ICM on the condition that I conduct all my activities in accordance with procedures outlined by the United States Department of Justice. It seemed logical that Justice would deny my registration if there were to be a problem with my representation of ICM and its client the Government of Libya.

Brendan assured me that ICM was a U.S. Company incorporated in the state of Delaware. I was sure that as long as I represented, and was paid by, a U.S. corporation there would not be any problems with the Justice Department. I signed a twelve month agreement with ICM for a fee of $120,000.

Upon my return home to California, I immediately filed my registration as a Foreign Agent pursuant to Section 2 of the Foreign Agents Registration Act of 1938, as amended, with the United States Department of Justice.

The next order of business for my new client, ICM, was a trip for me to Geneva to meet Youssef El Debri, Head of Libyan National Security and a member of the Libyan Committee to Resolve the Lockerbie Dispute. Youssef was to be in Geneva beginning on October 25th. He wanted to meet with me in his suite at the Noga Hilton

AGREEMENT

This agreement is made this date between International Communications Marketing, Inc., a Delaware Corporation (ICM) and The William Chasey Organization (TWCO).

ICM hereby employs the services of TWCO to provide Washington Representation on behalf of ICM and its client, "The Government of Libya". In its role, TWCO will provide relationships with key Members of the United States Congress to assist in the development of normalized relationships between the United States Government and the Government of Libya. All activities of TWCO will be in complete compliance with the Foreign Agent Registration Act under TWCO Foreign Agent Registration #4221.

The term of this agreement is for twelve (12) months beginning October 8, 1992 and terminating October 7, 1993. ICM agrees to pay TWCO $120,000.00 for its services as follows: $20,000.00 upon the signing of this agreement, $20,000.00 on or before December 5, 1992, and $20,000.00 on or before the following dates: February 7, 1993, April 7, 1993, June 7, 1993 and August 7, 1993.

Personal expenses will be borne by TWCO except for any international travel related to the success of this contract.

We agree to the above.

Brendan J. Kelly
Managing Partner, ICM

Gerrit P. Van De Bovenkamp
Managing Partner, ICM

William C. Chasey
President, TWCO

October 8, 1992
Date

October 8, 1992
Date

43

Hotel on Tuesday, the 27th. Gerrit would meet me at the hotel along with what he called his Libyan consultant, Mohammed Bukhres, a Libyan/American living in Washington, D.C.

I began a personal crash course on Libya and the events surrounding the crash of Pan Am 103. It was very possible that my flight to Geneva would take me over the little town of Lockerbie.

An American Airlines First Class prepaid ticket to Geneva, Switzerland was waiting for me at the San Diego airport the morning of October 25th. I was off to meet "Uncle Ben," code name for Youssef Debri.

Chapter Four

Geneva—The Libyan Connection

Youssef El Debri was a short, round black Libyan, whose ancestors came from Kenya in East-Central Africa. I remember how surprised I was when I first met him on October 27, 1992, as he opened the door to Suite 600 at the Noga Hilton Hotel in Geneva, Switzerland. I was not expecting a black Libyan. It had never crossed my mind that Libyans were anything but yellowish, brown-skinned Arabs.

Suite 600 was rented yearly to Youssef Debri. He used it to get away from Libya to conduct governmental and personal business. I found out later that evening that he was quite a ladies' man and the suite was used to entertain some of Switzerland's ladies of the evening. The suite has one of the best views of beautiful Lake Geneva, and the Jet d' Eau, the famous fountain that is the trademark of the city. It is visible for miles around from April to September and throws water 460 feet into the air above the lake. The Genevese call the fountain the "jeddo."

Debri was wearing an African wraparound robe, with a tie around the middle. The robe just reached around his rotund body. He wore no shoes. The suite reeked of cigarette smoke and a lighted, unattended cigarette burned in an ash tray next to the large picture window. Dirty dishes, waiting for a room service pick up, were stacked against the walls. Empty wine and beer bottles were everywhere.

A glass table, with four chairs, was covered with the remains of a late night card game. Peanuts and pretzels were strewn about the glass top. Playing cards were stacked on top of each other. The room smelled as if it had been closed up for days and the cigarette smoke almost made

45

me sick. The bed was king sized and dominated the room. Although it was almost noon, the bed had not been made. It was obvious that Debri had just gotten up after a late night of card playing.

Gerrit carried a gift for Youssef under his arm. The neatly wrapped package contained a large pictorial book of the United States. Gerrit had told me earlier when we met for breakfast that he had selected this gift because Debri had never been to the United States. He wanted desperately to visit America but was barred from obtaining a visa because of his alleged terrorist activities. He had tried to obtain a visa many times to no avail.

"Hello Gerrit, do you have good news for me?"

Gerrit responded, "Yes, of course. I brought you Dr. Chasey from Washington, D.C., eeh!"

Youssef shook my hand as he closed the door to the hallway behind me. "Hello Chazzy, did you have a good trip?"

"Yes, very nice thank you," I responded.

"Come in and sit down Chazzy." He picked up the telephone and asked, "What do you want to drink, wine, water, whatever you like?" Gerrit and I moved further into the suite. Youssef didn't wait for our response and sat on the corner of the bed and ordered sparkling water, wine and beer from room service in French. "I will order lunch later," he told us.

I pulled the drapes back and peaked out at the beautiful panorama the large window provided. It was Fall and the trees that lined Lake Geneva had started turning color.

It was a warm, sunny day and I was reminded of how much I love Switzerland, and of the many wonderful times I had shared there with Virginia and Katie. The last remaining flowers of the season were evident in the Quays of Geneva. The quays, with their luxuriantly planted flower gardens, dotted with ancient buildings, are a sight to behold. The usual aquatic population of sea gulls, ducks, and swans was visible from the window, among the fleet of small boats called "Mouettes Genevoises." These boats shuttle visitors from one quay to another, from spring until autumn's blasts become too chilly.

I had walked past the Noga Hilton many times on those trips. However, this was my first time staying as a guest. I had insisted that I not register under my name and Bovenkamp had obligingly made arrangements so that I didn't need to check in when I arrived. I simply picked an envelop containing my key from the reception desk. I thought it best that no record be kept of this trip and I was assured that I wouldn't get stuck with the bill.

Gerrit was extremely upset. He began to fidget as we waited for Youssef to join us. He explained that he was to have met his Libyan consultant, Mohammed Bukhres, the previous evening at London's Heathrow Airport. He explained that Bukhres was to have flown into London from Washington's Dulles Airport, while Gerrit departed New York's JFK. They were to have met in Heathrow's British Air Club and completed their journey to Geneva together. While traveling together, they were to plan their strategy for the meetings with Debri. I found out later that their major agenda item was to firm up a consulting agreement with the Libyan Government. Gerrit had searched for Mohammed at the airport to no avail, and continued on to Geneva alone. As I would find out later, the mysterious Mohammed Bukhres had a special way of disappearing.

Youssef Debri joined us at the table after clearing away the remains of the previous night's party. He grumbled under his breath as he stacked the dirty dishes and ash trays against the wall with the other dirty dishes that had accumulated. He used a bath towel to clean the remaining crumbs from the glass table top. He sat down, lit another cigarette and attempted to cover his rotund shape with his robe.

The first order of business, was Gerrit's gift book. Youssef opened it with obvious embarrassment. He quickly looked at it and said thanks, as Gerrit tried to explain the purpose of his selection. Youssef laid the book on the floor next to his chair with no more discussion.

"Why do you think you can help me, Chazzy? We have been paying big money to your elected officials for a long time, and what do we have to show for it? Nothing! I have paid hundreds of thousands of dollars to people right inside of the White House. I filled their Swiss accounts and never heard from them again. My people are hurting badly from this embargo. We need medical things—supplies! Sorry, for my bad English. We can't talk to anybody in the United States. We have tried for months to talk to someone in power."

"Gerrit says you know lots of Congressmen and can get someone of authority to talk to us. What do they want from us? I have sent letters to the Secretary of State, the President—what more can I do?" Youssef became more and more angry as he spoke.

"My 'Leader' is tired of no action. It makes me crazy, Chazzy. He wants something to happen now. He can't wait. My Leader blames me for this. I need your help now Chazzy."

I found it interesting that Col. Muammar Muhammad al-Qadhafi has no official title such as President or Prime Minister, nor does he have any statutory executive power in Libya. He is referred to simply as the "Leader" of the Great Socialist People's Libyan Arab Jamahiriya, Libya's official name. However, for those of us in the cloak and dagger business, he is merely referred to as "Charlie."

As I listened and watched Youssef I tried to draw upon the little information I had about Libya's history and how Qadhafi had come to power. To understand the power Qadhafi exercises over the people of Libya—one needs to know a little Libyan history.

Chapter Five

Libya

(Three of the best sources of information about the Libyan past that proved helpful were: Geoff Simmons' *Libya: The Struggle for Survival,* 1993, Ruth First's *Libya; The Elusive Revolution,* 1974, and John Wright's *Libya,* 1969.)

Berbers are believed to have been the earliest inhabitants of Libya. In the 600's B.C., Greek colonists settled in the northeastern part of the region. Their province became known as Cyrenaica. In the 400's B.C., the ancient city of Carthage, in what is now Tunisia, established trading centers in the northwestern part of the region. This province became known as Tripolitania. The Romans destroyed Carthage in 146 B.C. and Tripolitania became part of the Roman province of Africa Nova.

Later on, during my time in Libya, I was amazed to see the large number of Roman Ruins and the vast collection of Roman artifacts in the home of Youssef Debri. These items had to be worth a small fortune and would equal in number and quality the Roman artifacts found in some of the world's most famous museums.

A Germanic tribe called the Vandals captured the region in A.D. 431. In the sixth century, Byzantine forces conquered the region. Rebellions by Berber tribes created instability that aided Arab entry into the region.

Arab soldiers, spreading their new religion of Islam, entered Cyrenaica in 642 and occupied Tripoli in 643. A succession of Arab and Berber dynasties then controlled what is now Libya. The culture of northwestern Libya developed along with the political units just west of it, while

51

development in the east was strongly influenced by neighboring Eqypt.

In 1551, Ottoman Turks captured Tripoli. They incorporated Tripolitania, Cyrenaica and the southwestern region known as the Fezzan into their empire, which was centered in Asia Minor (now Turkey). But local rulers had almost complete freedom. For three-hundred years, private ships commanded by Barbary corsairs preyed on European and U.S. shipping in the Mediterranean. The United States fought a war against the corsairs in the early 1800's.

Italy invaded the coastal regions in 1911 and took control of the three provinces. During the 1920's and 1930's, the Italians sponsored many improvement projects, such as towns, roads, and irrigation systems, luring thousands of European immigrants to the country. But in Cyrenaica, the Sanusi brotherhood, a Muslim religious and social reform group, organized stiff opposition to Italian rule.

During World War II, members of the Sanusi brotherhood cooperated with the British in Egypt against Italy, their common enemy. In 1942, Great Britain established a military administration in the north. French forces captured and took control of the Fezzan. In December 1951, the United Nations called for the independence of all of Libya.

A united kingdom came into being, with Muhammad Idris al Mahdi as-Sanusi, leader of the Sanusi resistance, as king. The three provinces - Cyrenaica, Tripolitania, and the Fezzan - had considerable authority to rule themselves. But their separate geographical and cultural development fostered an atmosphere of localism and rivalry that complicated the nation-building process. The provinces were abolished in 1963 and Libya became a monarchy controlled largely by the central government.

The discovery of oil in Libya in 1959 transformed the country from a poverty-stricken nation into one of the wealthiest in the world. However, widespread discontent resulted because the ruling class controlled the wealth.

In September 1969, a group of officers known as the Revolutionary Command Council (RCC) overthrew King Idris and seized power. Colonel Muammar Muhammad al-Qadhafi, who led the revolution, became the head of Libya's government. Under his rule, the government took control of most economic activities. One of Qadhafi's top lieutenants was a young military officer by the name of Youssef El Debri. Qadhafi tried to forge unions with a number of Arab states, but none of these efforts succeeded for more than a brief period.

During the 1970's, oil revenues were used to fund ambitious social and economic development projects. Existing political institutions were replaced by popular assemblies. Despite the appearance of democracy, Qadhafi's government tolerated no political opposition.

Under Qadhafi's rule, Libya supported a number of radical movements throughout the world, particularly the Palestine Liberation Organization (PLO). It involved itself in rebellions in Chad and Morocco. Libya also supported Iran's declaration of an Islamic Republic in 1979.

Chapter Six

More Involved

Youssef seemed to calm down somewhat as two room service workers delivered drinks and began to tidy up the suite. The bed was made and the dirty dishes were removed as the three of us made small talk. Frankly, I was relieved that this brief interlude gave Youssef a chance to collect his emotions. After all, I was meeting with one of the world's most sought after terrorists and irrationality had no place in that room that day.

He wanted to know about my family and asked if I had a picture he could see. I showed him a picture that I carried in my briefcase of Virginia, Katie and myself sitting on a corral fence with Katie's horse looking over our shoulders. I told him about Katie's riding prowess, and all the championships she had won.

I noted Gerrit's dissatisfaction with all the attention Youssef was paying to my picture, realizing that Youssef had just almost totally ignored the gift that Gerrit had brought for him with such pride. I explained that the picture was used on our Christmas card the previous December.

Youssef grew excited as he told me how much his own daughter loved to ride horses and that our daughters had a lot in common. He talked with fatherly affection about his three children, two girls and one boy. "Maybe someday our children will ride horses together. When our countries are friends again, our children will be friends again." He became very introspective, almost sad. "It will be my pleasure to have you, Virginia and Katie come to my home in Tripoli, Chazzy."

My anxiety dwindled as his demeanor radically changed from the rantings of an international terrorist to the warmth of "father of the year." He actually became a rather pleasant fellow, and it was hard to imagine a guy like this committing terrorist acts on behalf of any cause.

I had a similar feeling when I had the opportunity to meet and spend time with one of the PLO's top Officials, Mr. Bassam Abu Sharif, during the summer of 1989.

Virginia, Katie and I were invited to Cap Antibes, in Southern France by Roger Edde, a wealthy Lebanese, who was running for the Presidency of Lebanon. We had met Roger at a reception at Senator Larry Pressler's home on Capitol Hill a couple of months before.

Roger and his wife Alice, an American, were enthralled with us and with the exciting life that we led. I had dinner with Roger and Alice at the Dancing Crab in Northwest Washington a couple of weeks after we met.

Roger wanted me to consider representing him in Washington as his liaison to the U.S. Congress. He felt that he needed lots of powerful people on his side as he sought the Presidency of Lebanon. Roger and Alice would be leaving for their summer home in France in a few days. I told them that Virginia, Katie and I would be in France in the next few weeks. They invited us to visit with them there to discuss my involvement with Roger further in a more relaxed environment.

Unknowningly, our time in Cap Antibes turned out to be anything but relaxing. Upon our arrival we were encouraged by the house staff to freshen up and join the rest of the guests at the tennis court for the finals of the doubles tournament. Roger holds a tennis tournament each summer for some of his closest friends and house guests. It is topped off with the "Grand Evening," a dinner party held

*in honor of the tennis winners on his magnificent patio
overlooking the blue Mediterranean Sea.*

*We were among some 30 or so house guests staying
in the main residence of the Edde estate. Virginia and I
were provided with a lovely room next to a tree-lined court
yard. Katie had her own room just down the hall. I had
never seen such a villa. It was beautifully situated on a
hill with expansive views of the enormous white yachts
seen cruising along the coast most of the day.*

*We had left Paris that morning by train and arrived
at the Cap Antibes Train Station about 4:00 P.M. We were
travel weary and therefore very happy to join the tennis
festivities. We sipped champagne as Queen Farah, the wife
of the late Shah of Iran, and her partner, David Sanbar, a
wealthy industrialist from London became champions. (We
ran into David the following winter in Vail and shared
some special ski time with him.)*

*Those attending the dinner that night represented all
facets of the French summer community. The one common
thread running through all those invited to honor the win-
ning couple was—wealth. I doubt if we have anything in
the United States to compare with the wealth represented
in Southern France during the summer months.*

*The language of choice was French, with Arabic a
close second. At one point during dinner, our poor American command of the French language led us astray. We
believed that we were engaged in a conversation with a
group of Frenchmen in the security business, only to find
out later that what they really did was provide security—
not sell securities. They were Queen Farah's bodyguards.*

*Lunch the next day was set at a long table under an
olive tree facing the Mediterranean. The guest list consisted of Israelis, Lebanese, PLO representatives, the Ed-
des, Virginia and me. The language of the day was Arabic
with a bit of French interspersed. The years I spent learn-*

ing the Spanish language for my work in Central America didn't help much. Virginia and I felt a little left out, but fortunately Alice sat close by and did a little translating for us. She did her best to make us feel comfortable in a difficult situation.

At one point between courses, the table erupted into laughter. An Israeli had been engaged in a discussion with Bassam Abu Sharif, Yassir Arafat's top Lieutenant. Sharif seemed to be a very nice man. I can admit now that I had no idea at the time what a powerful force he was within the PLO. We had first met the night before at the "Grand Evening;" Sharif was not easy to forget—his face was badly scared, and he was missing fingers from his hand.

I waited until dinner that night to ask Roger's brother what had been the cause of the laughter earlier in the day. He explained that Sharif had been the victim of a letter bomb a few years earlier. The Israeli he met for the first time at lunch that day was the man who had sent the letter bomb to Sharif. I guess in a very strange way, only those personally immersed in the Middle East situation could fully appreciate the special bond the two men shared.

As the room service crew was leaving, Youssef got up and removed a stack of new, crisp, U.S. one-hundred dollar bills from a brown paper grocery bag standing next to his night stand. I watched as he removed two $100 bills from the bank wrapped stack and gave one to each of the two room service people with a pleasant smile and *merci beaucoup*. From where I sat, I could see that the bag was full of stacks of $100's. I was dying to see if the other two grocery bags standing next to this one were full of similar denominations.

Before Youssef could sit back down, there was another knock at the door. He opened it with one hand as he picked up the telephone with the other and called room service again. I couldn't see who was at the door, but I heard Youssef become engaged in a discussion with another man in Arabic. Gerrit looked over at me from across the table and whispered, "It's Mohammed. The S.O.B. did come after all."

Now Mohammed looked exactly like what I thought a Libyan would look like—with the exception of the expensive Italian suit he was wearing. Gerrit stood to greet him as he entered the suite. The moment was full of confusion. Muhammed tried to communicate with Youssef in Arabic. Youssef tried to order lunch from room service in French, and Gerrit tried to find out where in the hell Mohammed had been, in English. I waited patiently, knowing that things would calm down and someone would get around to introducing me to Mohammed. When Gerrit finally did, Mohammed had already convinced him that it was Gerrit's fault that they missed each other in London the previous night.

I was very much aware that Mohammed had a difficult time looking me in the eye as we exchanged pleasantries. He was nice enough, but my first impression was, in a word, "sneaky." He had some story about getting a telephone call from "Charlie," (code name for Qadhafi) just before leaving Washington and missing his flight. He took the next scheduled flight to London arriving in Geneva just an hour before and hadn't even checked into the hotel yet. He needed a shave and seemed quite frail. His suit was loose fitting as if he had recently lost weight. He wore dark, stylish, horn-rimmed, tinted glasses. I guessed his age to be about 40.

We all sat down at the table. Youssef was obviously upset again, this time at Mohammed. He raised his voice and waved his arms as he seemed to scold him in Arabic. They exchanged words, foreign to me, and then all became silent. Youssef had the last word as he mumbled under his breath, "Mohammed, you make me crazy."

59

Youssef turned toward me and asked, "Chazzy tell me how you can help. What does lobbying really mean? You Americans like to take our money but we never see results. My Leader asked me to tell our story to decision makers of your country. He has set up this committee, Committee to Resolve Lockerbie. I am a member of the committee, and we want to make our Leader happy."

Gerrit began to talk before I could answer Youssef's questions. "Dr. Chasey is the best lobbyist in Washington. I have been to Washington with him and I am very impressed with whom he knows. I heard about Chasey, and was introduced to him by our mutual friend Senator Larry Pressler, a member of the Foreign Relations Committee and the Ranking Republican on the Committee on Terrorism, Narcotics and International Operations."

I was impressed that Gerrit remembered his lessons well. I had briefed him earlier on the key committees he would need to lobby. He continued, "Senator Pressler thinks Chasey is the best man to help us resolve this Lockerbie situation. He has represented lots of foreign governments and clients in Washington for 20 years. We are lucky to have him here!"

I interrupted and began my standard sales pitch. I told Youssef and Mohammed about my life as a lobbyist and foreign agent. Most people in the United States know very little about what I do for a living. What they do know about lobbyists they learned from the Presidential campaigns of Ross Perot and Bill Clinton. They were pretty hard on my profession. Perot called us those "Awful Foreign Lobbyists," and Clinton said that if elected president, "He would put us out of business."

Chapter Seven

My Life
As A Lobbyist/Foreign Agent

As a Washington lobbyist, I am required to register with the Clerk of the United States House of Representatives, for work that I do for clients before the House. In similar fashion, I am required to register with the Secretary of the United States Senate for work that I do for clients before the United States Senate. In reality, I personally register with both Houses when I take on a new client, because I usually involve both houses of Congress in my efforts.

Washington representatives number in the thousands. The 1994 list of Washington representatives estimates that there are as many as 15,000 lobbyists in Washington. The largest element (about 5000) are officers of the 2,200 trade and professional associations and labor unions which keep a permanent presence in the nation's capital. Another 1,500 are representatives of individual corporations who, as distinguished from their marketing colleagues, are responsible for government and public relations.

About 2,500 are advocates of special causes from the ERA to environment, from handgun control to prison reform, from saving whales to saving unborn children. Lawyers who have registered as lobbyists or foreign agents, or who have been identified as representing clients in regulatory matters and legal confrontations with the government, currently number about 3,000. Public and government relations consultants and professional managers of client associations and interest groups also number about 2,500. Another 200 persons are officers of political parties or political action committees and 350 others are active in policy think tanks which make their views known on a wide variety of domestic and foreign policy issues.

The profession of lobbying in this country dates from its earliest days as a logical expression of the constitutional right of citizens to "petition the government for a redress of grievances." Lobbyists work both the Executive and Legislative Branches of government, dealing directly with legislators and policy makers in Washington's corridors and cocktail parties of power.

To many, their personal charm and persuasive powers are still major assets. More important to most lobbyists is their ability to collect and present, factually and fairly, vital information for a Member of Congress trying to sort his way through the diversity and complexity of issues on which decisions must be made. I pride myself on being well versed in the industry I represent; articulate, believable and known for my integrity. I think that I am informative and credible in the job I have been doing for more than 21 years.

Despite criticism from the media and the Administration in recent years about the corrupting influence of lobbyists and special interests on the political process, it is important to remember that all Americans belong to these so-called "special interest groups." Today, every worker from mechanic to physician, every cultural group from Native America to retired senior citizen, every issue from cigarette smoke to owning a gun, is represented by lobbyists in Washington. The President himself has a large staff of lobbyists who roam Capitol Hill everyday. The American public has been sold a bill of goods on the role of Washington lobbyists. In fact, while a Congressman represents his constituents, very often it is the lobbyist who gives voice to the "special interests" and concerns of those same constituents.

Many governments, businesses and other organizations of foreign countries, in addition to their diplomatic missions, retain representation in Washington. When I represent a foreign entity, I register as a Foreign Agent with the Criminal Division of the Justice Department. This is just what I did, the day after I signed the $120,000 contract with Gerrit's International Communications Marketing Inc., (ICM) on October 8, 1992. I was assigned the Foreign Agent Registration Number 4221.

Although it was debatable if I needed to register with Justice, I felt that I should register because of the chance that the Government of Libya might benefit from my activities on behalf of ICM. I was representing a Delaware Corporation and, as far as I was led to believe, I would be paid by this U.S. Corporation. In any event, I wanted to be sure that I wouldn't run afoul of the Justice Department. My connection with a highly visible country like Libya was bound to attract attention.

I was right. My registration did attract not only attention but publicity. On December 7, 1992, *O'Dwyer's Washington Report*, a newsletter that keeps the PR and lobbying professions aware of current activities, carried a front page story about my registration.

The title was *"Chasey Organization gets $120,000 pact to push Libya ties with the United States."* The article went like this:

> The William Chasey Organization registered a $120,000 one-year contract to help Muammar el-Qadhafi's Libya establish normalized relations with the United States.
>
> This newsletter made two attempts to reach TWCO President, Bill Chasey, at his Washington Office, seeking comment on his work for the terrorist state.
>
> Neither call was returned.

According to the November 12 Foreign Agent Registration Act (FARA) filing, Chasey plans to write letters and arrange meetings with Members of Congress on behalf of the Libyans.

His goal is to "assist in the development of normalized relationships between the U.S. Government and the Government of Libya." The contract runs through October 7, 1993, and calls for TWCO to receive six $20,000 payments every other month.

It is signed by Chasey and two managing partners—Brendan Kelly and Gerrit P. Van de Bovenkamp—of International Communications Marketing Inc., a New York outfit with an unlisted phone number, which calls Libya a client.

TWCO's Libyan connection marks the second recent effort, filed at Justice, promising to improve the diplomatic standing of the North African country.

Former Congressman John Murphy (D-NY) filed a $200,000 pact for a worldwide media campaign for Libya (July 6), which was aborted on September 10.

Fortunately, no one of any importance reads the *O'Dwyer Newsletter* and there were no immediate repercussions resulting from the article. To date, I have not been contacted by the Justice Department other than to request the quarterly reports required by all active foreign agents.

Chapter Eight

Plotting the Strategy

I don't know how much of what I said had meaning to Youssef, or if he really cared. He sat, smoked and listened.

Mohammed seemed especially interested in my discussion. He told me that he was a U.S. citizen and represented a group of U.S. citizens interested in resolving the Lockerbie situation. Mohammed went on to say how much the United Nations sanctions were hurting the people of Libya. He was personally involved because his own mother needed specialized medical attention. Due to the sanctions she was unable to fly to Switzerland for help. She could not live through such a long trip by surface transportation to get the medical assistance she needed.

We were joined by two Libyan men who had participated in the previous night's card game. They made a grand entrance but sat quietly during our discussion. The first man was rather large, with a mustache. I didn't catch his name and he offered no business card. Youssef said that he had been Libya's ambassador to Switzerland. I suspected the smaller man, Mohammed Abulgassem Algaidy, to be a Libyan secret agent working for Youssef. There always seemed to be undercover agents positioned in strategic positions in close proximity to Youssef. He ignored them most of the time but they were always around.

I asked Youssef to give me his Government's side of the Lockerbie incident. Gerrit had told me before we made this trip that Youssef would prove to me that Libya was not responsible for the bomb that blew up Pan Am 103. He said that by the time I left Switzerland, I would know the real truth. I hoped that this would be the case but my real interest was in helping get to the bottom of the stalemate that had caused so much heartache, for so many people, for so many years.

During lunch of "cow's scalp stew," with a good bit of the cow's hair still attached to the scalp, Youssef appealed to me to bring a Member of Congress to Libya to meet with the Libyan Committee to Resolve Lockerbie. I explained that it would be almost impossible to get a Member to go to Libya. He asked if I could get someone to come to Switzerland, or to Malta for a meeting. I said it would be a lot easier to do this, although it would be a real challenge to do so, even for me. He said the only way for him to regain his credibility with his Leader was to get a Congressman or Senator to meet and discuss the situation they faced in Libya.

I tried to explain how difficult it would be to get an individual Member to come, and that it might be easier to get a small group to come. I suggested that the Libyans organize an international conference on Pan Am 103, under the auspices of the League of the Red Cross or some other organization. Libya might consider giving a major donation to one of these groups as a token of good faith. I knew I could get congressional participation in such a conference.

I thought that it might be a good idea if the Libyan Committee to Resolve Lockerbie—run by Youssef—could join forces with the U.S. Committee to Resolve Lockerbie—run by Mohammed—and jointly sponsor such a conference. Youssef liked the idea, but my plan did not fit his time frame. "Can you bring a Member of Congress to Geneva next week? I will pay all the expenses. He can fly here one day and fly home to Washington the next. I don't care who comes. I just need someone right away. You know how my Leader is. He wants action now. It will only take a few hours."

Mohammed took up the cause. "What is the problem? It would only take a few hours. He could fly the Concord from New York or Washington and be here in a few hours. I will charter a plane if you like. You can bring an entire delegation if we use a chartered jet. A G-4 can carry 10 people across the ocean with no problem. They can bring their wives. They can shop in Geneva while we meet with the Congressmen. It should only take a few hours."

Gerrit started in on me. "Do you think we can get our good friend Larry (Pressler) to come for a few hours? I know he likes to travel. We can let him bring his wife if he likes, eeh? It would be a very private meeting, and no one would ever know that it took place. What do you say, eeh?"

This badgering continued for more than an hour. I tried to explain the political realities of the situation and how it would look for a Member of Congress to meet with Libyans. I suggested another scenario. They might invite Senator John Kerry's Subcommittee on Terrorism, Narcotics and International Operations to do an official congressional site visit of Libya. There would be a lot for them to investigate, including the presence of training camps for terrorists, chemical and biological warfare factories, etc. This would give the Members of the Senate a chance to investigate Libya and take back recommendations to the entire Congress and the Clinton Administration.

"Another great idea Chazzy, but we don't have that much time. The United Nations will be meeting again in a couple of weeks to discuss further sanctions against us. We need to show them that we are not the world's bad guys. We need to move fast. Gerrit says you can do anything with the U.S. Congress. Why not this simple request? How much will it cost? Money is no object. Just get someone here."

I spent a few minutes explaining that a Member of Congress could not accept any type of remuneration or

67

gifts from a foreign entity. All travel expenses have to be paid by a U.S. citizen or U.S. Corporation. I continued that this is a very important part of political life and all Members of Congress are aware of the limitations under which they must operate.

Mohammed sounded in that he was a U.S. citizen and that he could pay for the trip or have his own company, U.S. Medical Supply, pay for it. "I can get the members of our Committee to Resolve Lockerbie to pay for it. They have lots of money. You just arrange to get someone to a meeting and I will see that the payments are made legally."

This first meeting with Youssef broke up after about four hours. I was ready to get away from the mounting pressure from Youssef, Gerrit and Mohammed. Youssef said that he wanted to join us for dinner but that something had come up for that evening and he wouldn't be able to make it. He was sorry.

I got on the elevator to escape to my eighth floor room. An American gentleman in his 40's got on with me. I recognized him immediately as a CIA operative I had often seen going in and out of the U.S. Embassy in Costa Rica. I never forget a face. What a remarkable coincidence that the two of us would end up in the same elevator in Geneva, Switzerland.

I confronted him directly. "I know you from Costa Rica, don't I?" He responded that he had never been to Costa Rica. I persisted, "What brings you to Geneva?"

He sheepishly replied, "I work for Dupont in Delaware—you may have seen me in Washington."

I went in for the kill, "How did you know I'm from Washington?"

Before he could answer, the elevator stopped on the seventh floor. He nervously exited with a quiet, "Good night."

I was brought down to earth by my visit with Mr. "Dupont." I knew I would see him again. At least I was relieved to know that the CIA didn't take me too seriously. If they had, they would have sent a professional, not just an agent who knew what I looked like.

Gerrit, Mohammed and I ate a late dinner that night in the Chinese Restaurant on the second floor of the Noga Hilton. As the pressure on me to get a US Congressman to Geneva grew from my two dinner companions, Youssef Debri walked in with a young white girl, no more than 20 years of age, on his arm. He seemed surprised to see us and didn't take the time to introduce us to his young friend. He passed by us and proceeded directly to his reserved table in the back of the restaurant.

Youssef was well known in the hotel and, after observing his $100 tips earlier that day, I was not surprised that he was so well taken care of by the hotel staff. I noticed that the relationship with the young lady was not platonic and I was sure that it wasn't his daughter. I kept them in sight from time to time out of the corner of my eye.

I left the restaurant about 11:30 P.M. with Gerrit and Mohammed at the table sipping their coffee and eating chocolate covered strawberries. I went directly to my room.

I was just about to doze off when Gerrit and Mohammed knocked on my door. They entered my room and tried once more to convince me to bring a U.S. Congressman or Senator to meet Youssef. Gerrit explained that Youssef was in real trouble with "Charlie," and he had to have this meeting to save face. Gerrit pulled out a hand written contract. He and Mohammed would pay me a $200,000 bonus if I could deliver a Member of Congress to meet Youssef in Libya, Switzerland or Malta within the next seven days. I agreed, and said that I would do my best. Gerrit and Muhammed signed the agreement. I did not sign the agreement, but took it with me.

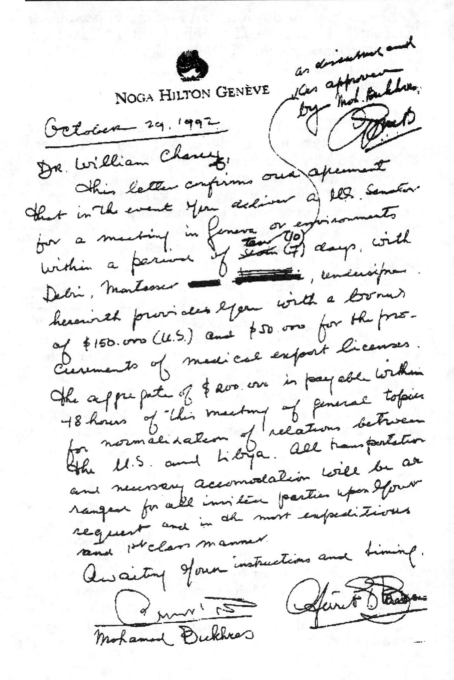

NOGA HILTON GENÈVE

as discussed and
has approved
by Mod. Bukhres

October 29, 1992

Dr. William Chasey,

This letter confirms our agreement that in the event you deliver a U.S. Senator for a meeting in Geneva or environments within a period of ten (10) seven (7) days, with Debri, Montasser ~~————~~, enclosiper. herewith provides you with a bonus of $150.000 (U.S.) and $50.000 for the procurements of medical export licenses. The appropriate of $200.000 is payable within 48 hours of this meeting of general topics for normalization of relations between the U.S. and Libya. All transportation and necessary accommodation will be arranged for all invited parties upon your request and in the most expeditious and 1st class manner.

Awaiting your instructions and timing.

Mohamed Bukhres

I asked Gerrit to provide me with official letters, signed by Debri, that I could hand deliver to three key members of the United States Senate. I was leaving early in the morning for New York and then on to Washington and, since time was of essence, I would need these letters before I left for the Airport. I asked that these letters be addressed to:

Senator John F. Kerry, Chairman,
Subcommittee on Terrorism,
Narcotics and International Operations

Senator Hank Brown, Ranking Republican,
Subcommittee on Terrorism,
Narcotics and International Operations

Senator Larry Pressler,
Senate Committee on Foreign Relations

I noticed that Mr. "Dupont" was up early. He was sitting alone in the lobby. He looked away as I caught him watching me leave the hotel

I left the Noga Hilton for the Geneva Airport with the three letters in hand.

I had arranged to meet with my good friend Ralph Wright, Director of Public Affairs for the League of the Red Cross, for breakfast at the Geneva Airport. Ralph is an American who began his Red Cross career in the United States and was now assigned to Geneva where he had been living for the past few years.

I had worked closely with Ralph to develop a major Red Cross promotion for one of my clients, Simple Green. In return for using the Red Cross Symbol, the most widely known symbol in the world, on their bottles, Simple Green would contribute a percentage of their sales to the League

71

of the Red Cross. I made a similar deal for Simple Green with the American Red Cross.

I shared my experiences of the past two days with Ralph during breakfast in a small snack bar at the Airport. He is a real humanitarian, and pledged the help of the League of the Red Cross. He really wanted to get Lockerbie behind us.

I told him that I would keep him informed of my progress and would include him when the time was right. I also told him that I was beginning to suspect that not all of the information was in on Lockerbie and that there could be an international cover up.

Ralph warned me to be careful and to watch my back. He knew that the Libyans played rough and thought that our intelligence forces could play rough also. A word to the wise. . .

I flew Swiss Air to Zurich. There I changed planes to my home away from home, American Airlines Flight 65. As always, I was met in Zurich by the American Airlines Special Services folks who made sure I was well settled in my usual first class seat, 3B, enroute to New York's JFK Airport.

As we leveled off over the North Atlantic, I opened the package Gerrit had slid under my door sometime during the early morning hours as I slept.

The first document was somewhat of a surprise. It was a letter addressed to me, Gerrit and Brendan Kelly on Official Libyan stationery and dated October 28, 1992.

لجنة الجمامهيرية العربية الليبية الشعبية الاشتراكية
لجنة لدى الأمم المتحدة بجنيف
بالبعثات الدولية بسويسر

ل ــ ـ ا ث
.....

Dr. William C. CHASEY
Mr. Brendan J. KELLY
Mr. Gerrit P. VAN DE BOVENKAMP
INTERNATIONAL COMMUNICATIONS
MARKETING, INC.
666 Fifth Avenue
NEW YORK

N.Y. 10103, U.S.A.

October 28th, 1992

Messrs. CHASEY, KELLY AND VAN DE BOVENKAMP :

This letter authorizes the above named persons to act as official
agents representing the People's Government of Libya in its quest
to normalise relations with the Government of the United States
of America.

Cordially,

Youssef EL DEBRI
The Head of National Security
People's Republic of Libya
Member of the Committee to resolve the Lockerbee Dispute.

The package also contained three very official looking, identical letters addressed to the three Senators. This
is the letter to Senator Kerry.

*Mission permanente
d'Aljamahiriya arabe libyenne populaire socialiste
auprès des Nations Unies à Genève et des
organisations internationale en Suisse*

بعثة الجماهيرية العربية الليبية الشعبية الاشتراكية
المقيمة لدى الأمم المتحدة بجنيف
والمنظمات الدولية بسويسرا

Senator John F. Kerry,
Chairman of Subcommittee on
Terrorism, Narcotics and
International Operations

421 SROB

Washington, D.C. 20035
U.S.A.

October 28, 1992

Dear Senator Kerry,

The Secretariat of the Libyan People's Congress on behalf of the
Libyan people is pleased to address you with respect to a
prospect for improvement of bilateral relations between the
American and the Libyan people, as well as relations between the
U.S. and the Libyan Government.
It is the view of the Libyan Arab Jamaheriya that, as long as
contacts between our two nations are suspended and the means of
communication virtually nonexistent, the specter of distrust
between our nations will never be far from the surface.
Separation can generate accusation and accusation may eventually
lead to conflict.

Such has been the atmosphere which has pervaded our countries'
relations for almost a decade.
In fact we neither wish nor desire such mistrust. On the
contrary, we honestly and seriously are seeking an opportunity to
dialogue and negotiate through your good offices of Foreign
Relations, a positive change toward better relations between our
peoples and nation based on mutual respect and understanding -- a
new page in our history marked by good and honorable intentions.

It is in this spirit that we are willing to discuss and come to
an agreement on :

1) Libya's willingness to renounce all world terrorism ;

2) Libya's willingness to pledge not to engage in anti-government
or destabilization tactics ;

3) Libya's willingness to open its borders to United Nations
inspection teams in order to assure that weapons of mass
destruction are not being manufactured ;

- 2 -

4) Libya's willingness to deliver its two citizens accused of the
   PanAm 103 disaster provided that an international acceptable
   neutral country, will be used for the trial.

Libya further extends an invitation to you and your Committee on
Terrorism, Narcotics and International Operations to visit Libya,
in your official capacity and to experience firsthand our recent
accomplishments. I will personally work with you through our
representative Dr. William C. Chasey, to arrange this fact
finding mission. Hopefully we can meet face to face to plan your
agenda.
These accomplishments are decisive proof that Libya has never
intended to threaten anyone and in particular your country, the
United States of America, whose great assistance in our fight for
independence we shall always remember.

It is our appreciation for your kindness, honesty and integrity
which has led us to extend this invitation. We are sure that what
you will witness in our country will prove to you that the moral
philosophy of our system is deeply rooted as well.

We are confident that you and your Committee will return with the
firm belief that the time has come to mend the sorrowful rift
between our two countries.
We initiate with this letter a dialogue for the road to better
relations.

Sincerely Yours,

Youssef EL DEBRI
Head of Libyan National Security
Member of the Committee to resolve
the dispute of Lockerbie

75

I was amazed that Youssef had gone so far to reach out to the Senators. I had been told by Gerrit that Libya had sent similar letters to President Bush and to Secretary of State Jim Baker, but had never received a response. I couldn't imagine that I couldn't get one of the Senators to respond favorably to this kind invitation.

I carefully read each of the three letters to be sure that I hadn't missed anything. The letters were identical. I felt for the first time that maybe I would be able to deliver a Member of Congress to meet with Youssef in the next seven days.

After checking in to the New York Sheraton Towers at 7th Avenue and 53rd Streets I began my telephone calls. First, I called Ramona Gustafson, Senator Larry Pressler's Scheduling Secretary. I wanted to begin with Larry, since he had gotten me into this deal in the first place.

I was surprised to find that Larry was in New York serving as a United Nations Special Representative for the month. I arranged to meet him at his office on the 4th floor of the United States Mission to the United Nations, 799 United Nations Plaza, at 10:15 the next morning, October 29th.

I had dinner that evening with Dick Corey at the 21 Club just down the street from my Hotel. Dick worked for J.C. Bradford, Co. He was a specialist in doing big municipal bond deals, one of which was for a Senior Living Center at Brandermill Woods, Virginia. I chaired the Board of this center. J.C. Bradford had brought a $1 million lawsuit against the Board, and me, over the defeasance of some B Bonds owned by one of the investors, Allan Bird.

Corey and I had agreed to discuss the matter and see if there was a way to work things out without further litigation. We had a great dinner but made little progress in settling the lawsuit. As we left the 21 Club I ran into an

76

old acquaintance from years past, a rather rotund, red-cheeked gentleman, by the name of Rush Limbaugh. Rush had the number one talk show and the number one book in the country. We spoke briefly. I introduced Rush to Corey. Dick had never heard of Rush Limbaugh and wondered why he deserved all the attention he was getting from the restaurant patrons.

The next morning I went to the United States Mission to the United Nations. After I passed through a metal detector, a squared-away Marine Lance Corporal, sitting behind a wall of bullet proof glass, waved me into the reception room. I was escorted into Senator Pressler's office on the 4th floor of the U.S. Mission. It was 10:20 A.M. October 29th.

Larry seemed glad to see me and asked what had brought me to New York. I told him I had been in Geneva with Gerrit meeting on the Pan Am 103 issue. Larry became a bit uneasy discussing such a controversial topic in his UN office and suggested that we walk together to his hotel, the Waldorf Astoria, a few blocks away. He apologized for not being able to have lunch with me as he already had plans to meet a Park Avenue Japanese businessman for lunch.

We strolled to the hotel and went directly to Larry's suite on the 23rd floor of the Waldorf Towers. The suite is used by the U.S. Government for those dignitaries who serve in the short-term Presidential appointment as Special U.S. Representative to the United Nations. The telltale remnants of what had been the contents of the mini bar were strewn about the room. The maid obviously hadn't gotten there yet. I commented that it looked like his perpetual diet had once again gone astray.

I told Larry about my meetings in Geneva and the invitation for him to meet with Youssef Debri. Larry answered his telephone. It was Ramona, calling from his

Washington Office. He began recording a list of messages on a scratch pad on a small end table next to his sofa. From his body language, I could tell that he was preoccupied with our discussion and was most anxious for Ramona to finish her list.

"How could we make such a meeting happen?" he asked, as he abruptly hung up the phone. "No one could ever know that I met with Qadhafi's people. What do you think the voters of South Dakota would think if they knew? It is probably a worthwhile thing to do, but the fallout would be devastating. I need to get back to the UN and pick up my *Washington Post*. Did you know that it is the only place in New York City where you can get *The Washington Post* the same morning?"

We continued our conversation as we walked back to the Main United Nations Building. Larry first said that he couldn't participate in a meeting with the Libyans, but warmed up to the idea when I suggested Malta as a potential meeting site.

Malta is a Mediterranean island country sixty miles south of Sicily. Its proximity to North Africa would not only make it a convenient spot for the Libyans, but its mild climate in November might just be the ticket for the Senator.

Larry became even more enthusiastic when I suggested that he take Harriet and her daughter, Laura, on the trip. He and Harriet were looking for a warm spot to take Laura over the Congressional Thanksgiving Recess, and Malta appeared to have the right appeal. Laura was at college in Boston and had given the Presslers specific instructions to find a warm, sunshiney place for the upcoming vacation.

We proceeded to devise a plan for Larry, Harriet and Laura to travel to Malta as guests of the Knights of Malta, a Catholic men's organization of which Larry was an active member. I would arrange to have Youssef Debri and Omar Muntassir, the new Libyan Foreign Minister, meet secretly with Pressler sometime during his stay on Malta.

We discussed the possibility of Libya making a contribution of $1 million dollars to the Knights of Malta for their assistance in this matter. The money could be used in their relief hospitals located in Third World countries around the world.

Larry also asked if I could arrange for him to get an honorarium from The University of Malta if he were to give a speech or to meet with faculty and students. He reminded me that I had done just that for him with National University in Costa Rica.

Because of Libya's pressing interest in resolving the Lockerbie situation, and the discomfort the UN Sanctions were creating for them, I didn't think that any of these requests would be unreasonable. The Libyans were desperate to meet with any U.S. Official, and a United States Senator on the Foreign Relations Committee would be more than they could imagine. I clearly remembered Youssef's words in Geneva, "Do whatever it takes to get a meeting."

We discussed the trip further over coffee in the UN Diplomatic Reception Room. Larry now had his *Washington Post* on the table in front of him and had a most difficult time keeping his eyes off the front page as we talked. We took great care not to be overheard by the other dignitaries in the room.

At an opportune time, I handed Larry the letter from Youssef Debri. Without comment he slid the letter into his inside coat pocket. His eyes once again shifted to his newspaper as he said, "I will read this in private."

We agreed to discuss our arrangements further early the following week. Larry wanted time to discuss the trip with Harriet and to be sure that she and Laura approved of the prospects of a Maltese holiday. He suggested that I call him directly at the Waldorf and avoid Ramona and his Washington office staff. He wanted our discussion to be strictly confidential between the two of us.

79

Thanksgiving was more than seven days away and according to the time constraints imposed by Gerrit and Mohammed in my contract, I couldn't collect the promised $200,000, even if Pressler decided to go to Malta. I reminded myself to call Gerrit in Geneva and negotiate a time extension to my contract.

I checked out of my hotel for the trip back to Washington. Before leaving New York, I made a call to Senator John Kerry's office in Washington. Kerry was not in his office. I was told that he was chairing a hearing in the Hart Office Building concerning our missing MIA's and POW's in Vietnam. His Appointment Secretary, Pat Gray, told me that I needed to hurry to Washington if I wanted to catch a few minutes with the Senator. He would be rushing from the hearing to Dulles International Airport enroute to Vietnam. He would be out of the country for a week. The race was on!

I caught the next Delta shuttle back to Washington where Paul was waiting to drive me to the Capitol. When I arrived at the Hart Building, Kerry had already left the hearing. I had just missed him. I rushed to the Russell Senate Office Building only to see him leaving his office with his luggage in hand. I caught up to Kerry in the hall outside his office and walked the short distance with him to the fourth floor elevators.

I quickly explained that I had a very important letter for him from Youssef El Debri, Chief of Libyan Intelligence, concerning Pan Am 103. As the elevator doors began closing Kerry said that he wanted to read the letter when he had time to give it his full attention. He apologized for his haste, but asked that I give the letter to his Administrative Assistant David Leiter to review. "Bill, if you have a few minutes, could you give David a quick briefing on the matter before I get back? Maybe you can do it now."

David and I met for about thirty minutes. I gave him a very superficial briefing. Because of the sensitive nature of the issue, I didn't want an Administrative Assistant to know too much. I had spent the past four years developing a special relationship with John Kerry and didn't want to jeopardize that trust.

Leiter read the letter with great interest and said that Kerry's Subcommittee on Terrorism, Narcotics and International Operations had no immediate plans to discuss Libya. He did say, however, that the full schedule for the new Congressional Session (beginning January 3, 1993) had not been set and that he would discuss the possibility of a visit to Libya with the Senator. He suggested that I arrange a meeting with Kerry as soon as possible. There was nothing more I could do until Kerry returned from Vietnam.

I called Senator Hank Brown's office in the Hart Building. Hank was the Ranking Republican on the Terrorism Committee and one of the Senate's most conservative members. His secretary said he would be returning to Washington the following week, but that I could reach him at his home in Colorado. I talked to Brown on the phone for quite some time that evening. I made rather broad references to Lockerbie in our discussion, to avoid pushing his hot button or turning him off altogether. I really didn't know what his personal feelings were about the issue.

One thing for sure, I wanted to give Brown Youssef's letter in person. By doing so, I would have ample opportunity to lobby him about meeting with Youssef and his Lockerbie committee. I offered to fly to Colorado to meet him that night, or the next day. After discussing several meeting options, we agreed to meet in Brown's Washington office the next week.

I have known Hank Brown since he first represented the 4th district of Colorado in the House of Representa-

81

tives. He was elected to the United States Senate in 1990 filling the seat that had belonged to my very dear friend, Bill Armstrong. Armstrong, a true Christian and man of his word, retired from the Senate because he had promised his constituents that he would only serve two terms and then return to Colorado to live under the laws he had passed. I, like so many of his friends, tried to get Bill to change his mind but, as the man said, "a promise is a promise."

I sat quietly in Senator Brown's office the following week and watched him read the letter with great care. "Amazing." He gathered the pages together once again, and read it just as carefully a second time. "Amazing," he said again. "I would say this was some kind of a joke, if I didn't know you so well, Bill. How did you get this letter?"

I recounted my visit with Youssef in Geneva the previous week. I gave him a little insight about Youssef, and the Libyan Committee to Resolve the Lockerbie Dispute.

"Do you believe this guy, Youssef? Does he really speak for Qadhafi? What is your take on this situation?" Brown was really caught off guard by the letter. "Have you shown this to John Kerry? He Chairs the Terrorism Committee, you know."

"Yes, I do know," I responded quickly. "I gave John a similar letter last week. He was rushing off to Vietnam and didn't get to read it before he left. We did discuss it briefly. His staff has the letter but I don't know if he has read it yet. I plan to talk with him this week."

"Kerry is focused on the POW/MIA situation right now," Brown said. "He has the attention of the National Press and is not about to give it up without milking it for all it is worth. It's hard to get him to think of anything else. The Special POW/MIA Committee he chairs is scheduled to disband at the end of the year. He is compelled to get to the bottom of the situation while he has time.

"I want to talk to John about this letter before I respond to Mr. Debri. He (Kerry) and the Terrorism staff may have something on this that neither you nor I know about. They play it pretty close to the chest. It is a matter of information control for them. If you control the information, you control the situation."

His voice reflected the frustration I have heard so often from minority party members on Capitol Hill. Total control of the very important committee structure in the United States Congress was in the hands of the Democrats, the majority party. It had been this way in the House for 43 years and in the Senate for all but two of the past 26 years.

Committees are the engines of the Congressional lawmaking machinery. The 16 Senate and 22 House standing committees take initial jurisdiction over legislation and can move, stall or stop it. Without committee approval, a bill has little chance of reaching the full House or Senate for consideration.

While the House and Senate determine standing committee jurisdictions and provide money to run their respective committees, these legislative engines, once running, almost have an independent power and life. Special, select or ad hoc committees, created for specific investigation or oversight function, are more apt to die or have functions routed to a standing committee. Such was the case of the POW/MIA Special Committee that was absorbing so much of Senator John Kerry's time.

In addition, there are a number of what I call "Power Committees." Members generally seek membership on committees related to their personal interests and background and to the economic interests of their district or state. Many, however, particularly if given an opportunity

83

early in their careers, will choose the powerful Appropriations Committees. These control the flow of money to programs authorized by other committees. The Senate Finance and the House Ways and Means Committees that consider tax legislation are also very popular. The respective House and Senate Budget Committees, which now allow Congress to compete with the White House in establishing national priorities through a national budget, also are attractive to most members.

Senator Brown discussed the possibility of Mr. Debri coming to Washington to deliver his message in person. This, of course, would have been my first choice but the State Department wouldn't issue him a visa. Unfortunately, I explained, Youssef was on the State Department's short list of international terrorists and the possibility of a visa for him was out of the question. I suggested, with a little chuckle, that this could change if a powerful U.S. Senator on the Foreign Relations Committee, like Hank Brown, were to intervene for him with the Republican-run State Department.

As a Foreign Agent, I have always preferred to have my clients come to Washington to deliver their own sales pitches. First, no one knows the pertinent issues better than the foreign principal; and second, Heads of State make great lobbyists. This is especially true when they can lavishly entertain Members of Congress in their own Washington Embassies.

I have represented some 23 different foreign governments and businesses during my career. The smallest country I represented was Costa Rica (two different presidents, two and a half million people), and the largest was India (Prime Minister Rajiv Gandhi, 850 million people). Each presented me with uniquely different challenges on how best to represent their interests before the United States

Congress. Being able to use a Washington Embassy for social functions and dinner parties is a great arrow for a Foreign Agent to have in his lobbyist quiver.

Costa Rica had very little in the way of financial support to enable its Ambassadors to be a part of Washington's diplomatic inner-circle. More importantly, poor, little Costa Rica had no embassy for me to use as a political attraction. The lovely, old rustic home on "S" Street in Northwest Washington, that had adequately served this valuable function for many years, was now gone.

Late one night in 1988, a fire of unknown origin gutted the structure and left it useless. The Ambassador, Federico Vargas, and his family narrowly escaped with their lives. Unable to afford repairs, the building went on the auction block. Future Costa Rican Ambassadors were left with no more than a small suite of offices in a rather ordinary looking office building on Connecticut Avenue as the focal point of their diplomatic stature.

On the other hand, the Indian Ambassador to Washington lives in opulence. The historic residence, which backs up to the National Zoo in Northwest Washington, is a beauty to behold. It is full of typical Indian art, furnishings, and the trappings of years gone by. Indian houseboys, fitted out in their white Nehru jackets with white pants and shoes, presented a striking image of the genteel Indian life style. I used the Embassy and the Ambassador's residence frequently in my lobbying activities.

On a monthly basis I would submit an invitation list to Ambassador P. K. Kahl, of key Members of Congress I thought should be invited to his residence for a small dinner party. The Indian hospitality, cocktail talk and delicious food made for an evening to remember. The food at the Indian Embassy is well known in diplomatic circles around Washington and, after my tenure as the Indian Foreign Agent, it was also well known around Capitol Hill. These dinner parties became a must. When the word started

85

to get around Congress, I had no trouble getting Members to attend and even had some lawmakers asking me for an invitation.

Senator Brown asked, "Why would Libya make such a magnanimous offer? The only real hang-up over the Lockerbie situation is where to try the two suspected terrorists. Why won't we agree to a trial in a neutral country?" Without waiting for an answer, he said, "Does the President know about this offer from Qadhafi?"

I answered, "I have been told that numerous letters had been sent to President Bush, Secretary of State Baker and various Members of Congress, with no response."

"I don't know how you got involved in this situation, Bill, but I hope you know what you are doing. I have learned a great deal about the terrorist world since joining this committee. You may know something about traditional warfare from your Marine Corps days, but there are no rules with these guys. Have you registered with the State Department on this?" Hank asked.

"The Justice Department. I registered with the Justice Department," I corrected him. "It's under their jurisdiction."

He looked down at the letter on his lap and said, "I am going to talk to Kerry and find out what I can. I will get back to you when I know something. In the meantime, be very careful, my friend."

As I left his office, Hank offered me four seats to the Clinton Inauguration. I graciously accepted. Hank had no interest in attending the ceremonies, and I had clients who would love to go. By January 20th, I had rounded up an additional 18 tickets for clients and friends to see Bill Clinton sworn in as the forty-second President of the United States.

Chapter Nine

A Congressman Agrees To Go

I paged through my handy, pocket Congressional Pictorial Directory on my flight back to California. I had a feeling that my good friend, Larry Pressler, would probably change his mind about the trip to Malta and I needed a ready backup waiting in the wings. My history with Senator Pressler was that he was always first in line for a free trip, speaking fee or a fund raiser, but rarely did he ever help me with a legislative issue.

I laughed under my breath, as I visualized the ridiculous situation in which I found myself. I was about to start calling my congressional friends with an "offer they couldn't refuse." The coward's approach would have been to send them an invitation by fax. I jokingly composed this one in my mind:

```
Dear Joe:
     You are cordially invited to join me on
an overnight trip to Geneva, Malta or
wherever, to meet in a hotel room with two
Libyan agents. One agent is high on the list
of the world's most sought after terrorists.
These Libyans represent the most disliked
man in the world, Muammar Qadhafi. I want
you to come hear them say that Libya didn't
blow up Pan Am 103. It will only take (to
use Gerrit's words) a "few hours"of your
time. Since we need to depart in the next
four days, please cancel all of your pending
appointments, speeches and fund-raisers. By
the way, we don't want anybody to know that
you made the trip. I look forward to our
time together.

     Best regards,

               Bill
```

I had taken on challenges in the past, but this one qualified for the Lobbying Hall of Fame. There had to be one out of the five-hundred-thirty five Members who would be available, interested and crazy enough to make the journey with me.

I first considered asking some of my closest congressional friends, especially those who owed me a favor. Since Gerrit and Mohammed didn't stipulate any specific individuals or committee responsibilities, my hand was free to select any Member that I could persuade to go.

I made a few phone calls and, as expected, ran into various obstacles along the way. Congressman Duncan Hunter, Republican of California, said that he wanted nothing to do with that "Mad Man" Qadhafi. Congressman and Minister Floyd Flake, Democrat of New York, had to preach to his 5,000 member Allen A.M.E., African-Methodist-Episcopal Church in Jamaica-Queens, New York on Sunday morning. With national elections only three days away on November 3rd, some were unreachable on the campaign trail, while others that I did reach didn't want to discuss any travel plans until after the election.

With the pending meeting with Youssef and Omar only one week away, it struck me that my best bet would be to target Members who would not be returning for the 103rd Congress. This decision would narrow my search to those who had either lost their primary race or who would be retiring at the end of the 102nd Congress.

I would also be meeting the requirements of my contract. These individuals were now Members of Congress and would remain Members until the following year. It would be better to take a Member who would be returning next year but that option didn't look good at this point. With the elections coming the following week, there was no sure way of knowing what Members would be returning anyway.

I called three close friends who met my new criteria. Representative Bill Lowery, Republican of California, had announced his retirement. He was forced out of his own district by fellow Republican, Randy "Duke" Cunningham, and also found himself in the middle of the House Bank scandal. Unfortunately Bill was on an airplane when I called and we didn't make contact until it was too late.

Congressman Bill Alexander, Democrat of Arkansas, had lost his primary fight to his former Washington receptionist, Blanche Lambert. Bill said that he had vacation plans that he couldn't change at this late date, but that if I needed his help later, for a fee, he would be available as a Washington Lawyer.

Beryl Anthony, Democrat of Arkansas, had also lost his primary race. He expressed his regrets because he was reluctant to leave the country. He was confident that his good Arkansas buddy, Bill Clinton would be elected President of the United States on Tuesday. Governor Bill would need his help as he prepared for his move to Washington.

My next call hit pay dirt. I phoned my good friend, and primary election loser, Carroll Hubbard, Democrat of Kentucky. He was not in the office, but his secretary said that he had nothing on his schedule the following week. Carroll and his wife, Carol (no joke), were scheduled to vacation back home in Mayfield, Kentucky. I left a message that I wanted him to go to Geneva with me the following week. She promised to give him my message.

We were having dinner at home in California when Carroll returned my call. I immediately recognized his slow, deliberate Kentucky drawl. "What does my good friend Bill Chasey want me to do, go to Geneva? Next week? Well, that sounds great!" Without even knowing the purpose of the trip, he asked, "Can Carol come with us?"

I knew his secretary had made the call for Carroll when he asked me where I was. "Are you in your beautiful home in La Jolla overlooking the Pacific? La Jolla, Wow! La Jolla is one of my favorite places in the world. I want to thank you again for letting me use that beautiful home. I will never forget the two weeks I stayed in that beautiful home. Tell Virginia and Katie thanks again for me. What a beautiful home. People in Mayfield, Kentucky only see homes like yours in the movies."

In 1987, I had mentioned to Carroll that the Chasey family would be spending the month of August in England. We had arranged for a flat in the Little Boltons section of London proper. Carroll jumped at this opportunity in a flash. He asked if he and Carol and their two children could use our home for a week while we were out of the country. He was looking for a place to go during the August recess. We agreed, and Carroll made plans to vacation in Southern California.

We were shocked to receive a phone call a few days after arriving in England from our longtime Vietnamese housekeeper, Dong. She reported that Congressman Hubbard did arrive, but not with his family. There were three young women staying in the house with him. He told Dong that the women were members of his Congressional staff. Dong was most concerned that the Congressman was smoking in the house. She knew we wouldn't like it. I had known Carroll for ten years and never knew that he smoked. I assured Dong that he would be leaving in a couple of days and that she should do the best she could.

Carroll called me in England a day or so later to ask if he could extend his stay in our home another week. After a rather long heart to heart discussion, I acquiesced only when Carroll agreed not to smoke in the house. I was the lobbyist responsible for eliminating smoking on domestic airline flights and most members of Congress knew it!

"I'm not on the Foreign Affairs Committee," Hubbard responded when I told him the nature of the meeting in Geneva. "I'm a real good friend of Congressman Lee Hamilton, the new Chairman of the Committee, though. I can report the results of our meeting to Lee when I come back to Washington."

I explained that Youssef was interested in meeting with a Member who would champion his cause of normalizing relations between the U.S. and Libya. Committee membership was not that important.

We discussed the trip at length. I suggested that we maximize our time in Geneva, by flying over on the Concord. "The Concord. Wow! You sure do things right my friend, Dr. Bill Chasey. We have never been on the Concord. It's real expensive I hear. Can you afford to pay for the tickets?"

I told Carroll that all expenses were being paid by a New York based public relations company called ICM. Actually I wasn't really sure if the trip would be paid for by ICM or by Mohammed's Committee to Resolve Lockerbie. I was certain to assure him that all expenses would be paid from U.S. accounts; by U.S. citizens or Companies. No Libyan monies would be used.

I couldn't have been happier! I had my man!

Youssef, Gerrit and Mohammed would be delighted with the news. Regrettably, I did have a major problem. I couldn't make the seven day time limit specified in my contract. I called Gerrit in New York and asked that he change the time limit from seven to ten days. I also asked for permission to have a Congressman in place of a Senator. When he heard that I actually had a Congressman willing to go to Geneva, he immediately made the changes to the contract and faxed me a copy.

I was feeling pretty smug. I couldn't imagine anyone else in my business being able to overcome so many ob-

91

stacles and actually get a sitting Member of Congress to take the trip.

I did come off my high perch long enough to reflect on my responsibilities to the Justice Department. It had been almost a month since I registered as a Libyan Foreign Agent. I had not been contacted in any way by the Justice Department. I assumed that all was well on that front. No news is good news. I would be required to report the forthcoming trip when I filed my next Justice supplemental report, which was due in about sixty days.

These reports are rather exacting. One needs to list all of the contacts that you make on behalf of a foreign principal. You are also required to report all monies received and expended on behalf of a client. All political activity has to be reported, as do all political contributions.

The Justice Department is particularly tough on political propaganda, which they define in their typical bureaucratic jargon as:

.... including any oral, visual, graphic, written, pictorial, or other communication or expression by any person which is reasonably adapted to, or which the person disseminating the same believes will, or which he intends to, prevail upon, indoctrinate, convert, induce, or in any other way influence a recipient or any section of the public within the United States, with reference to the political or public interests, policies, or relations of a government of a foreign country or a foreign political party or with reference to the foreign policies of the United States or promote in the United States racial, religious, or social dissensions....

On top of this, according to Rule 205—all forms must be filed in triplicate!

Carroll called with panic in his voice more than once the following week. Each time the phone rang, I knew in my heart that he was calling to cancel. Most of the anxiety emanated from his wife's questions about travel plans, i.e., what to wear, what clothes to take and what free time we might have to shop or sightsee. I was surprised at their naivete about traveling to Europe. Most Members of Congress travel quite a bit during their careers. Their wives often get to travel with them, either on official business, or on the now famous Congressional "Junkets." I was especially surprised at Carol Hubbard's lack of sophistication in preparing for this trip.

Carol Brown Hubbard, a former Miss Kentucky in the Miss America Pageant, was much more politically astute than the average Washington political wife. She had just been defeated in the Kentucky Democratic Congressional Primary. If she and Carroll had both won their primaries, they would have represented adjoining districts in the United States Congress. This would have been the first time that a husband and wife team would have served in Congress concurrently.

There was some obvious bitter feeling over her defeat. Part of the reason given for Carroll's defeat in his own primary was the amount of time he devoted to campaigning for his wife. There were some rumblings about illegal campaign practices during both of their campaigns. I didn't take them very seriously. After all, Carroll, 56, had been investigated once before for illegal campaign practices. When he ran for Governor of Kentucky in 1979, the F.B.I. investigated whether he used members of his Congressional staff to work on that campaign but no charges resulted from the inquiry.

I was convinced that Carroll had lost his primary to Tom Barlow, a Paducah businessman who went on to win the general election, because he had gotten caught up in

93

the House Bank Scandal. He had 152 overdrafts at the House Bank from July, 1988 to October, 1991. Another factor was voters' perception that, as a senior member of the House Banking Committee, he had not been vigilant in monitoring the savings and loan industry. The real truth would be known later.

Chapter Ten

Geneva and Points Unexpected

All tickets in hand, I departed San Diego for Washington on Friday, November 6th, 1992. I was to meet the Hubbards at Washington's National Airport early the following morning.

Our American Airlines Flight 4989 to New York was scheduled to depart at 6:35 A.M, but I planned to be in Washington much earlier in case there was a problem. I had offered to have Paul pick the Hubbards up early that Saturday morning. Once they were in the car, they were mine. With $200,000 riding on getting them to Geneva, I wanted to cover all of my bases.

I was pleased when they arrived in plenty of time to make our flight. I hadn't seen Carol in some time and immediately noticed her obvious weight gain. She had a very pretty face but controlling her weight had always been a problem. She was wearing jeans and a turtle neck sweater, both of which exaggerated her lack of self control. Carroll had always been heavy but to see the two of them together in casual clothes was more than I expected. My guess was that they had suffered from post-primary-defeat-syndrome and had eaten their way to full recovery. Oh well, my contract said nothing about how large or small they needed to be, only that I get them to Geneva in ten days. The prospect of doing so was becoming a reality.

We transferred from the American flight to the British Air Terminal at JFK. We were graciously escorted to the Concord Lounge. The fact that breakfast was being served didn't go unnoticed by the Hubbards. I checked the three of us in at the reception desk, while my travel companions fortified themselves for the three hour transatlantic flight.

The flight over the Atlantic was uneventful. As we began to disembark from the plane at London's Heathrow Airport, I couldn't believe what I saw next. As a thank you British Air had given us a small silver pill box with the Concord logo embossed on the lid. It was neatly wrapped in a little gift box. Most passengers left the empty box behind on their seats or in their seat backs. As I made my way down the aisle behind the Hubbards, I watched as they stopped and opened each little gift box to be sure that some unsuspecting Concord passenger hadn't inadvertently left their pill box behind with the gift wrap.

We left London at 8:00 P.M. on Swiss Air 837, arriving in Geneva at 10:30 P.M. Waiting for us at the baggage claim was one Gerrit P. Van de Bovenkamp with William, Youssef Debri's Swiss Chauffeur. Gerrit, always the gentleman, warmly welcomed us to Geneva. He briefed us on our schedule as we drove the ten minutes to the Noga Hilton Hotel.

It was almost midnight when we all sat down in the lobby cocktail lounge to discuss plans for the following day's meeting. Gerrit suggested that we meet in the lobby at 10:00 A.M. and go to the meeting room together. I had insisted that we use a hotel meeting room. I didn't want to expose the Congressman and his wife to Youssef's messy suite. The Hubbards retired for the night.

Gerrit and I spent a few more minutes discussing the details of the next two days. I was informed that the Libyan Foreign Minister Omar Mustafa al-Muntassir had called Youssef and said that he would not be able to come to Geneva as planned. He requested that we fly to Jerba, Tunisia, the following morning on Youssef's jet and hold our meeting at the Jerba Airport. "Where in the world is Jerba?" I asked. Gerrit answered that he understood it was a small island off the coast of Tunisia.

"It will only take a few hours," he said. Gerrit also told me that Mohammed, the guy who was to host this party hadn't arrived as yet and that he had not heard anything from him in a couple of days.

I was most upset with Gerrit. I accused him of deception. "Why wasn't I told about Omar? How am I going to explain all this to the Hubbards?" I asked.

They were getting nervous as it was. I could feel the tension grow on the last leg of our flight from London. They asked me a lot of questions about Youssef, Omar and Mohammed. Now I was going to have to face them in the morning, and tell them that two of the three people we came to see would be missing. I didn't like the way this smelled.

Gerrit apologized profusely as he tried to ease my temper. He didn't know until just a few hours before that Omar couldn't come. Youssef had told him earlier in the evening. Youssef wasn't concerned at all, so why should we be concerned? He tried to explain that Mohammed was always late and that he might still show up before the scheduled meeting the next morning.

I spent a rather uneasy night collecting my thoughts. How would all this look to Congressman Hubbard? Would he be willing to fly to Tunisia? I had told him that Mohammed represented the U.S. Committee to Resolve Lockerbie and the guy doesn't even show up for his own meeting. On a more personal note, Mohammed was supposed to pay me $200,000 within 48 hours of our meeting. Tomorrow would tell!

Gerrit and I had breakfast together early the next morning. We had just one hour before the Hubbards were expected. Gerrit gave me some more bad news. Youssef wanted to meet in his suite instead of a meeting room. Mohammed hadn't checked in to the Noga during the night. It seemed Mohammed had disappeared again. While there wasn't anything I could do about Mohammed, I vehemently protested the room arrangements. Gerrit agreed to call Youssef and make appropriate arrangements.

97

The Hubbards appeared in the dinning room neatly dressed in business attire. I had to admit that they looked quite striking. They joined us for coffee, indicating that they had had breakfast earlier in their room. We discussed the day's activities while Gerrit left to call Youssef. Mrs. Hubbard was anxious to get started so there would be sufficient time to get some Swiss shopping in before dark. I had decided to let Youssef break the news about Omar's absence and to let him make the suggestion that we fly to Tunisia.

Much to my surprise, Gerrit reappeared at the dinning room door accompanied by Youssef Debri. We were caught off guard. No one was quite ready to meet the Chief of Libyan Intelligence at this point. The tension level at our table heightened as they approached.

This was not at all what I had in mind in the way of introductions. What happened to the formal introductions of Youssef and the Libyan Foreign Minister over the neatly prepared conference table? What had happened to the writing pads and sharp pencils? Where were the pitchers of ice water and the green table cloth? There was no chalk board. It was time for this Foreign Agent 4221 to be creative.

"Youssef, it is so good of you to join us for breakfast," I improvised. "We are honored with your company." I made introductions and waited to see what would happen next. Much to my great delight, Youssef took complete charge of the situation. He was neatly dressed in a tan, short sleeved leisure suit type outfit. He was completely relaxed as he graciously welcomed Congressman and Mrs. Hubbard to Switzerland. They were obviously charmed by him and I could see the tension release from their bodies.

I could almost read their minds. "This was no way for an international terrorist to act." They didn't know exactly what they had expected but were delighted with what

98

they got. Everyone began to relax and all of a sudden we were a group of new friends sharing a lovely Swiss brunch.

Before Carroll and Carol knew what had happened they had agreed to spend the balance of the day in Jerba, Tunisia. All of my worrying the night before had gone for naught. Not only had they agreed, but Youssef had convinced them that it would be an exciting thing to do. Youssef explained that Omar had been detained in Tripoli, but had requested that we meet with him in Jerba. As the man said, it would only take a few hours.

Youssef looked directly at Gerrit and asked, "Will Mohammed be going with us?" Gerrit was embarrassed as he explained that he had had no contact with Mohammed in the past two days. Youssef grumbled under his breath as he left the table, "Mohammed makes me crazy."

William, Youssef's driver, was waiting for us in the hotel drive, in a brand new Mercedes 600 SEL. How interesting—I saw my old friend, Mr. "Dupont" talking with the hotel doorman just outside the revolving front door!

Since we took no belongings with us, we simply got in the car and were off to Geneva's General Aviation Airport. We were greeted by our friendly flight crew consisting of two male pilots and two female flight attendants. We boarded a Falcon 500 jet that, unbeknownst to us at the time, would take us on the adventure of our lives.

It was like stepping into a Hollywood stage set. It couldn't have been more perfect. The plane was beautifully appointed with magnificent art works and furnishings. The seats were large and comfortable. There were two cabins with four seats in each. The galley was replete with modern kitchen equipment and conveniences. Some seats in the second cabin had been removed to accommodate Youssef's personal belongings and gifts for the folks back home. A red toy electric car was strapped securely to the starboard bulkhead. I guessed that this car would be enjoyed by Youssef's eight year old son. Since the 1991 United Nations air embargo was imposed such items were scarce in Libya.

I sat directly across from, and facing, Youssef. The Hubbards were seated across the aisle facing each other. Gerrit sat aft in what I jokingly referred to as "coach class." He sat with a mysterious man in a black leather jacket named Zouhair Chirif. His business card said that he was in the construction business in Beirut, Lebanon. I remember thinking at the time that next to medical supplies, construction was the business to be in, in Beirut. Youssef introduced Chirif as his longtime friend. I thought he was just "hitching" a ride to Libya. "Omar Chirif" as I jokingly called him, confided in Gerrit that he was actually Chief of Syrian Security on a secret mission to Libya. I hoped that I wasn't the mission!

The flight attendants served drinks, Russian caviar and a most scrumptious lunch with a choice of roasted lamb, chateaubriand or salmon. I focused on my favorite, the caviar. It was a beautiful, clear day. We were afforded a magnificent view of the Swiss Alps, Italian coastline and the Island of Malta.

Our casual conversation turned serious when Youssef began discussing Libyan/U.S. relations. I was always amazed at how much the Libyans knew about the political situation in America. Youssef said, "Libya has been the victim of a major U.S. disinformation program brought against our Leader, Col. Qadhafi. In 1986, President Reagan approved a strategy of disinformation and deliberate deception against Qadhafi and our people. We are still the targets of this campaign, and Lockerbie is the latest attempt to discredit us in the eyes of the world."

I took notes as he talked and filled in blanks in his story later, after doing some research. As in other places in this book, Geoff Simons' book, *Libya: The Struggle for*

Survival, was very helpful in piecing together this background material.

Youssef didn't refer to notes during his discourse. "Did you know that your National Security Advisor, Admiral Poindexter, advocated a plan in 1986 that was a combination of real and illusionary events through a disinformation program? The basic goal was to make our Leader think that there was a high degree of internal opposition to him within Libya, that his key trusted aides, like me, were disloyal, and that the U.S. was about to move against him militarily. I have seen this memo. It was reported in *The Wall Street Journal,* August 25, 1986, by Bob Woodward of *The Washington Post.* This was just a few months after the United States bombed my country. I wish I could take you to see the destruction the bombs caused."

As I recall the situation, the memo was leaked to the press and created a major uproar in the White House and in the press. In self-defense, the White House sought to draw a distinction between practicing deception toward Qadhafi and using the American press for disinformation. The White House admitted deception but denied disinformation!

At one White House briefing in mid-November, 1986, President Reagan acknowledged Poindexter's memo and said he wanted to keep Qadhafi off balance. Poindexter insisted, "We did not intend and did not plan or conspire to mislead the American press in any way." The problem was that many White House reporters felt, with good reason, that they had already been patsies for a planted story line about a phony crisis with Libya.

A high State Department official said that some of Poindexter's national security aides fed false information to the American press about Libya, thinking (on the basis of an August 14, 1986, meeting with Reagan, Poindexter,

101

and others) that a planted story "might be smiled upon" by Reagan. That August 25, 1986, The Wall Street Journal story asserted that Qadhafi "has begun plotting new terrorist attacks" and "the U.S. and Libya are on a collision course again" (though Poindexter's mid-August memo had said there was no evidence of imminent terrorist attacks).

For the record, Larry Speakes, Reagan Press Aide, had "no comment" on the Journal article, but Speakes insured that its version would be widely repeated, by telling other reporters that the story was "authoritative." In short, the White House promoted its planted story but kept its hand hidden, leaving reporters furious when the bogus crisis was later exposed by Bob Woodward of The Washington Post.

Secretary of State George Schultz added to Reagan's image problems by defending the principle of deception. "Frankly, I don't have any problems with a little psychological warfare against Qadhafi," Schultz declared. He recalled Winston Churchill's justifying deception against Hitler during World War II: "In time of war, the truth is so precious, it must be attended by a bodyguard of lies."

But the Libyan disinformation plot was an inside-the-beltway tempest. The devastating disclosure of Reagan's duplicity on his secret dealing with Iran was the coup de grace, *echoing elements of the Watergate scandal, with some abuses of executive power, official attempts at cover-ups, shredding documents, and above all, the president's personal policy of deception. Across the nation, this affair shattered Reagan's carefully crafted political image. I, in a small way, had contributed to creating this image while serving on Reagan's National Campaign Staff in 1980.*

Two hours and ten minutes after departing Geneva, we began our final approach into Jerba. Youssef said that Omar would have a lot more information for us at the airport.

We were met at the plane by a group of plain-clothed Libyan Secret Intelligence Agents of the Jamahiriya Security Organization (JSO). They had the familiar "Secret Service" look right down to the dark sun glasses and hand held radios. It was obvious that Youssef was their boss, as they attempted to anticipate his every need. The agents escorted us through the side door of the small terminal building as Youssef began a rather animated radio conversation with someone. It was hot when we departed the plane and the terminal's air conditioning was most welcome.

Youssef was very angry as he joined us in the terminal. He was hot and sweaty from standing on the tarmac talking on the radio. "That was Omar on the radio. He can't get here. He wants us to come to Tripoli to meet with him in his office. He is very sorry and sends his sincere apologies."

This was not good news. I began to wonder if we were being had. It was like they were drawing us in—closer and closer every step of the way. Now we were being asked to actually go to Libya!

We had two very distinct choices at that point. We could either return to Geneva, or follow Youssef's suggestion and go to Tripoli. Unfortunately it wasn't quite that simple. To be perfectly honest, I knew nothing about travel restrictions for U.S. citizens to Libya.

We were told that it was a three hour drive to Tripoli. If we decided to go, we would be forced to spend the night. The Geneva airport closed from 10:00 P.M. till 6:00 A.M. each day and we wouldn't have sufficient time to travel to Tripoli, meet and return to Jerba in time to fly to Geneva before the airport closed. Mrs. Hubbard quickly pointed out that we had no luggage and spending the night would create a real hardship for her.

Under U.S./UN sanctions against Libya, no air traffic is permitted into or out of the country. I found it humorous that we Americans were ourselves victims of our own sanctions.

Youssef suggested that we drive to Tripoli. He would call his wife and have her prepare a very special dinner for us in their home. He would make arrangements for us to spend the night at the El Mahari Hotel in Tripoli. Whatever items of clothing or personal effects we might need would be provided. Our meeting with Omar could be arranged for the early morning in order for us to return to Geneva before the air traffic deadline the following evening. He would be sure that we would not have any passport stamps from Libya. The trip would be top secret.

I remembered that no one knew where we were anyway. All those who cared thought that we were at the Noga Hilton in Geneva. Youssef made it sound very inviting and, personally, I hoped that Congressman Hubbard would agree to his plan. I was enchanted with the idea of visiting Libya. After all, as Youssef had said, "It will only take a few hours."

I huddled with Caroll and Gerrit to discuss our options. Carroll's first concern was safety. He suggested that we might be the target of a Libyan kidnap plot. "Why not?" he said. "Look what they went through to get us this far." I wondered out loud how President Clinton would feel about launching a military raid to rescue us from Libya, just as Jimmy Carter did trying to rescue our hostages from Iran in 1980. Carroll didn't think my comment was particularly funny. He started getting a little testy with me, almost as if I was a part of the Libyan plot. So much for levity. . . .

I think everyone in our party was intrigued with the idea of going to Libya. We knew that we would be traveling at our own risk and that, without the benefit of diplomatic relations between the U.S. and Libya, we couldn't expect help from our own government if we got in a jam. "Let's do it," Congressman Hubbard announced to the group.

A surge of excitement spread throughout my body. It was similar to the feeling I had when, two years before on July 16, 1990, I agreed to fly on a reconnaissance mission with the Salvadorian Air Force. Virginia and I were guests of Salvadorian President and Mrs. Alfredo Cristiani while on a humanitarian mission in that country.

Earlier, in 1989 and 1990, I had lobbied Congress for support of a prosthetics relief program in El Salvador by a large prosthetics company (Orthomedics) located in Brea, California. When the company was sold, Virginia and I, along with Roy Snelson, former owner of Orthomedics, established the Third World Prosthetics Foundation to enable us to continue the work we had started with the amputee population of children and soldiers in that war torn Central American Country. We were in El Salvador with a team of volunteer prosthetists fitting land mine victims with new arms and legs. We actually contributed over one-thousand such devices to these great people over a three year period.

On this July day I was invited by a U.S. Air Force Advisor, Major Jim Kelly, to be the machine gunner on the French-made Salvadorian Alouette helicopter that was about to leave on a reconnaissance mission. The mission entailed flushing out FMLN guerrillas reported operating in the northern part of the country.

We were attending a lovely outdoor luncheon at the home of a very prominent Salvadorian, Billy Sol, when Kelly arrived in full battle gear in an armored car. He took me and three of my team members, Roy Snelson, Bud Smith and Nick Apostle, to a takeoff site located in a cane field about three miles down the road. We hid in the bushes

105

while Kelly, with the aid of a Salvadorian military trans-
lator, directed the Alouette to our position. As soon as the
helicopter landed we quickly slid into our body armor and
scrambled aboard.

    An M-60 machine gun was thrust into my hands which
I loaded with little help from the flight crew. I had used the
M-60 frequently during my Marine Corps days and, even
after such a long time, the loading process seemed rather
automatic. We focused our two hour search on an area in
which the FMLN had been recently reported conducting
operations. Unfortunately, thunder storms brought our
mission to an abrupt end. Although we did encounter three
FMLN patrols, we drew no enemy fire from below. I have
to admit, the event brought out more than a little of the
John Wayne in me—at least for a couple of hours.

    Youssef made a couple of phone calls and gave some
instructions to the men who were unloading the Falcon
500. We got in our designated limos and hastily departed
the airport for Tripoli. The sense of adventure was very
much alive.

Chapter Eleven

The Desert and Tripoli

As I peeked through the curtain of the black Mercedes limousine, I wondered, *"What is the son of a milkman from Trenton, New Jersey doing in a place like this?"*

There were two other men in the limousine with Gerrit and me. The driver, Abdel, spoke no English. I estimated him to be in his late 40's. In the right front seat sat Khaled, a very handsome young man wearing an Armani suit and a silk shirt open at the collar. The bulge under his neatly tailored suit jacket presented the obvious tell tale sign of an automatic 9mm pistol. He had spoken to us in acceptable English at the Jerba airport, but now he barked orders from his open car window to his subordinates in Arabic. These men were highly trained JSO (Jamahiriya Security Organization) Agents. Later they were assigned to us as bodyguards while we were in Libya. They were now loudly engaged in an animated discussion outside of our car with armed Tunisian border crossing guards. We were just a few hundred feet from the Libyan Border and there seemed to be a problem with us leaving Tunisia.

Gerrit was like a little kid in the back seat of our car as the commotion continued outside. He said, "This would make a great book." Little did he know! He asked repeatedly, "What's going on out there? Why are we being delayed?"

Our car was part of a three car caravan. The black Mercedes directly behind ours contained Congressman and Mrs. Carroll Hubbard. They were also assigned two Libyan Security guards, one driving and the other in the right front seat of the car. The third black Mercedes contained the

107

Chief of Libyan National Security, Youssef Debri, and his friend from the plane.

Khaled sat back in his seat and turned around to face us. "They want to see your passports," he said.

"I thought we had it worked out that they wouldn't ask for our passports," I responded. Gerrit and I got out of the car to talk privately. We were carefully observed by the border guards as we walked back to Congressman Hubbard's car. He joined us and we walked away to an area where we couldn't be heard. Mrs. Hubbard remained in the car. She was extremely tense and was obviously afraid of all the commotion. We had a rather long discussion about giving up our passports to the Tunisian guards. After all, we had been told earlier that afternoon by Debri that our visit was to be secret. A passport stamp would let the cat out of the bag.

None of us were sure about the legalities of a trip into Libya. I hadn't been in a U.S. sanctioned country since I spent time in Cuba as a Marine Corps Officer some thirty years before. We hadn't planned to go to Libya and were totally unprepared for the events taking place.

Carroll Hubbard was traveling on a diplomatic passport with very few stamps. This indicated that he had not traveled very much or that it was a new passport. I checked page two of my well worn passport to see what it said about travel to Libya. The only prohibited country listed was Cuba. We all knew that we would be traveling at our own risk, but none of us ever guessed that the U.S. Government could punish such travel. It really didn't matter since the trip was secret and we were well protected by Youssef's crack agents.

By this time Youssef Debri had left his car and approached us. He was obviously disturbed by the delay. "What's the problem Chazzy?" I told him that we had been asked for our passports by the Tunisian Guards. He stormed off toward Khaled mumbling under his breath, "This makes me crazy." Debri quickly became involved in the debate between his intelligence officers and the Tunisian border guards. They were out of ear shot but we knew that there was a major disagreement over the passports.

Youssef returned to our group and explained that it would be alright to give the border guards our passports, but not to worry when we got to the Libyan border. We would not enter Libya on our U.S. Passports, and there would never be a record of our visit. We reluctantly gave our passports to Khaled, who took them into a small room in the immigration office.

There was a very long line of Libyans waiting to leave Tunisia. It is the custom for Libyan merchants to sell their wares in Tunisia each day. The trip through the border was tedious, both entering Tunisia early in the morning and reentering Libya in the late afternoon and evening. We had moved quickly past all of the little trucks and no one seemed to mind.

Khaled returned with our stamped passports and distributed them to each of us.

I never thought that entry would come back to haunt me years in the future. That passport entry in Arabic creates a major problem every time I leave Poland where I am now engaged in business activities. The immigration officers always flag the entry with a variety of questions and a suspicious manner.

With passports in hand we were waved through the Tunisian border crossing at Ra's Ajdir. We stopped a few hundred yards further ahead at the Libyan border crossing. All of a sudden three Libyan police cars with flashing blue lights positioned themselves in front of our motorcade and three more police cars took up positions at our rear. The police officers had obviously been waiting for us with engines running. No time was lost as our tires squealed from a standing start to 160 kilometers per hour (100 M.P.H.) in a few seconds.

The fact that I was actually in Libya did not go unnoticed. My heart rate increased and Gerrit and I simultaneously looked at each other without a word. My first thought was, it was too late to turn back now. I also felt some comfort knowing that I had been in similarly scary situations like this in El Salvador, Nicaragua and elsewhere around the world and had always made it through before.

One trip in particular stood out in my mind. I went to El Salvador in the spring of 1982 to sign a contract to represent the Salvadoran Freedom Foundation (SFF) as a Registered Foreign Agent in Washington. The Foundation was a right wing group composed of wealthy Salvadoran land owners. Some members were descendants of the original thirteen families who at one time owned all of El Salvador. That was, of course, until new land reforms were instituted by the Salvadoran Government in the early 1980's. The SFF was later accused of operating a number of "Death Squads" in El Salvador, since many of the SFF were also members of the right-wing Republican National Alliance Party (ARENA). I was accompanied on the trip by one of my employees, Ambassador Alvaro Rizo, former Nicaraguan Ambassador to the United States.

As was customary in that war-torn country, the SFF provided us with an armored car and a contingent of heavily-armed bodyguards who remained close at hand during the day and stationed outside of our hotel rooms at night. Our first meeting with the SFF was held over lunch on the veranda of a magnificent plantation owned by a handsome young Salvadoran by the name of Orlando de Sola. What I remember most about the plantation was the iron gate, barbed wire security fences, farmers working the fields with automatic weapons over their shoulders and large, colorful Spanish pots filled with hand grenades stationed strategically around the veranda.

Each of the six SFF members joining us for lunch that day had been wounded at least once sometime during the country's struggle against communism. The kidnapping of rich Salvadorans for ransom was in vogue at the time and each lunch guest had come in an armored car with a small army of bodyguards. The three days we were in Salvador were marked by torrential rains leaving over 300 Salvadorans dead from landslides and floods. The bodyguards who surrounded the main house in the pouring rain and fog made for an eerie sight.

In spite of the rains and the precarious political situation in El Salvador, I was able to see a little of the country. I even had time to buy Katie a little Salvadoran red and white jumper. Although she was just a baby, I figured that by the time it fit her it would be a rather unique conversation piece.

After lunch, our personal security team was reinforced by a second team of six bodyguards for the drive to the airport. The ride was considered especially dangerous at the time. Not only had the rains washed out many of the main roads, but some Catholic nuns had been ambushed and killed on the same road just a few weeks earlier.

The rain fell so hard that our driver had a most difficult time following the road. This was exacerbated by the condensation that built up inside due to the double thickness of bulletproof glass windows. We were following closely behind a Salvadoran military six-by-six truck used to carry troops. The rain, and the truck's canvas cover, prevented us from seeing if soldiers were actually riding inside. Both Ambassador Rizo and I were extremely nervous. It seemed like we would never reach the airport.

As we approached the exact spot where the Catholic nuns had been ambushed and shot, our car was hit hard by something. The roof above me crushed in, just missing my head by inches. Our driver slammed on his brakes and our car came to a sliding stop. I was thrown to the opposite side of the back seat, landing with my head on Alvaro's lap. As I brought my head up our driver and the bodyguard in the right front seat jumped from the car with weapons drawn. As Alvaro shouted, "We are going to die!" I could see the canvas on the back of the truck in front of us open up and armed, uniformed soldiers jumping to the ground.

The little dress I had purchased for Katie was lying underneath me on the seat. My first thoughts were that she would never wear the dress and I would never see Virginia or Katie again.

After a great deal of shouting and commotion, the guards opened our doors. We got out of the car. As we stood in the downpour, what had occurred became immediately evident. The rains had washed out the road. The rushing water coming down the hillside above us had uprooted a telephone pole which had fallen, full-force, on our vehicle. The Salvadoran soldiers in the truck had seen the pole fall and jumped from the truck to rescue us from what they knew had to be a crushed car full of mangled bodies. Luckily, the roof of the armored car had been reinforced with steel.

Now, here I was again in an armored car, surrounded by armed security police. Although I had exchanged the rain forest of El Salvador for the desert of Libya, I had no doubt that another adventure awaited me.

The sirens began to howl from the lead police cars. The noise was deafening. As we approached the first major intersection in a town called Zumarah, two of the lead police cars moved into position to block the progress of the cars approaching from our right and left. We sped through the intersection without slowing down. Almost like clockwork, two of the police cars from our rear sped past with sirens blaring and switched positions with the cars that had stopped in the intersection. I wondered how fast those cars would have to go to be able to catch up to our motorcade. This process was repeated at each intersection on our three hour ride to Tripoli.

The two-lane highway ran parallel with the Mediterranean Sea. Cars that happened to be in our path were nudged off the road by our advance men. One poor fellow meandering down the highway in a tiny little car was pushed off the road, through a small fence enclosing goats, sheep and chickens, by our crack security force. It was comical to see the dust, feathers and fence posts fly as we sped by. At 100 miles per hour the drive was treacherous.

United Nations Security Council Resolution 748 came into effect on April 15, 1992, and provided for a series of sanctions to be imposed upon Libya for its failure to turn over the two Libyans suspected of planting the bomb that blew up Pan Am 103. An air embargo was key in trying to bring Qadhafi to his knees. The resolution stated that all UN member states:

...deny permission to any aircraft to take off from, land in or overfly their territory if it is destined to land in or has taken off from the territory of Libya, unless the particular flight has been approved on grounds of significant humanitarian need by the Committee established by . . .

Libya told the UN Security Council that because of the international aircraft boycott, heavy road traffic led to 10,200 accidents since April 15, 1992. They resulted in the death of 1,622 people, serious injury and permanent disability of 4,220 others, slight injury of 3,124 people,

113

and destruction of more than 9,200 motor vehicles. I prayed that our Mercedes wouldn't be number 9,201!

The radio in our car began to crackle as I heard the familiar voice of Youssef shouting instructions in Arabic. Khaled responded briefly and turned to tell us that it was alright to open our black window curtains and enjoy the view of the Mediterranean. Our view thus far had been through the front window of the car and things brightened up considerably as we drew the curtains back.

Libya is in northern Africa. It lies on the coast of the Mediterranean Sea. The country is bordered by Egypt and Sudan on the east, Chad and Niger on the south and Algeria and Tunisia on the west. Tripoli, which was our destination, is Libya's capital and largest city. We could see the Mediterranean to the left and the vast, dry Sahara Desert, which covers most of Libya, to our right. We passed little villages named, Zuwarah, Sabratah and Az Zawiyah.

Libya has about 5 million people. About 80 per cent of them live along the Mediterranean coast or in the upland regions just south of the coast. About 70 percent of Libya's people live in urban areas. About 30 percent live in rural areas, mostly in villages or desert oases like the ones we were passing at great speed. Some nomads move with their sheep, goats and camels in search of pasture. We noticed many single family dwellings in the rural areas, with most people living in stone or mud-brick houses. Khaled told us that often families have a single room for all activities. Farm animals are the substance of life and live as well as some of the farmers who own them.

Most of the men we saw were wearing a loose cotton shirt and trousers covered by an outer cloak. They wore flat, brimless, tight-fitting caps. Women were wearing the traditional full-length robe. Khaled told us that some people in Libya's cities wore these garments to indicate their regard for traditional values and practices but that most city dwellers wore Western-style clothing.

Only the areas we were passing are inhabitable and useful for agriculture. Huge sand dunes make up most of the inland desert region of Libya. The Mediterranean Sea strongly influences the climate of the coastal region. The area has warm summers and mild winters. In January, temperatures in Tripoli average 52 degrees F. Tripoli's July temperatures average 81 degrees F. The coast receives more rain than the inland desert, about 16 inches annually. The desert climate is characterized by extreme high and low temperatures. Rainfall in the desert averages less than two inches each year.

Every now and then we could see sheep grazing on a desert oasis near a large sand dune. People were riding camels and shepherds were moving their goats or sheep down the sides of the road. After almost two hours of deafening sirens there was the sound of Youssef's voice on the radio again. Khaled acknowledged this message on the hand-held microphone and our motorcade slowed down as we entered a little village called Sabratah. Khaled said we were going to stop for water.

We pulled to a halt in front of a small store. Men, wearing their traditional garb, were sitting at small tables in front of the store in a sort of makeshift cafe. They were smoking their hooka pipes (bongs) and drinking what appeared to be goat's milk. They looked at us with great curiosity as we all got out of our cars to stretch our legs. Some of our guards and most of our drivers went into the store. My driver couldn't wait to light up a cigarette, having been confined in the same car with me for two hours. I am sure he was warned of my contempt for smoking and had obliged me accordingly.

I couldn't believe what I saw next. Congressman Carroll Hubbard was circulating between tables in the little outdoor cafe, handing out his business cards with the official gold seal of the United States Congress embossed on them. He shook each hand and gave a card with the greeting, "Hi! I'm Congressman Carroll Hubbard from Kentucky," just as he worked the crowd back home in eastern Kentucky. The mostly elderly Libyans looked with bewilderment, as they viewed the official looking cards and the fat man in the western business suit handing them out.

Hubbard was well known on Capitol Hill for giving business cards to people, no matter how many times he saw them during a given day. There were times when I would find 3 or 4 of Hubbard's cards, as I emptied my pockets when I returned home from a rough day in the Capitol.

He also loved to have his picture taken on the Capitol steps with a constituent or friend. The House photographers were sure to have plenty of film in their cameras when Hubbard was in town. A few days later you would find a large brown envelop in your mail with the franked congressional signature of Carroll Hubbard where the rest of us would place a stamp. The enclosed picture would have the inscription, "To my good friend Bill Chasey or Joe Blow, from Carroll Hubbard, MC, (Member of Congress), Kentucky. There have been many Christmases when I would receive 5 or more congressional calendars in the mail from you guessed it, "Your Good friend, Carroll Hubbard, MC, Kentucky."

The drivers and guards returned with grocery bags of bottled water under their arms. Three bottles were placed in each car as we climbed back into our caravan. The sirens began again as we peeled out of the little village, leaving behind a confused group of bong smokers in the dust as we headed east toward Tripoli.

As we entered Tripoli we saw large billboards with pictures of "The Leader," Col. Muammar al-Qadhafi, every few blocks. Tripoli looked like most North American and Western European cities. High-rise office and apartment buildings filled the downtown areas. Suburban areas seemed to have more spacious, single-family dwellings than those we had passed enroute to Tripoli. Expensive European automobiles were seen everywhere. There were no visible signs of poverty.

The lack of poverty was no surprise. Petroleum serves as the basis of the economy of Libya. It accounts for about 50 per cent of the value of Libya's total economic production and for almost all the country's export earnings.

Youssef had told us earlier in the day in Geneva that Col. Qadhafi planned to distribute half of Libya's oil income in cash grants to the people of Libya. Under his plan, each family would be given $7,000 to $10,000 beginning early in 1993.

We were also told by Debri that there was a severe economic crisis in Libya, resulting from the United Nations sanctions over the Lockerbie situation. I assumed the grants were intended to ease the pain of the economic embargo on the Libyan people. Qadhafi actually announced his grants scheme a week later on November 19th.

It was 8:00 P.M. and almost dark, as we pulled into the drive of the El Mahari Hotel, on Hotel El Mahari Road of El Fath, Tripoli. We were directly across the street from Tripoli Harbor, one of the most beautiful harbors I had ever seen. The harbor is the major route for all shipping into Tripoli and a large ferry boat was making its way through the harbor entrance as we entered the lobby of the hotel.

The El Mahari lobby came alive as our entourage entered. The bellboys that rushed to our cars to help us were obviously confused not to find luggage in the trunks. They

117

were, as we were, even more surprised to see the arsenal of machine guns, rocket launchers and various other heavy weaponry neatly arranged in the trunks of each car. Hotel guests standing in the lobby were caught off guard as we made our grand entrance. Most eyes focused on me with my California sun tan and blond hair, not often seen in Libya in recent years.

The lobby was modern and resembled most western hotels. We were escorted past the reception desk to the bank of elevators at the far end of the lobby. Several of our security guards picked up keys from the reception desk and joined us on the elevator. We were all taken into my suite and given a briefing on the hotel and the special features of each room.

In addition to the usual bedroom and living room, we were told that each suite had its own office, dining room, full kitchen and three baths. There were fresh flowers in all of the rooms and a large tray with fruit, cookies and cheeses was neatly placed on the living room table. Being a Muslim country there was no mini bar but the refrigerator was well stocked with juices and soft drinks.

We were told by Khaled that we would have about 15 minutes to freshen up before we should be in the lobby to be transported to the home of Youssef el Debri for dinner. The Hubbards were then taken to their suite on the top floor of the hotel and Gerrit was taken to his suite down the hall from mine to prepare for the evening's activities.

Youssef's home was a 10 minute ride from the hotel. It was in what appeared to be a wealthy neighborhood of large expensive homes. Youssef's house was distinguishable by the large security force stationed outside the front entry court yard. Armed guards in uniform were evident in all directions, and the addition of our security guards upon our arrival made for an armed camp in this quiet neighborhood.

We were escorted through a courtyard containing a swimming pool. I was amazed to see pieces of Roman ruins neatly situated around the yard and up the long path leading to the main entrance of the house. We were told by our escorts that the Romans conquered much of the region in 74 B.C., and ruled it as a province. To the Romans the Mediterranean was Mare Nostrum (Our Sea) and, on the southern shore, Roman Tripolitania developed over two centuries until the collapse of the Roman Empire.

On our tour, Khaled had told us that Leptis Magna, an hour's drive from Tripoli, surpasses any set of monuments in the Roman Empire, including Imperial Rome itself. Libya was the breadbasket of that empire, and Khaled pointed out to me and the members of our party that Libya's ancestors provided many of the best artists and craftsmen of Ancient Rome. Khaled said that he would take us to Leptis Magna if we had time on our way back to Jerba.

Youssef met us at the door with a warm greeting. He was anxious for us to come upstairs with him to meet his family. He introduced his wife, who was white skinned compared to Youssef. She was dressed in a western skirt and blouse and greeted us warmly to her home. His two daughters looked very much like Mrs. Debri and were obviously dressed up for our visit. They made every attempt to make us feel welcome. Youssef said that it had been many years since they had entertained Americans in their home and his family was very happy to do so. He thanked me with great enthusiasm for making this evening possible.

Islam is Libya's official religion. Almost all Libyans are Muslims and belong to the Sunni branch of Islam. As a matter of fact, the 1977 constitution ordered that all legislation must agree with Islamic Law. The Muslim law against the consumption of alcoholic beverages went unnoticed that evening. Youssef had a bar that would equal any in non-Muslim countries. Most of us drank red or white wine.

119

We became more at home with each other as the evening wore on. The house was well decorated and had all of the modern conveniences we have at home in La Jolla.

As we sat and made small talk we were joined by one of Youssef's closest Libyan friends, Salah El Fituri. Salah was President of Fitex, S.A., a Swiss Corporation located in Geneva. I later found out that this company was used by Youssef as a mechanism to do business with the West. They were into international trade, construction, resorts and banking. Salah lived in Geneva with his family. He traveled back and forth between Switzerland and Libya frequently.

He had left Geneva that morning using the route of most Libyans since the United Nations air embargo against Libya was instituted in April 1992. He had flown to Malta and transferred to a ferry boat which brought him into the Harbor of Tripoli. Salah was a very pleasant man I guessed to be forty-five years old. He spoke very good English with hardly an accent.

It was after 10:00 P.M. and I didn't think I could make it another minute unless we ate something. Mrs. Debri finally told us that dinner would be ready about midnight, which was their usual hour for dining. The Hubbards were very gracious, although I knew they were starving.

Youssef's daughter left the room to get something for me. She brought me a picture of herself and her horse. She told me that her father had told her about my daughter Katie and her love for horses. We had quite a conversation about horses in general and her riding specifically. She was a lovely young woman and I enjoyed my visit with her. I promised that I would bring Katie to Tripoli with me and they could ride together. The older daughter was very busy helping her mother in the kitchen and I didn't spend much time with her.

Mrs. Debri brought their young son in to meet us before he went to bed. He spoke very little English and was

120

quite shy. Youssef related the story of his son's reaction to the April 14, 1986, bombing of Libya by the United States. Some of the bombs landed fairly close to the Debri home. As a result his son had nightmares for months that followed. He would wake up and cry out, "Reagan is going to kill me, Reagan is going to kill me."

All Libyan children from 6 to 15 years of age are required to attend school. The free state education system provides six years of primary school and three years each of preparatory school and high school. About 10 per cent of the people attend one of Libya's five universities or attend school in another country. Youssef indicated that his older daughter would be attending Libya's largest university, Al-Fatah, in Tripoli

When dinner was finally served it was well worth the wait. Youssef had called ahead to his wife from Jerba and told her to prepare her best meal for his new friends from America, and she had.

The status of women in Libya has changed dramatically in the late 1900's. Women once received little or no education and were largely confined to the home. Today, they have the legal right to participate fully in Libyan society. Libyan women make up only about 10 per cent of the work force but this percentage is increasing as more women become educated. Youssef's wife was obviously well educated and had traveled extensively throughout the world, with the exception, of course, the United States of America.

We arrived back at the El Mahari at 2:30 A.M. after finishing dinner and saying our good-byes. It is the practice for at least the rich Libyans to eat late and sleep late. Youssef told us to sleep in and be ready to meet with Foreign Minister, Dr. Omar Muntassir, at 10:00 the next morning. Youssef said he would have his people pick us up a few minutes before 10:00.

121

Having gotten to know Youssef's disdain for promptness over the past couple of months, I doubted we would see him even close to the designated time.

Chapter Twelve

Recollections

The El Mahari Hotel lobby was deserted when we returned from dinner at Youssef's home. I wanted desperately to call Virginia in California, but I didn't want any records, including phone records, of my visit to Libya which might be disclosed at a later date. I kind of chuckled when I wondered if the El Mahari had ATT USA Direct. In all my years of traveling the world, this was the first night that I had been away from Virginia that we didn't communicate either by telephone or fax.

I knew that she would be worried about me and concerned that she hadn't heard from me. She wasn't overjoyed with my involvement with Libya, but she felt that I might be useful in bringing the Lockerbie situation to a logical conclusion. Virginia would be restless and awake most of the night checking the fax machine and voice mail. I hoped that she wouldn't try to call me at the Noga Hilton and find out that I wasn't in my room all night. I was sorry that I couldn't communicate with her, but I was sure that all communications from Libya to the U.S. were intercepted by the National Security Agency's (NSA) satellites and I wasn't about to take the chance.

I went directly to bed and had a most difficult time getting to sleep. The last time I looked at my watch, it was 3:30 A.M. I couldn't believe what happened next. I was startled out of a deep sleep by the sound of morning prayers coming from the loud speaker in the mosque outside and below my balcony window. It was barely light outside. I jumped out of bed to see if what I was hearing was real or the result of too much to eat and drink a few hours earlier.

123

It was real. My chances of sleeping longer were gone for the rest of the night.

I lay there for a while trying to collect my thoughts. I reviewed in my mind what I knew about Lockerbie and the circumstances that led to the indictment of the two Libyans. Youssef mentioned that he wanted me to meet these two men during my visit but I had no idea that it would actually happen. Could it be that they really were being framed to take the pressure off the Administrations of the American, English and French Governments, as Youssef had suggested to us on our flight to Jerba the previous day? As I lay there in the dark room my mind bounced back and forth between where I would get clean underwear and a tooth brush for the day's activities and who blew up Pan Am 103.

If Libya was really guilty, why would they go to all this trouble to try to open a new dialogue with the West? I decided to focus my thoughts on what I knew so that I could ask intelligent questions when we met with the Libyan Committee to Resolve the Lockerbie Dispute in a few hours.

All of the reading I had done about the circumstances leading up to the Lockerbie disaster seemed to lead investigators closer and closer to the indictment of agents of Syria and Iran. Some of the earliest books and articles written about Lockerbie didn't even mention Libya as a suspect nation. It wasn't until November 14, 1991, that U.S. and Scottish prosecutors released a twenty-nine page indictment charging two Libyan men with carrying out the attack. This was almost three years after the Boeing 747 was blown out of the sky.

Named in the indictment were Lamen Khalifa Fhimah, thirty-nine, whom prosecutors said had used his job as an airline employee to store Semtex explosives at the

Malta airport, and Abdel Basset Ali Mohammed al-Megrahi, fifty-five, who had been identified by a shopkeeper in Malta as the man who bought an assortment of clothing found at the crash scene from Mary's House, a clothing store on Malta. The indictment stated that both men were agents of the Libyan intelligence service, Jamahiriya Security Organization (JSO), the Organization headed by Youssef Debri. Prosecutors charged that the Libyan government had provided them with Semtex high explosive and detonators and that other conspirators, not named in the indictment, also were involved.

It was late in 1990 when reports began to surface implicating Libya in the Flight 103 attack. Many of those with a special interest in the case viewed this turn of events with skepticism. Most feared the investigation was being forced in a direction that better suited the Bush Administration. Details implicating Libya seemed to coincidentally emerge at a time when the President was building a coalition against Iraq, prior to the war in the Persian Gulf.

The United States and Britain wanted Syria to join the U.S. led alliance against Iraq, after Iraqi leader Saddam Hussein invaded Kuwait in 1990. A cornerstone of the alliance against Iraq was Syria, home of Ahmed Jibril and headquarters of his Popular Front for the Liberation of Palestine-General Command (PFLP-GC). The PFLP-GC had been the number-one suspect in the Lockerbie bombing prior to 1990. All of a sudden the heat was taken off the PFLP-GC and Iran in the investigation.

There were also reports that U.S. and British authorities overlooked the possible Syrian and Iranian connection to the bombing in return for the 1991 release of Britain's Terry Waite and America's Thomas Sutherland who had been held by pro-Iranian forces. Waite was released soon after Foreign Secretary Douglas Hurd repeated in the House of Commons that Syria was not involved in the Lockerbie bombing. Shortly thereafter, Sutherland was also released.

I called the front desk of the El Mahari and requested shaving gear and a toothbrush, which they quickly provided. I dressed in my day-old clothes and went down to the lobby for breakfast and a quick walk around Tripoli Harbor. The lobby was full of Germans who had entered Libya illegally, against UN sanctions, to make what I suspected was some major oil deal. I had been told by Youssef the night before that there were as many as 5,000 Americans also living in Libya illegally. They were working on the oil rigs left behind by American companies when they were forced to leave Libya. I listened from afar at breakfast while two Americans engaged a Libyan in a business discussion. I was also very aware of two Libyan men sitting nearby. They seemed to have a special interest in me, and my actions.

The hotel staff was very friendly. They went out of their way to greet me as I passed through the hotel lobby and out the front door. I noticed that the two men who had been so interested in me at the restaurant left the hotel just after I did. The day was beautiful and the water in the harbor was a sparkling blue green color. The temperature was in the 70's. The air was clean and fresh, in spite of the cars racing past me on the harbor-side drive. The two men following me immediately split tracks after leaving the hotel. One fell in place just behind me at about 50 yards and the other about 100 yards behind me, but on the opposite side of the street. When I stopped, they stopped, either looking in a store window, lighting a cigarette or propping a leg up on the sea wall to view the large ferry boat just passing through the breakwater leading into the harbor.

I hoped that they were part of Youssef's Libyan undercover Jamahiriya Security Organization and not the CIA. I wondered if their purpose in following me was to gather intelligence or to be sure that nothing happened to me in their country. Later on Youssef told me that none of his agents were assigned to follow me that morning.

I returned to the hotel with the two agents close on my heels, just in time to see the Hubbards getting off the lobby elevator. They were on their way to breakfast and asked if I would join them for coffee. We began to discuss what the day held for us. We were quite open in our discussion until one of the men tailing me earlier came and sat at the next table. I could see his partner on a lobby telephone just outside the restaurant entrance. We decided to talk later in a more secure environment.

Chapter Thirteen

Business in Tripoli

Youssef was at the wheel of his personal Mercedes as he drove up in front of the hotel on mean Libyan time, which is always a half hour late. Youssef asked me to ride with him. He asked the Hubbards and Gerrit to ride in the black Mercedes limo that was just pulling up behind his car. The usual contingent of JSO personnel was close at hand: three separate unmarked police cars, one in front of Youssef's car and two behind the limo. The annoying sirens that guided our path the night before were silent as we finally made our way to our meeting with the Libyan Foreign Minister.

It was a short drive to the headquarters of the Foreign Ministry. Youssef had arranged for the two of us to drive together so that we could talk in the strictest confidence. Much to my shock, he told me that he had arranged for me to meet with the two Libyan suspects indicted by the United States and Scotland for the 1988 bombing of Pan Am 103. He asked me not to discuss this meeting with the Hubbards or Gerrit or, for that matter, anyone else.

The two men, Abdel Basset Ali Mohammed al-Megrahi and Lamen Khalifa Fhimah, were under house arrest in Tripoli. Youssef said that the two suspects had not been interviewed about the Lockerbie disaster other than by their Libyan and Western lawyers. Youssef said, "If you are going to lobby for them in Washington, you should get to know them personally. I want you to look them in the eye and ask them if they did it." He wasn't quite sure how he would arrange the meeting without the others finding out but assured me that it would occur before I left Libya.

I wondered why the Libyans were placing so much trust in me. I felt a surge of excitement as I pondered a visit with these men—the "terrorists" allegedly responsible for murdering hundreds of people and responsible for holding normalized relations between Libya and the West at bay for the past year.

As we pulled into the driveway of the Libyan Foreign Ministry there were small groups of people staring at us from the windows of what appeared to be an office building directly adjacent to the Ministry building. I was quite uncomfortable with their watching our arrival and wondered how they knew we were coming. I asked Youssef to drive up as close to the front door as possible so that we could exit our cars without our faces being exposed to the curious onlookers. He obliged. I made a quick, unrecognized exit from the car, moving directly into the Ministry Building. I waited anxiously for Congressman Hubbard to follow my lead.

Wonders never cease! I was aghast as I saw Congressman Carroll Hubbard of Mayfield, Kentucky slowly open the back door of his limo, deliberately turn to face the office building and begin waving to the crowd of people in the windows above. It reminded me of an arrival ceremony for a head of state at the United States Capitol, or the arrival of a celebrated starlet at the Academy Award Ceremonies in Hollywood. How would his act play on the hidden CIA cameras that I knew had to be recording all arrivals at this strategic government facility?

This was the same Carroll Hubbard that would tell *The Washington Post* a little over a year later, on December 11, 1993, that he traveled to Libya with me and met with the Libyan leader, Col. Muammar Qadhafi, in the course of his work as an FBI informer. How proud the FBI must have been of Hubbard's performance if, by any stretch of the imagination, his story were true.

I couldn't hide my anger toward Hubbard as he joined me in the entrance lobby of the Ministry. I reminded him of our agreement to avoid all public exposure during our stay in Libya. He laughed and said in true Washington political style, "You never know when you might run into a voter from the 1st District of Kentucky, Ha-Ha!"

We were graciously escorted into the office of Libyan Foreign Minister Omar Mustafa al-Muntassir. The small office reeked of cigar smoke. Dr. Muntassir sat behind a large, disorganized, governmental-issue brown desk, piled high with papers and reports. He was a serious looking man, who appeared to be in his fifties. He was rather round and wore large horned-rimmed glasses. A large, unlighted cigar protruded from his mouth as he stood to greet us.

A conference table extended away from the desk at a right angle so that he could remain seated behind his desk while participating in a group discussion with those sitting at the conference table. There were just enough chairs to seat the Hubbards, Gerrit, Youssef, myself and the Libyan Ambassador to Tunisia. There was also a chair for a thin middle-aged gentleman I assumed to be Dr. Muntassir's personal assistant.

After a warm welcome, Dr. Muntassir lit his cigar and eased back in his swivel chair. "To begin," he said in perfect English, "I want to thank you for your bravery in coming to Libya. Looking directly at Carroll, he said, "You are the first American government official to visit here in many years and the first since the Lockerbie indictments. I know that you have all come at great personal risk and I want to express my thanks and the thanks of our leader, Col. Qadhafi." I could see that Mrs. Hubbard was a bit uncomfortable with Omar's reference to personal risk.

He looked directly at me and said, "I have heard a great deal about you Dr. Chasey. Youssef has gotten to know you and has checked you out carefully." *(I wasn't sure I liked the "checking out" part.)* "We have a lot in common," he continued. "We both come from academic backgrounds. I studied at the University of Michigan.

"I love the States and hope to be in New York in a week or so. That is, if I can get a visa from your government. I understand that you can make things happen in Washington. You know the right people. The fact that you brought a sitting Congressman to Libya is very impressive. I thank you on behalf of my fellow countrymen and Col. Qadhafi for bringing Congressman and Mrs. Hubbard to meet with me. I trust good things will occur from our meeting here today.

"Our Leader, Col. Qadhafi, established The Committee to Resolve the Lockerbie Dispute. I am the Chairman of the Committee and Youssef Debri and our Ambassador to Tunisia are members of the Committee. We are anxious to discuss the Lockerbie incident with you in hopes that you will be able to help us open a dialogue with the United States Congress and your President-elect, Bill Clinton. We look forward to the new Clinton Administration with great optimism. The Libyan people are very happy with your President-Elect. We watched with great interest the results of your elections. We think that there is an opportunity for us to reestablish normal relations with your new President."

He reached over and picked up a sheet of paper that looked, from where I sat, to be a photocopy of a news clipping. He read a few lines of the paper to us. "On September 17, 1992, Clinton said, if elected he would make sure that all questions regarding Syrian and Iranian involvement in the Pan Am 103 tragedy are addressed and fully answered. I hope that you, Mr. Hubbard, and you, Mr. Chasey, can be of help in making this happen."

I thanked Minister Muntassir for his hospitality. I told him that we were looking forward to our discussions concerning U.S./Libyan relations, and the Lockerbie situation.

I thanked him for his generous comments about me and with tongue in cheek, I also thanked Youssef for his insightful, and accurate description of me to Omar.

Congressman Hubbard expressed his interest in doing what he could to help in the Lockerbie stalemate. He apologized that he wasn't a member of the Foreign Affairs or the Intelligence Committees that had jurisdiction over the Libyan situation. He stated that, "Congressman Lee Hamilton, the new Chairman of the House Foreign Affairs Committee is my very good friend, and I will be happy to relate our discussions to him when I return to Washington. Lee is from Indiana, and I am from Kentucky, but our districts adjoin each other. We fly back and forth to Washington together a lot. If you want me to give him a letter or something like that, you can count on me. We are here to help."

Our discussion quickly turned to an historical discussion of U.S./Libyan political relations. We were certainly outclassed during this discussion by the Members of the Committee to Resolve the Lockerbie Dispute. The Libyans knew times, dates and places for events that, in some cases, I had not heard of previously.

Dr. Muntassir provided us with a large, green magazine sized publication entitled, *The Hostile and Terrorist Actions Carried Out By The US Administration Against The Arab People Of Libya*. This large, four page publication listed 47 hostile acts by the United States against Libya between 1972 and 1991. (I have drawn heavily from the publication when researching this story and when I needed to fill in many details while writing this book.)

At that point, the conversation could have digressed into a nasty debate. But the Libyans presented their case very effectively and we were totally unarmed to retort logically. We mostly listened to the Foreign Minister. It was as

133

if he had all these facts pent up inside him for years, just waiting for right opportunity to let them out.

I didn't want to believe what I was hearing. After all, I am the right wing conservative who joined the United States Marine Corps when I was 18 years old. *My country, right or wrong*—had always been my motto.

The Chasey Family in one of our favorite spots for Christmas 1994, Vail, Colorado. This picture was taken on the sixth anniversary of the Lockerbie bombing.

To Bill Chasey
With best wishes,
Marilyn Quayle

Vice-President and Mrs. Quayle greet me at a reception at the
Vice-President's Home.

To Bill
Thanks for
all you have
done for
the
Dem.
Party.
Love.
Fritz

I greet Vice-President Walter Mondale in the U.S. Capitol. U.S. Secret
Service Agent Jim Varey is in the foreground.

We are joined by our good friends Joanne and Jack Kemp. San Diego
Congressman Bill Lowery is on the right.

Me as a young Marine Corps First
Lieutonant.

Senator Larry Pressler, Repulican of South Dakota, addresses a fund-raiser we hosted for him in our La Jolla home.

Senate Republican Whip Alan Simpson of Wyoming (center) introduces Senator Steve Symms of Idaho to a fund-raising audience at our home in La Jolla. Ann Simpson is in the center.

Senator Larry Pressler and I stand in front of the Costa Rican flag during a series of meetings in San Jose, Costa Rica.

For Bill Chase, with very best regards from his friend, Jim Wright 4/12/88

I am caught between two Speakers: Speaker of the California Assembly, Willie Brown, and Speaker of the U.S. House of Representatives, Jim Wright. That's my faithful driver, Paul Williams, on the right.

Me with Reagan close friend and former U.S. Attorney General, Edwin Meese.

I took this Congressional Delegation to Costa Rica where we met with President Oscar Arias. From left to right: Myself, Augustin Penon (Arias' Brother-in-law), Congressman Mickey Edwards, Congressman Bill Lowery, President Arias, Congressman Jerry Lewis and Carlos Marin of National University. President Arias gave a two hour briefing on his Central American Peace Plan for which he would be awarded the Nobel Peace Prize the next year.

The Chasey Family all dressed up for the Bush Inaugural Ball.

Dr. Robert Schuller was a big hit on Capitol Hill. My driver, Paul Williams, is on the left.

A little time with President George Bush during an official visit to San Diego.

Foreign Agent 4221 in Geneva. The Jet d'Eau
is in the background.

The winners of the Cap Antibes tennis tournament in Southern France: David Sanbar, in left foreground, and Queen Farah, fourth from the left. Host Roger Edde is the fellow in the middle with the moustache and Alice Edde is in the center.

A not very famous (at the time) Congressman Newt Gingrich stops by a reception in the U.S. Capitol I put on for my client, the Indian Embassy.

This was the picture I gave to Libyan Chief of National Security, Youssef Debri.

Me with President Reagan at the White House at a thank you lunch for his 1980 campaign staff.

The countryside of El Salvador as seen from the door of our Alouette helicopter. That's my machine gun, which was our first line of defense on our reconnaissance mission.

The First Lady of El Salvador, Mrs. Margarita Cristiani, presents Virginia and me with a silver tray for helping the amputee population of El Salvador through our Third World Prosthetic Foundation.

Bud Smith of Texas (on the right) joins me in a discussion with Salvadoran President Alfredo Cristiani in San Salvador. We contributed 1,000 prosthetic devices to the victims of war in that country.

A group of Salvadoran Army amputees waiting to be fitted with new legs. After being fitted with a device, they were able to stand— and then walk away on their own.

Congressman Carroll Hubbard and I on the Capitol steps. Capitol photographers were sure to have plenty of film when Hubbard was on the Hill.

Congressman Carroll Hubbard with the Chasey Family in 1989. Hubbard was the most photographed Member of the U.S. House of Representatives.

This picture was taken at my meeting with
Muammar Qadhafi in Tripoli, Libya.

The Libyan Leader,
Muammar Qadhafi
signs a copy of his
Green Book. The
fellow to the left is
Gerrit P. Van de
Bovenkamp,
President of ICM.

Qadhafi gives me a
copy of his *Green
Book* as a gift.
Gerrit waits to have
his copy signed.

My friend, Congressman Merv Dymally, is greeted at a reception I gave in the U.S. Capitol for my client, the Embassy of India.

Sergeant-at-Arms Jack Russ, on the right, sees that Prime Minister Benazir Bhutto of Pakistan meets two of my Indian clients prior to her address to a Joint Session of Congress. I am standing in the rear.

Virginia and I greet Barbara Bush in the U.S. Capitol. Sergeant-at-Arms Jack Russ is to the right.

We joined the Quayles at a reception at the Vice-President's Residence.

Virginia and I hosted U.S. Senator Pete Wilson for a fund-raiser in our La Jolla home. Pete moved on to become Governor of California.

A little time with, then, U.S. House of Representaives Majority Leader, Dick Gephardt, in California.

Chapter Fourteen

Introspection

I began to reflect on how the United States could find itself in this standoff with Libya—the most powerful nation in the world at loggerheads with this tiny North-African state of five million people. Was there a real likelihood of a Lockerbie cover-up? I wasn't ready to believe all I was hearing from Omar, but I suspected that there was probably *some* truth in what he was saying. It wouldn't be the first time that U.S. Officials had taken us down a long, winding international primrose path, only to find that there was no way back.

Virginia and I had made a thoughtful decision eleven years before not to make Washington, D.C., our permanent home. (Thus my weekly commute between California and D.C.) We would raise Katie in the world outside of the Washington Beltway. We didn't like the transient lifestyle which made Washington a stopover duty station for people on their way to bigger and better things. There is no accountability when you serve for two or three years in a particular position and then move on. We really disliked the temporary nature of Washington where friendships are fleeting and short-lived. It was Harry Truman who once said, "If you want a friend in Washington, buy a dog."

More importantly, Washington has become a city of overload. The government has grown all out of proportion to what the framers of the Constitution had in mind. Washington has usurped more and more of the responsibilities—and authority—reserved for the States. In the process, government has grown and work loads of employees have exacerbated. Under a deluge of mounting regulations and paperwork, elected officials have not only lost control of their own lives, but also control of the lives of the thousands of staff members hired to relieve some of the burden of their labor.

Unfortunately, over the past twenty-plus years, I have observed, first hand, the emergence of a new power structure in our nation's capitol which I call the *unelected second-tier.* It would come as little surprise to me if a cover-up of the Lockerbie situation got its start with a small lie by one of these second-tier officials which then quickly grew into an international incident, the ever expanding tale being passed on to one, two or more of the official's successors. To believe that this could happen one just needs to recall the elaborate cover-ups designed by one maverick Marine Lt. Colonel by the name of Oliver North, over Iran. Why not Lockerbie and Libya?

The American people have gotten a small taste of what this group can do from the painful revelations emanating from some well-known scandals like Watergate, Irangate and, most recently, Whitewatergate. There just isn't enough time in the day for elected first-tier people like the President of the United States and Members of the United States Congress to wield appropriate oversight control over their unelected second-tier appointees. These appointees, for the most part, seek and secure government jobs with grandiose titles and prestige just to have their professional resume tickets "punched" by serving a couple of years in lofty positions. An all too frequent scenario is that an unelected official will make a mistake and, rather than face up to his error, will cover up his actions knowing that he will shortly leave government.

Many of the second-tier appointees of the Reagan and Bush Administrations were less than honest with the American people when it came to foreign policy matters. Some were found out and forced to pay their price to society. I have no doubt that there were just as many, or more, guilty of similar crimes and blunders who were never found out. Many of the Reagan and Bush appointees were in positions of authority and deeply involved in other conspiracies and cover-ups when, in 1986, the United States bombed Libya. Some of the same people were in power when, in 1991, the blame for Lockerbie was conveniently shifted from Syria and Iran to Libya

What made me think that they hadn't orchestrated a very successful U.S. disinformation program aimed at Libya? Was it beyond them, or others like them in the White House, to lie to the world about Libya, Qadhafi and Lockerbie?

While White House appointees have grown more powerful, so have congressional staffs. I have observed over the years how the political process on Capitol Hill has changed. Mostly due to the increase in work load, more and more power has shifted from the elected Members of Congress to their unelected second-tier. The day of the citizen legislator has disappeared. Members of Congress, no matter how much talk there is about term limits, have become full-time, professional legislators, with enormous support staffs of bright young people, constantly looking for ways to better serve their masters.

As knowledge doubles every two years, so does the work load of the elected Washington politician. Since information is power, staff members who have the information have become increasingly more powerful in the corridors of the United States Congress. The unelected staff have become a major political force because elected officials just don't have the time nor the energy to devote to the voluminous data required to function in Washington.

Over the past twenty years of my service on Capitol Hill (10 Congresses), more than 200,000 bills have been introduced in the U.S. House of Representatives—more than 20,000 bills introduced during each two-year term! Only slightly more than ten percent have been reported from the twenty-two standing committees to the House floor. Of the 20,000 introduced, the average number that become law per Congress is under five percent.

Each bill introduced, whether passed or not, has a sponsor, a constituency and a special interest group, that requires attention by the various congressional offices. It is obvious that the elected Members cannot deal with each bill, each issue and each person who calls or writes during the course of a Washington business day. The responsibility for dealing with this vast work load falls on the shoulders of the 35,000 Capitol Hill Staff members, referred to as "Staffers" or "Hillies."

Because of this immense work overload, staff members often find themselves making major decisions that were previously reserved for our elected representatives. I have spent most of my waking hours positioned outside the doors of either the House or Senate Chambers. I have seen it all. When you are as visible as I am in the U.S. Capitol, Members and staff regard me as part of their team, and often speak and act openly in my presence, with a total disregard for secrecy or my reactions.

I can't count the number of times I have watched a staff member, not much more than 25 years old, brief a senior U.S. Senator on the merits of a floor speech or an upcoming vote as together they ride on the Senate's underground subway to the Senate Chamber. Or, the number of times I have heard a staffer yell, "Vote aye, you are for this!" as the Senator rushes from the "Senators Only" elevator to the Senate floor to record his vote within the fifteen minute time limit permitted under Senate rules.

Chapter Fifteen

The Briefing Continues

Our discussion with the Libyan Committee to Resolve the Lockerbie Dispute continued for more than three hours. Omar's initial remarks dealt with some early attempts by the United States to assist his government. Later he switched to what he termed the history of U.S. aggression against Libya. He often referred to his notes and a copy of the Green Magazine he had given us. (I have researched the various points and added to the information presented by Omar. Geoff Simons' book, *Libya: The Struggle for Survival*, was most helpful.)

When Qadhafi assumed power in Libya in 1969, he enjoyed U.S. support. He was allowed to purchase U.S. and other western weapons. The U.S. was responsible for warning Qadhafi of several coup attempts. However, Qadhafi turned out not to be a pliant puppet of the West. The U.S had been prepared to offer Qadhafi a measure of protection immediately after the fall of the Idris monarchy but it seems that Qadhafi paid no attention to this offer in organizing his domestic and foreign plans.

For a brief period after the fall of the pro-West Idris monarchy in Libya there were elements in the U.S. administration who saw Qadhafi as a nationalist and anti-Communist and, as such, a force that could be viewed with sympathy. The U.S. and Western European intelligence services protected Qadhafi from his enemies and helped him to remain in power. In the early days of the Libyan Revolution some factions in Washington were pleased to note that Qadhafi was taking a number of anti-Soviet and anti-Communist actions.

139

In his early speeches he criticized the Soviet Union for being a self-proclaimed atheistic society. He had condemned the involvement of the Soviets in the 1971 Indo-Pakistan war as signaling "Soviet imperialist designs in the area." He was also critical of the 1972 Soviet/Iraqi treaty, even though Qadhafi himself had signed a trade and technical treaty with the Soviet Union a short time earlier. The U.S. was pleased that Qadhafi had applauded Anwar Sadat's expulsion of Soviet military forces from Egypt in July of 1972. There were even signs in these early days of CIA protection of Qadhafi's regime and person.

The evident U.S. protection of Qadhafi was demonstrated when splits began to appear in the Revolutionary Command Council (RCC) soon after the fall of the Monarchy. Two Libyan colonels, late appointees to the RCC, were arrested after the U.S. had warned Qadhafi that they were plotting against him. The CIA warned Qadhafi that the two men, Adam al-Hawaz and Ahmed Musa, pro-Western officers, could not be trusted.

Around the same time an Arabic translation of a Soviet book highly critical of Islam began circulating in Tripoli. The Soviets did not deny the book's authenticity but that it had only been intended for use in the Soviet Union.

Qadhafi had sent aircraft to Pakistan to counter the Soviet support for India in the 1971 war. He had forced down a plane over Libya carrying Communist coup plotters against President Numeiri of the Sudan. They were subsequently hanged in Khartoum. Such events combined to create the impression that Qadhafi was prepared to conspire with U.S. schemes in the region. To some limited extent, the impression was accurate.

Qadhafi himself banned all political parties and prohibited all political meetings between socialists, communists and other groups hostile to the United States. This all had a pleasant ring to Washington. Perhaps Qadhafi was a bit wild in his support for the Palestinians and terrorists elsewhere but there were influential factions in Washington prepared to see Qadhafi's authoritarian anti-Communism as one of the blessings of the area. In such circumstances it was surely worth protecting Qadhafi from attempted *coups* in his own country.

The Libyan leader was also greatly assisted by CIA operatives and a series of "free enterprise" initiatives that eventually incurred the wrath of Washington. These initiatives relied upon the relationship between the CIA and Nugan Hand Bank, based in Sydney, Australia. The bank had been an employer of several retired CIA agents and was heavily involved in drug trafficking. The Nugan Hand Bank had a branch conveniently located in Libya. This operation became involved with a network of former CIA agents run by Edwin Wilson. Formerly with the CIA, Wilson prospered in the arms business in the private sector. Between June and September, 1976, Ed Wilson supplied Libya with thousands of CIA-designated bomb timers and in excess of twenty-one tons of Composition C-4, the most powerful nonnuclear explosive in America's arsenal.

Wilson also recruited U.S. Green Berets to train Libyan commandos. He is even said to have arranged assassinations in various countries for Qadhafi. The CIA was informed of Wilson's activities by a CIA employee, Kevin Mulcahy, but Theodore Shackley, then CIA Deputy Director of Clandestine Services and an old friend of Wilson's, blocked an internal investigation. In such a fashion the CIA, against policy thrusts of other departments of the U.S. administration, protected Qadhafi and sanctioned his acquisition of the accouterments of modern terrorism.

In April, 1977, *The Washington Post* publicized Wilson's activities and commented that, "he may have had contact with one or more current CIA employees." The article stimulated the new CIA Director, Admiral Stansfield Turner, into launching his own inquiry, which in due course led to the transfer of the high-ranking Thomas Clines and Theodore Shackley to lower-grade jobs. Soon afterward Clines resigned from the CIA, borrowed a half million dollars from Wilson to create his own company and won a $71 million contract with Egypt for the delivery of arms. Shackley also resigned to become a consultant. Wilson himself was eventually convicted of supplying Qadhafi with explosives, timing devices and military training.

Elements in Washington flirted with the idea that Qadhafi could be promoted as a useful anti-Communist tool. During this time, some small quantities of military hardware were exported by the U.S. Government to Libya. In 1970 we supplied eight Lockheed C-130 Hercules aircraft. In 1978 Libya received a Bell-121 helicopter, and in 1981 two, C-130 Hercules aircraft.

Omar continued his discourse in true academic style, "Our countries first came into conflict in 1801 when your country refused to increase payments to Tripoli for protection against pirate raids." Trade between Europe and North Africa (the Barbary states) was flourishing during that time.

The discussion continued with each Libyan adding his own bits and pieces of information about the historic plight of Libya against the powerful United States Government.

The Barbary States derived a substantial income from their pirate ships. The activities of the pirates were supported by local rulers, who provided political support and an effective market for the pirate loot. It was difficult to defeat the pirates in naval confrontations since they were relatively close to their own bases and in any case enjoyed the protection of the local tribal leaders.

The other option was for traders to pay protection money. President John Adams began paying annual pay-

ments of $18,000 to the local rulers in North Africa to guar-
antee immunity for U.S. merchant ships. The payments
soon increased to $250,000. When Thomas Jefferson be-
came President he objected to having to pay protection
money to pirates. Jefferson sent a fleet of U.S. ships to
engage the Barbary pirates in 1804. The U.S. ships failed
in their efforts to blockade Tripoli Harbor and the rest of
the Libyan coast. The U.S. frigate Philadelphia hit a shoal
and the ship and crew were captured by the Libyans.

*The discussion brought to mind my Marine Corps his-
tory, so well taught to me by Captain Bob Mason during
my Officer Training Program, at The Basic School in Quan-
tico, Virginia, thirty years ago.*

*I remembered now that it was a Marine Corps com-
mando raid led by Lieutenant Stephen Decatur that succeeded in infiltrating the harbor at Tripoli and blowing up
the Philadelphia, so rendering it unusable by the Libyans
as a gunship guarding the harbor. This raid inspired the
inclusion of the words "to the Shores of Tripoli" in the
Marine Corps Hymn.*

*My walk earlier that morning around Tripoli Harbor
with the two unknown Agents on my tail, gave a new meaning to the words, "to the Shores of Tripoli," to this former
Marine.*

*In the end, the U.S. ended up paying $60,000 ransom
for the crew of the Philadelphia. The pirates continued to
operate off the Barbary coast, and all U.S. military operations in the area were stopped.*

Chapter Sixteen

More History

In 1977 the U.S. Government learned about a Libyan-supported assassination plot against Herman Frederick Eilts, the U.S. Ambassador in Cairo. Eilts was working with Henry Kissinger on Anwar Sadat's ground-breaking shift to collaboration with the United States. Qadhafi was upset at what he saw as a betrayal of the Arab cause.

One theory was that a mole in Qadhafi's terrorist organization had learned of the assassination plans and informed Washington. President Carter thereupon sent a personal letter to Qadhafi informing him that he knew of the plot and offering details to substantiate the claim. It was hoped that this communication would be enough to thwart the scheme. For a while Qadhafi hesitated. He then protested that the charge was absurd; there was no such plot; the accused Libyans were innocent, and Qadhafi himself was obviously the victim of disinformation. Whatever the truth, "Operation Eilts" never got off the ground, but it served to establish the framework within which U.S./Libyan relations would be conducted in the years ahead.

In March, 1978, the Libyan Foreign Liaison Bureau launched a series of "people to people" visits which it hoped would improve the U.S./Libyan diplomatic climate. Qadhafi was particularly keen to secure the granting of U.S. export licenses for Boeing 727's, which the American government insisted had military potential. It was these circumstances that led to the Billy Carter Hearings and to President Carter's declaration of policy differences with Libya.

The Libyan Bureau had contacted President Carter's brother, Billy, in the hope that his opinions would carry weight with the Carter Administration. The contact was made via a circuitous route by the former Libyan Ambassador to Italy, Jabril Shalouf, who had worked at cultivating Billy's business partners.

Billy naively accepted an invitation to Libya, having been told that such a visit would be useful to his own business ventures. In January, 1979, he hosted Libyan dancers in Georgia and established the Libyan Arab Friendship Society. At the same time, by chance, the U.S. administration decided to issue export licenses for the Boeing 727's.

In November, 1979, the Libyan government attempted to influence the Iranian authorities into releasing the U.S. hostages in Teheran. It was an effort to patch up relations with the United States. The attempt failed and relations between Libya and the United States went into a steep decline. One key factor was the burning of the U.S. embassy in Tripoli on December 2nd, a reaction to the U.S. decision to freeze Iranian assets.

Omar failed to mention that, at that time, Qadhafi was doing all he could to help destabilize U.S. foreign policy efforts in Central America, Africa and Asia. I made no issue of Omar's failed memory.

Carter decided that Qadhafi could not be trusted. At the beginning of 1980 he wrote:

> There are few governments in the world with which we have more sharp and frequent policy differences than Libya. Libya has steadfastly oppressed our efforts to reach and carry out the Camp David Accords between Israel, Egypt and the United States, signed in 1978 and 1979. We have strongly differing attitudes toward the PLO and the support of terrorism.

On May 7, 1980, Washington expelled members of the Libyan People's Bureau (Embassy) on the grounds that Libya had been persecuting dissident Libyan students. In August of 1980, Washington announced—as an obviously provocative act—that it intended to hold Sixth Fleet exercises in the Gulf of Sirte, which Libya claimed as sovereign waters. However, one month later, in September, the exercises began. The fleet was ordered to stay outside the zone claimed by Libya. A U.S. C-135 electronic surveillance plane flying at the edge of Libyan airspace, escorted by F-14 fighters, was confronted by Libyan jets twice in one week. The aim of these exercises was to send a clear warning to Qadhafi about his aggressive behavior, without starting a military conflict.

When Ronald Reagan took over the White House in January of 1981 (which may not have happened had Qadhafi been able to secure the release of the U.S. Hostages), the relations between Libya and the United States, already on the slide, worsened still more.

Washington was already smarting from a number of foreign-policy reverses: the humiliating failure of our helicopter rescue mission in the Salt desert; the fall of the Shah of Iran; the collapse of the Somoza dictatorship in Nicaragua; the burning of the U.S. embassy in Pakistan; and a pro-Soviet coup in Afghanistan, followed by an invasion by Soviet troops. Ronald Reagan came to the White House in an atmosphere of chauvinism and militancy, determined to ensure that the United States walked tall again.

Omar seemed to grow angry as he delivered this history lesson to us.

The scene was set for a dramatic reassertion of the global authority of the U.S., which in practice meant no less than bullying weaker nations into acquiescence when confronted with American demands. A key goal of our foreign policy in the 1980's was to establish American dominance over the developing countries and to demonstrate the unambiguous power of the U.S. over the Third World.

At the start of the Reagan Presidency this may have seemed a daunting task given the existence of a still powerful Soviet Union, prepared to fund anti-West subversion. One of Reagan's first tasks was to launch a campaign against Soviet-sponsored terrorism. At the same time Qadhafi came in for special attention as a pawn of the Soviets.

Libya was dubbed "a base for Soviet subversion," and Qadhafi, "the most dangerous man in the world." Psychological pressure was put on Qadhafi by spreading rumors about assassination attempts against the Libyan leader. Provocative naval maneuvers were begun in March, 1981, off the coast of Libya.

This time the Sixth Fleet moved within the disputed Gulf of Sirte. For a period of four days exercises were conducted by two U.S. aircraft carriers, ten other ships and several squadrons of carrier based F-14 aircraft. The Libyans took care to avoid a military confrontation.

Next, Washington tightened the noose around Libya by promising to fund anti-Qadhafi forces in Africa. On July 8, 1981, Chester Crocker, the Assistant Secretary of State for African Affairs, declared to Congress that the U.S. government would provide arms for African opponents of Libya "to help those who see the problem as we see it."

The U.S. administration moved to supply arms to factions along Libya's borders that could be relied upon to present a military threat to Qadhafi. Thus Washington announced its willingness to provide Tunisia with fifty-four M-60 tanks. Frank Carlucci, the Deputy Defense Secretary, visited Algeria to whip up anti-Qadhafi feelings and offered to supply C-130 transport aircraft for the Algerian Air Force. American strategists also speculated on how the U.S. might take over the Libyan oil fields, observing

148

that it would be preferable to assume control of Qadhafi's oil resources than to take over the oil fields in the Gulf.

The mounting U.S. hostility toward Libya also had a broader purpose. Qadhafi, it was widely assumed, had funded anti-American subversive groups throughout the world, so any destabilization policy directed at the Libyan government would indirectly help American client states across the globe.

The U.S. administration had already witnessed the fall of Anastasio Garcia Somoza in Nicaragua and the Shah in Iran. To attack Libya would be seen as a worthwhile demonstration of Washington's commitment to surviving U.S. puppets. With a more robust government in Washington it would be harder, so the argument ran, for Qadhafi to encourage the collapse of unpopular pro-U.S. regimes in Central America, Africa, Asia and elsewhere.

Throughout the summer of 1981 the U.S. continued its Naval exercises off the coast of Libya. These provocative exercises seemed deliberately designed to lead to a military confrontation. In this aim they succeeded. A massive Sixth Fleet battle group, including the nuclear-powered aircraft carrier *Nimitz*, sailed into the Gulf of Sirte.

On August 19, 1981, two Libyan SU-22 bombers took off to monitor the movements of the U.S. battle formation. They were promptly shot down by Nimitz-based fighters. The Pentagon subsequently admitted that it had no evidence that the Libyan pilots had received orders to act in a hostile way. It has been suggested that the Libyans' MiG or Mirage aircraft would have been better suited than SU-22 bombers for offensive action. It was also significant that the Americans gave various inconsistent accounts about the U.S. Navy's proximity to the Libyan coast.

Having earlier declared that the incident occurred sixty miles out, Rear Admiral James E. Service later stated that, "The closest we came was about 25 miles of their coast."

Few independent observers doubted that the American posture throughout this period was intentionally provocative, designed to give Qadhafi a "bloody nose."

Omar carried the conversation with a little help from Youssef.

At the same time there was new evidence that Washington was encouraging a military confrontation between Egypt and Libya. President Sadat was said to favor a military incursion into Libya although some of his senior officers opposed the idea. When some of these same officers, including the Defense Minister General Ahmed Bedawi, were killed in a mysterious helicopter crash on March 2, 1981, Sadat's position was strengthened. French intelligence sources were quoted in July as stating that an Israeli working group was helping Sadat produce a plan for the invasion of Libya. It had already been made clear that Sadat could reasonably expect U.S. support in the implementation of such a plan.

When Sadat was assassinated in October, 1981, the idea of an Egyptian invasion of Libya was dropped. The new Egyptian President, Hosni Mubarak, who later became a friend of Qadhafi, was confronted with a domestic crisis and had no stomach for any inherited plan for hazardous foreign adventures.

On March 10, 1982, President Reagan, in a further move to isolate Libya, declared an embargo on the U.S. importation of crude oil from Libya. At the same time he also initiated a ban on the export to Libya of a wide range of technological products, a move designed to weaken not only Libya's military capability but also its capacity for industrial development.

It was suggested by U.S. authorities that "Libyan Hit Squads" were loose in the United States with a mission to assassinate President Reagan. The FBI later admitted that no such groups had ever been detected. Nonetheless, the import embargo and export ban remained in place in the hope that these would seriously impact the Libyan economy. Prior to that time the United States had been buying about a third of Libya's crude oil and it was assumed that Libya would be drastically affected by the loss of such a significant market.

U.S. oil companies were encouraged to bring home their personnel working in Libya. In due course the pressure from Washington was strengthened by a presidential edict. Three-thousand Americans came home, although workers and technicians had little sympathy with the pressure from Washington. The U.S. oil companies responded "reluctantly and under protest."

The Libyan Oil Ministry was soon recruiting Iranian, Canadian, Arab and European oil technicians to take the place of the departed Americans. Since the economic measures were clearly having little effect, the Reagan Administration again looked to the possibility of military action.

In February 1983, Reagan responded to Sudanese President Numeiri's claim to have uncovered a Libyan conspiracy against him by initiating a massive military confrontation with Qadhafi. AWAC surveillance aircraft were immediately dispatched to Cairo for reconnaissance missions over Libya. The *Nimitz* and its associated battle formation again sailed towards the Gulf of Sirte, encouraging speculation that this time an actual invasion would take place.

Suddenly, however, the U.S. backed off, amidst rumors of arguments with the Egyptian government. A senior Egyptian official commented: "We are furious. The Americans are trying to implicate us in things that do not involve us." In the same spirit, the Egyptian Defense Minister, Field Marshal Abdul Halim Abu Ghazala, declared that he could not see any sign of Libyan aggression against the Sudan. The Americans had made little effort to check the veracity of Numeiri's accusations against Libya. It was enough that the Sudanese leader had provided a pretext for a further U.S. confrontation with Qadhafi.

A few months later, the Americans were again mobilizing against the Libyan regime, this time using the excuse of Qadhafi's involvement in Chad. The USS *Eisenhower* sailed towards the Gulf of Sirte and AWACS planes were active. Yet the Egyptian government could not be relied upon to engage in military action against the Libyans.

In March, 1984, further Sudanese claims of Libyan hostility stimulated yet more U.S. maneuvers. On this occasion, Egyptian forces were sent to support Numeiri, but Mubarak still made it clear that he wanted to avoid a military confrontation with Qadhafi. There was also evidence that the U.S. was trying to lure Qadhafi into a confrontation with Numeiri so that Washington could righteously respond with a justified attack on Libya.

Egypt would be compelled to observe the terms of its 1975 defense pact with Sudan. One observer commented that Qadhafi prudently ignored the bait offered him.

By the mid 1980's, the Reagan administration had done all it could, short of a U.S invasion of Libya, to topple Qadhafi. At the time, as doubtless today, there did exist a plan for U.S. forces, with Egyptian support, to invade Libya. The Egyptian government was not prepared to cooperate in such a scheme. There were evident tensions between Egypt and Libya but Washington was never able to exploit these to the point of generating an actual military conflict.

In 1986 the U.S. continued to search for signs of Libyan-inspired terrorist activities. Washington claimed to have intercepted messages from Tripoli to various People's Bureaus, as Libyan embassies are called, leading to the suspicion that Libya was working to organize further terrorist attacks.

One message in particular, sent on March 25, 1986, was seen as crucially important. It was a coded message allegedly received by the Libyan People's Bureau in East Berlin and picked up by the German equivalent of our CIA, the Bundesnachrichtendienst, or BND. The information was passed along directly to the National Security Agency (NSA), the supersecret arm of U.S. intelligence that operates a worldwide network of electronic listening posts, headquartered in Fort Meade. American intelligence claimed that this message authorized Libyan security personnel in East Berlin to proceed with a terrorist operation against U.S. servicemen in West Berlin. The La Belle Discotheque in Hamburg was chosen as the target to be bombed.

The day before the bombing of the La Belle, in which one American soldier, Sergeant Kenneth Ford, and a Turkish woman were killed, and two hundred thirty others were wounded by the explosion, the Libyan Bureau in East Berlin had reportedly sent a message to Tripoli. The message informed the security authorities in Tripoli that they would "be very happy" when they saw the following day's headlines.

President Reagan claimed that the intercepted and decoded cables were "irrefutable proof" of Libyan involvement in the terrorist attack. However, sources within the U.S. administration and a West German translation of the intercepted cables testified that the Libyan leadership neither authorized the bombing nor specified the target. Additionally, Reagan's disclosures infuriated German authorities, who believed it was unnecessary to divulge the BND's electronic intercepts and the agency's obvious success in breaking the Libyan code.

U.S. authorities have been unwilling to clarify the precise nature of the Libyan involvement in the West Berlin attack, or to release the full text of the decoded and translated cables. Such reticence is conveniently explained by Washington in terms of national security. However, there is widespread suspicion that the U.S. administration deliberately sought to obscure the wording of the interpreted messages because they could not be relied upon to support an explanation that would justify the bombing of Libya.

In one interpretation, President Reagan merely inferred the responsibility of the Libyan leadership from evidence his advisors knew to be ambiguous. Washington tried to secure a trade embargo against Libya following the discotheque bombing, but could not secure the agreement of its European allies. The Bonn government, for example, expelled two Libyan diplomats but would not agree to a trade embargo. A frustrated White House decided that a military strike, Operation El Dorado Canyon, was the only option. Within a few days, Tripoli and Benghazi were bombed.

Chapter Seventeen

The U.S. Attack on Libya

My head was pounding as I listened to Omar and tried to assimilate what he was telling us compared to what I remembered from my own experience. Fortunately, it was time for a lunch break. Omar suggested to Youssef that he take us to visit the Bab Azizzia Barracks after lunch. He felt that we could learn a great deal about what actually happened on April 15, 1986, when American aircraft, flying from bases in Britain and carriers in the Mediterranean, bombed Tripoli and Benghazi.

On that morning in 1986, shortly before 2:00 A.M., thirteen F-111 fighter bombers, having flown from the UK, and three radar jamming aircraft from aircraft carriers, roared over Tripoli. Bombs and missiles hit the airport, the Bab Azizzia Barracks, where Qadhafi and his family were sleeping and various other civilian targets.

During a quick lunch at the El Mahari Hotel we decided to visit the Bab Azizzia Barracks on our way back to the Jerba airport. We needed to arrive in Geneva before 11:00 P.M. when the airport closed for the night. Our plan was to spend the night in Geneva and return to the States early the next morning.

The Barracks were located in the center of Tripoli, only ten minutes from the hotel. Youssef told us that what we were about to see would come as a shock. As we approached the Barracks, he pointed out various housing complexes and the French Embassy that were hit by the F-111 bombs. Col. Qadhafi had ordered the Barracks closed to visitors and had left the facility exactly as it was after the 1986 bombing. Very few people had seen the remains of

155

Qadhafi's home and Youssef said that we were the first Americans to visit the complex since it was open to the press just after the bombing.

Pilots who participated in the raid suggested that damage to the French Embassy in Tripoli and other civilian sites was caused by errant missiles fired by the Libyans. However, Western journalists in Libya at that time reported that the damage appeared to be too widespread to come from antiaircraft missiles.

U.S. intercepted messages suggested that the Libyan military response to the raid was weak and befuddled. Commanders at the Libyan air base near Surt, for example, ignored an order to launch their airplanes to repel the U.S. attack and suggested instead that the air base at Benghazi should respond.

Eight Navy A6 Intruder attack planes bombed the Benina airfield at Benghazi with 500 and 750-pound antipersonnel/antimaterial (APAM) bombs. The APAM cluster bombs scatter about 100 bomblets that can injure or kill people and damage airplanes.

U.S. bombers encountered heavy antiaircraft missile fire, but many missiles were sent astray by U.S. jamming and electronic misdirection equipment. In addition, Navy planes circling off the coast fired almost 50 missiles into Libyan targeting radars. U.S. bombers took advantage of surprise, darkness and low-altitude flying to evade the defenders as the bombers roared in at treetop level at about 400 knots. The F-111 has variable geometric "swing wings" and an all-weather target designator enabling it to fly at high speeds and low levels, hugging terrain to screen itself from radar detection. The F-111 was designed for surprise attacks and quick escapes. It did just what it was designed to do that April morning over Libya.

Just before takeoff, Air Force and Navy fliers chosen to bomb Libya, punched cockpit keyboards to tell their planes' computers the latitudes and longitudes of their flight's starting points. Otherwise, the pilots might miss their targets and become lost returning home. The F-111 fliers at two bases in Britain faced an exhausting, 14-hour flight of 2,700 miles each way. Their legs would go numb from sitting in one position that long. They would wiggle their hips, sit on one side of the hard seat and then the other to keep the blood moving while they flew. Some would return so stiff that they had to be lifted out of their cockpits after landing.

During the long run to Libya and back the F-111 was put on automatic pilot. But their human pilots had to stay alert to maneuver the swing-wing bombers to an exact place in the sky several times to meet a hose nozzle suspended from a flying gasoline station, an Air Force tanker.

Their Navy A6 counterparts had been taken so close to Libya on aircraft carriers that these pilots did not have to "plug" or refuel, like the F-111 flyers. After the bombing runs, however, the Navy pilots had to find their aircraft carrier in the dark, never an easy task, then land on its postage stamp deck, while plunging from the sky at 120 knots.

Air Force tankers took off first, forming a string of refueling stations along the circuitous F-111 route over the Atlantic and Mediterranean. The Air Force and Navy bombers were under orders to time their takeoffs and flight plans so they would rendezvous above Libya simultaneously in order to swoop in and away before the Libyan Air Force and antiaircraft gunners could respond.

Before takeoff, crews of both types of bombers had studied maps and pictures of targets around Tripoli and Benghazi. They marked check points along the route in hopes of flying a precise course, although the computerized wizardry of their planes' black boxes would do most of the navigating and bombing.

The heart of the A6 "smart" bombing system is in its big nose and a white basketball-like device hanging under it. The nose houses radar that can see a target more than 100 miles away. The heat-seeking and laser gear in the basketball does not come into play until the A6 is about 25 miles from the target.

F-111 and A6 radar see such big objects as buildings clearly in the dark and sketch their profiles on cockpit scopes. The radar cannot produce clear images of small targets, such as antiaircraft guns and fighter planes on the ground. If everything is working, the computerized bombing systems in each type of plane can hit a building with a single bomb but not destroy those near it. Secretary of Defense, Caspar W. Weinberger, said this was one reason that large buildings were chosen as targets in Libya, reducing the risk of "collateral damage;" a euphemism for hitting something, usually civilian, other than the desired military target.

The F-111 and A6 air crews were trained to follow elaborate procedures before dropping the so-called smart bombs. Those methods required the A6, for example, to match the radar profile of his target displayed from 100 miles away with one he had studied before takeoff. As the bomber, thundering at almost 500 M.P.H., moved within 25 miles of the target shown on the radar scope, the A6 would start "mixing paint." This consisted of activating the basketball's heat-receiving gear, which displays heat from the targeted building as a black-and-white profile on a separate cockpit screen.

The bombardier would maneuver buttons and knobs to fine-tune the radar and heat sensor, the latter called forward-looking infrared (FLIR). If the two sets of images matched those programmed into the computer as the target, the pilot would shoot a laser beam from the basketball when the plane came within five miles of the building. The building was now "painted."

With luck, the heat image would be so distinct that the bombardier could focus in his scope's cross hairs on a chosen window of the building. If the cross hairs slipped off the window as the plane maneuvered, he could move them back into position by jiggling a "joy stick" with his left hand. With the building "designated" by the laser beam, the pilot would punch buttons instructing the computer to take command of the bomb drop.

After the pilot and bombardier confirmed the target, the computer, calculating the plane's speed and drift, would release bombs at the precise moment required for a direct hit. A seeking device in the nose of a 500-pound, 1,000-pound or 2,000-pound bomb would find the laser beam and ride it through the building window before the bomb exploded.

If, in reading his radar and FLIR scopes, the bombardier mistook an embassy or a house for his target, the smart bomb would do what it was told and destroy the wrong target, causing the collateral damage that President Reagan said the attackers sought to avoid. Bombs struck buildings in Libya not on the target list, including the French Embassy, but whether the smart bombs went awry or these buildings were damaged by stray Libyan fire remains at issue.

There were charges that the raid could have been conducted more simply and at less risk with only Navy aircraft rather than the mix of Navy and Air Force warplanes. The carrier-based planes had to travel only several hundred miles, while the Air Force bombers that reached their targets had to fly 5,400 miles, a grueling round trip of 14 hours that required support by about 40 tanker aircraft for mid-flight refueling. The French were against the attack

159

and would not permit the planes to fly through French airspace.

It was reported in *The Washington Post* of April 16, 1986, that some Pentagon officials suggested that the Air Force planes based in Britain were included only to give that service a piece of the action or to demonstrate that at least one ally, Britain, supported the mission. The official Pentagon line was that there was a military need to use both the Air Force and the Navy planes to carry out a coordinated and simultaneous strike. Although the carriers USS *Coral Sea* and USS *America* together carry about 170 warplanes, each had only a dozen planes equipped for nighttime, low-level attacks, the A6 Intruder squadrons. Those planes could not have bombed all five targets simultaneously.

One F-111 had to turn back. Another, a plane that turned-up missing, never reached its target. A third F-111 completed its bombing mission but had mechanical troubles on the return journey and had to land in Spain for repairs.

A fleet of twenty large KC10 refueling planes and 22 KC135 tankers, some of which apparently took off from other allied bases in the region, kept the F-111's flying, with four refuelings each on their way to Libya. Their flying time, six hours down and eight hours back, was lengthened by the refusal of the French to permit overflight of their country.

Eight A6's carrying both unguided 500-pound bombs and 750-pound cluster bombs, attacked the Benina Military Airfield. They met no opposition and damaged five to twelve MiG23 fighters and several spare parts hangars. Six other A6's, encountering heavy antiaircraft fire, bombed the Al Jamahiriyah Barracks, described as a Libyan alternate command post, with 500-pound bombs. The Pentagon provided no damage assessment.

As the F-111's reached their targets around Tripoli, a fleet of fourteen A6 Intruders were approaching targets in the East. Meanwhile, other carrier based antiradar missiles and F/A18 Hornets were firing three dozen High-speed Anti-Radiation Missiles (HARM) into Libyan radars. E2C Hawkeye command planes were scanning the skies for hostile aircraft but none appeared.

Five F-111's, each carrying a dozen 500-poumd bombs, attacked the military side of the Tripoli Airport, destroying three to five IL76 Soviet-built cargo planes. Eight F-111's, each carrying four 2,000-pound laser-guided bombs, attacked the Bab Azizzia Barracks. The U.S. called this barracks the center of Libyan terrorism planning. The barracks were structurally damaged and the intelligence service headquarters, said to be located in the barracks, was virtually destroyed. Three F-111's, also equipped with four laser-guided bombs each, attacked the Sidi Bilal port west of Tripoli.

All attacks ended by 2:12 A.M. Libyan time, but the Libyans continued firing for some time thereafter. Radar at the SA5 site at Surt, which was not attacked, was turned on only after the U.S. planes had departed.

U.S. officials said the targets were chosen to hamper Libya's terrorist operations overseas while minimizing risk to U.S. pilots and possible harm to Libyan civilians. Attacks against inland oil facilities were considered and rejected, both because they would expose pilots to more antiaircraft fire and because Washington did not want to hit general economic targets. Officials also stressed in early briefings to Members of Congress that attacks on the Bab Azizzia Barracks where Libyan Leader Muammar Qadhafi lived, were not intended to kill him. "We were trying to send him a very clear message," one administration official said. "We were trying to make it clear that we would carry this directly to him and that we were prepared to impose the cost on him and his support operation, and thereby expose his ultimate vulnerability. . . ."

Targets also were chosen in an effort to damage military units loyal to Qadhafi without inflicting as much harm on regular military troops. Some Administration officials hoped that the attack would encourage military leaders, some of whom were already disenchanted with Qadhafi, to challenge him or his policies abroad.

Officials also said that the missing F-111, even if downed in the Gulf of Sidra, may not have been the victim of hostile fire. One of its bombs could have exploded on board, or it could have crashed for other reasons. No other planes were hit and there were no other U.S. casualties. Vice Admiral Frank B. Kelso, Sixth Fleet Commander aboard the *America*, said he was surprised that no Libyan planes challenged the U.S. force.

The U.S. claimed that in possible retaliation for the raid, Libya fired two surface-to-surface missiles at a U.S. Coast Guard navigation station on the southern Italian island of Lampedusa. There was no report of damage and information about the incident was sketchy. Also, in an incident that some U.S. officials feared would foreshadow future reprisals against Americans abroad, an employee at the U.S. Embassy in the Sudanese capital of Khartoum was wounded in the head on a residential street, during a burst of gunfire from a passing car. The shooting followed an anti-American demonstration by 1,000 protesters and came after U.S. Embassy employees were put on alert following the Libyan raid.

Chapter Eighteen

The Bab Azizzia Barracks

The Bab Azizzia Barracks are in the very center of a residential section of the city. It was hard to imagine that civilians wouldn't have been killed in the raid. We careened through a few back alleys and came to a stop in a small parking lot. Two uniformed Libyan police guards greeted our caravan, and waved us through a security gate. We had to use great care as we disembarked from our cars. Rubble from the bombs dropped in this place six years before was strewn about the parking lot. Carol Hubbard had the only camera in the group. She took a large number of pictures, including one with our party posed in front of the destroyed home of Muammar Qadhafi. (Despite repeated requests she never did give me copies of the pictures.)

I had trouble understanding why they called the Bab Azizzia a barracks at all. It appeared to be just another cement home in a residential neighborhood. Everything was just as it was six years before. The guards opened the front door. We entered, carefully stepping over scattered rubble, furnishings and personal items. Youssef escorted us from room to room and gave us a play-by-play description of the events of that infamous day.

We first entered a large reception hall. Despite the disarray, one could see immediately that it was a magnificent structure, well suited to receive Presidents, Prime Ministers, Kings and other Heads of State. I never expected to see what I saw next. Situated almost in the direct center of the room were the remains of the fuselage of the U.S. F-111 warplane shot down by Libyan antiaircraft guns during the 1986 bombing.

163

I was even more alarmed to see two flight suits and helmets inscribed with the names of the two pilots lost in the raid, Capt. Ribas-Dominicci and Capt. Lorence. This puzzled and shocked me greatly. We Americans had been led to believe the U.S. account of the downing of the plane. We were told that the swept winged, two-seat, fighter-bomber built by General Dynamics, had been hit over Libya, but crashed in the Mediterranean Sea, never to be found again.

The Washington Post reported the Defense Department version the day after the attack on April 16, 1986:

> An F-111 bomber and its two-man crew were lost at sea in the massive 12 minute raid on Libya, which officials otherwise characterized as a successful and complex mission involving 30 bombers and about 100 support planes. Libyan fighter jets, cargo planes, airport hangars and military barracks were damaged in the raid on five military targets in the port cities of Tripoli and Benghazi. But cloud cover over the areas bombed in Operation El Dorado Canyon interfered with U.S. photo reconnaissance missions and the Pentagon could provide no assessment of eyewitness reports that U.S. bombs also damaged embassies and residences and injured civilians.

> While Pentagon authorities and U.S. servicemen involved in the Libya raid expressed pride in carrying out the complicated and dangerous raid ordered by President Reagan, officials acknowledged that, it could be days before a more complete account of the damage is pieced together, and that the fate of the missing F-111 may never be known.

Well, the fate of the F-111 and the two-member crew was now known to me and the other members of our party. I reached into my memory to put the various parts of the story together. I wished that I could remember more about the details of the incident six years before. Were these really the flight suits and helmets the two men had worn, or was it one of the outlandish P.R. stunts Qadhafi was so inclined to pull?

Some of the pilots on the raid had reported seeing a fireball in the Tripoli area just before the bomber reached its target, although there was no official speculation on whether the plane had been shot down by Libyan antiaircraft fire.

Reportedly, U.S. search-and-rescue aircraft and vessels, including submarines, had searched the Mediterranean north of Tripoli late into the night. The searchers did not detect the electronic beeps that the gondola of an F-111 automatically emits if its crew is able to eject before a crash.

The Air Force identified the missing crew members as pilot Capt. Fernando L. Ribas-Dominicci, 33, a native of Puerto Rico and bombardier–navigator Capt. Paul F. Lorence, 31, a San Francisco native. Their plane flew from the Royal Air Force base at Lakenheath, England, where they were assigned to the Air Force's 48th Tactical Fighter Wing.

Lorence, who grew up in San Francisco learned to fly when he was 17. He was a classical pianist by avocation. He met his British-born wife, Dianne, while stationed at the Royal Air Force base at Lakenheath, England. The couple had been married for 18 months and had an 8-month-old son, Peter. Lorence had been in England the past four years.

Capt. Lorence was described by his stepfather as "quiet, unassuming," but assertive when the occasion called for it. His passion for flying mirrored that of his maternal grandfather, a pilot in Britain's Royal Flying Corps during World War I. Lorence enlisted in the Air Force out of high school and, after four years as a nuclear weapons specialist, he returned to college, earning a degree in history from San Francisco State University. He had rejoined the Air Force eight years before, in 1978. He was working toward a Masters Degree in international relations at Cambridge and expected to make the Air Force his career.

Capt. Ribas-Dominicci learned to fly while in college. When he wasn't going fast in airplanes he enjoyed the speed of power boats. He had been in the Air Force for ten years and had spent the past two years in England. Ribas-Dominicci was the youngest son of a furniture store owner and grew up in the central Puerto Rican hill town of Utuado. He graduated from the University of Puerto Rico with a degree in civil engineering. Ribas-Dominicci met his Mexican wife, Blanca Linda, while stationed in Texas. At the time of his death in this military action they had a 4-year-old son, named Fernando.

The ground floor of the barracks looked like a Hollywood set. Although the walls were still standing, there was very little left of the interior. I was surprised that there were no signs of a post-bombing fire. Every window in the house had been broken and had since been boarded up with plywood coverings. Everything was covered with dirt and dust that had accumulated over the past six years. We walked from room to room, only imagining the terror of that early morning raid. We climbed a shaky spiral staircase to the second floor. I wondered if the stair supports would hold our weight.

Youssef opened the door to a second floor room. Before I knew it, I was standing in the bedroom of Muammar Qadhafi. Most prominent in the large room was a round bed almost completely covered with debris from the ceiling above. In place of a headboard, the bed had a wrap around stereo system that one might expect to find in the Honeymoon Motel in the Pocono Mountains, or the Chicken Ranch Brothel in Texas.

I imagined Qadhafi and his wife sleeping in the bed as the attack began early that morning. The room was full of personal items including pictures of his children, an electric razor, perfumes, combs, brushes and closets full of Qadhafi's and his wife, Safia's, clothing.

Qadhafi's and Safia's three children were all victims of the attack. Two of the children were hospitalized in intensive care for many days, suffering from pressure shock from the 2000-pound bomb that made a direct hit on this structure they called home. Hanna, Qadhafi's adopted daughter, died a few hours after the attack from severe brain damage.

We went from bedroom to bedroom and saw where Qadhafi's two sons, Saef al-Islam and Khamees had been sleeping when the bombs fell. Khamees was rendered unconscious by the explosion and didn't regain consciousness for five days.

The most touching part of the tour was visiting one of the smaller bedrooms, which had belonged to Qadhafi's adopted sixteen month old daughter Hanna. I knew she had been killed in the raid, but like most, I had no idea of the circumstances.

Hanna's bedroom was not much different from those of American toddlers her age. Her toys were scattered about the room just as she had left them before she died. Now, however, they were covered with dust, cobwebs and ceiling plaster. Having three daughters of my own, I couldn't help but feel great sympathy for this innocent little girl I never knew. I felt deep compassion for the family which loved her. At her tender age, the world meant toys, a dog named Jay and a Mommy and Daddy.

Pictures of Qadhafi with Hanna were scattered on the floor where they had fallen. They were just lying there in broken picture frames. One in particular stands out in my mind. Qadhafi was pictured sitting on a large throne type chair, with Hanna sitting on his lap. Qadhafi held a small, pale-blue teddy bear in his left hand, in front of her face. It was evident that he was trying to make her smile for the camera. I choked up when, not more than five feet away, I saw the same little blue teddy bear lying with some of her other toys in the remains of her pink toy box.

Two pictures remained on the wall above Hanna's bed. One was of Hanna lying on a gurney type bed in the hospital after the bombing. She was already dead when the photo was taken. She was wearing only a diaper and her body was covered with open wounds. Incredible as it may seem, the second picture was a photograph of a young English girl in her early twenties.

As I stared, Youssef volunteered that she was Flora Swire, one of the victims of the Pan Am 103 bombing. In December of 1991, her father, Dr. James Swire, spent five days in Tripoli and met with Col. Qadhafi. Among other topics, the two men discussed their daughters both of whom had been indiscriminately killed. Dr. Swire, spokesman for the British Lockerbie relatives, offered, and Qadhafi accepted, a photograph of Flora. Qadhafi was touched by the gesture. He had the picture placed in Hannah's room as a symbol of the great personal loss both men shared.

Chapter Nineteen

International Response

The international response to the bombing of Libya was, to a large extent, predictable. President Reagan had made it clear, in characteristic fashion, what his purposes had been. He stated that he had bombed Libya as a way of "contributing to an international environment of peace, freedom and progress within which our democracy, and other free nations, can flourish."

The U.S. attack was denounced by most nations, but the president's popularity soared at home. The 1986 air attack on Libya was a brilliantly staged media event. It was the first bombing in history scheduled for prime-time TV, for the precise moment when the networks opened their national news programs. Anchor men were able to switch at once to Tripoli so that the exciting events could be viewed live. Then followed the carefully conceived news conferences and White House statements.

It was firmly explained that the bombing of Tripoli and Benghazi was "self defense against future attack," a measured reaction to the discotheque raid in Berlin ten days before. The media knew that the evidence for Libyan complicity in the discotheque bombing was slight but such an inconsequential detail was suppressed in the general applause for Reagan's decisive action.

In fact, a report from Berlin, just a half an hour before the U.S. attack, had stated that U.S. and West German officials had no evidence, only "suspicions," of Libyan involvement. This contradicted earlier government claims of "certain knowledge," again a minor inconsistency that the White House press corps resolutely ignored. Within a short time, leading West German publications, and obscure ones in the United States, carried the information that the German intelligence team investigating the bombing at the La Belle Discotheque had no knowledge whatever of any Libyan complicity. This information was largely suppressed in the United States.

There was more. Prior to the bombing, the U.S. administration put out a story that, having intercepted the Libyan messages, efforts were made to warn the U.S. servicemen at the discotheque but that the alert called in West Berlin had failed by fifteen minutes. The West Berlin police informed the BBC that no alert had been called—the American story was pure fabrication.

Setting the stage for the attack, President Reagan—famously fond of Rambo feature films—had been saying to aides for more that a year that he was looking for a "clean shot" against terrorism. Now he had the opportunity. Just days before the raid, on April 9, 1986, he attended a press conference where he denounced Qadhafi as "the Mad Dog of the Middle East."

Unbeknownst to the American public, the President's aides and military planners had been preparing for an attack on Qadhafi for some time, but they wanted to discourage speculation. Oliver North had set about creating the correct climate of minimum expectation, telling the NSC aide Johnathan Miller (who enjoyed good press relations) that action against Libya was unlikely: the United States did not want an incident, the right ships were not available and in any case the French would not approve overflights. Miller then called John McWerthy, the State Department correspondent for ABC News, to offer details of the story. The ABC anchorman included a report in his show stating that retaliation against Qadhafi was unlikely.

Oliver North remarked to Miller afterwards: "That was the best disinformation I've ever seen."

This systematic campaign of disinformation and news management achieved its purpose. Reagan's popularity in the United States soared as he was engulfed in a wave of adulation. The American people approved the specific air strike and the general strategy. Polls showed a 77% approval rating and President Reagan's foreign policy rating shot up, in less than a week, from 51% to 76%. There was regret that Col. Qadhafi had not been killed. High-technology weapons had been given their first trial by fire and, despite the unimpressive results, arms stock prices shot up immediately after the bombing. Liberal opinion in America might have been shocked by the U.S. onslaught on a sovereign state but the action had a chilling effect on state-sponsored terrorism and had demonstrated the President's resolve to the world.

The response in Britain to the bombing of Libya was mixed, with a substantial number of observers skeptical or disapproving. Even some committed Conservative columnists withheld their support from the Thatcher-approved American action. Thus, Ferdinand Mount, who had run Thatcher's policy unit for the two years bridging the 1983 election, ridiculed the idea that "carefully selected targets," designed to minimize civilian casualties, could include a site right in the center of Tripoli.

A resolution introduced in the U.S. Congress had offered Thatcher the highest praise and thanks for supporting the American action, but in the UK the episode made her deeply unpopular. There was concern that Libya would retaliate with terrorist operations. Right after the bombing, pro-Libyan activists killed two British hostages, Leigh Douglas and Philip Padfield, and the American Peter Kilburn in Beirut.

The response in Europe was deeply hostile. A round-the-clock protest was conducted outside the U.S. Embassy in London. Two thousand people held a candle-lit vigil

171

outside Downing Street. There were demonstrations out-side government buildings and at the four U.S. bases, Up-per Heyford, Lakenheath, Fairford and Mildenhall, from which the F-111 bombers had flown. About 10,000 people demonstrated in West Germany, and in Italy, 3,000 people attended a Communist Party youth protest. Polls suggested that 65 per cent of the people in Britain and 75 per cent in West Germany opposed the bombing. In France, 66 per cent were in favor, but 63 per cent approved the government's decision not to let U.S. bombers use French airspace. By the end of April, French opposition to the American attack had risen to 56 per cent with 79 per cent approving the ban on the use of French airspace.

On the day before the bombing, the European Eco-nomic Community had underlined the need for restraint on all sides. When the bombing occurred there was speedy condemnation from many European capitals. Bettino Craxi, of Italy, said that the action ran the risk of provoking a further explosion of fanaticism, extremism, criminal and suicide actions.

Other leaders joined the Italian Prime Minister in con-demning the U.S. attack. Spain, Greece, Austria, Denmark and the Netherlands expressed various degrees of criticism, with some, "deploring" the action. The Greek government accused Britain, with its foreknowledge of the attack, of "violating the moral rules of political cooperation," and Leo Tindemans, the Belgian Foreign Minister, demanded an explanation from British Foreign Minister, Geoffrey Howe.

The official French and West German reactions were more guarded. Perhaps the most predictable foreign reac-tion of all was the widespread Arab condemnation of the American attack. Most importantly, a veto by the United States was the only thing that kept the UN Security Coun-cil from passing a resolution condemning the United States for its surprise attack on Libya.

All of this negative reaction did nothing to dent the enthusiasm of the American public for President Reagan's resolute stand. The way was open for further anti-Libyan initiatives.

We stood in the large reception room of the barracks once again and continued to ask questions of Youssef. He told us how the raid had affected his Leader, Col. Qadhafi. Qadhafi became a changed man. He wanted to be a part of the world community again. "That is why this Lockerbie thing makes him crazy," Youssef explained.

Khaled responded to a crackling call on his hand held radio. It was obvious to us all that this was a very important call. Khaled abruptly handed the radio to Youssef, who began a rather long, animated discussion on the radio in Arabic. Youssef continuously looked at his watch, as if he had to rush off to a meeting. I began to be a bit concerned about our own time schedule. I knew that we had to leave shortly to make Jerba before dark or we would end up spending the night in Tunisia instead of Geneva. I really needed to catch my flight to Washington the next day.

Youssef finished his conversation. He handed the radio back to Khaled with a few instructions in Arabic. Khaled turned on his heels and rushed off to points unknown. Youssef turned to us and stated, "My Leader wants to meet with you today before you leave." It had been Qadhafi's personal assistant on the radio with Youssef. He had been instructed to do whatever possible to arrange a meeting between us and Qadhafi.

We walked out of the barracks and continued our discussion in the parking lot. We debated the pros and cons of extending our stay in Libya. On the one hand it would be most exciting to actually meet the "most feared man in the world;" undoubtedly a chance of a lifetime. On the other hand, the time available to make Jerba was about to run out and I wasn't sure what the consequences of that would be. I realized my return to Washington the next day was in doubt.

Youssef proposed a plan. By the look on his face, I could tell this was going to be another one of his, "it will only take a few hours" routines. He suggested that we take a walk through downtown Tripoli, and wait for his Leader to call for us. We could meet with Col. Qadhafi for an hour or so, return to the El Mahari for a few hours of rest, and then leave for Jerba at midnight. If we departed Jerba at 3:00 A.M. we would arrive at the Geneva airport right at its opening hour of 6:00 A.M. He would arrange for the pilots to be ready for our arrival at the Jerba Airport. And with a smile, he actually said, "It will only take a few hours."

By this time we had no choice. Even if we had left right then, we would have missed the arrival window in Geneva and ended up spending the night in the Jerba airport. The decision was collectively made. We were off to shop in downtown Tripoli. Hopefully I could find some unusual gifts for Virginia and Katie.

Chapter Twenty

The Libyan Marketplace

As it turned out, ours was anything but a typical shopping spree on a beautiful sunny afternoon in downtown Tripoli. Four Americans surrounded by a security force of twelve JSO agents was a sight to behold in the little winding streets of the central marketplace. It was obvious that we were the first Americans these people had seen in many years.

There was an excitement in the air as we strolled among the Libyan merchants squatting on the ground with their wares displayed in front of them on small linen cloths. My blond hair and California suntan was a point of curiosity for most midday shoppers. Carol Hubbard's long blond hair and fair complexion stood out in the crowd as we walked the narrow streets and alleys.

We saw a growing array of so called, "decadent" goods in the shops: French perfumes, Swiss watches and Japanese electronic goods were mixed in with traditional consumer goods such as clothing and rugs.

It seemed that the purchase of choice would be gold and silver jewelry. Most venders had an abundance of the precious Libyan metals. The majority of the merchants were dressed in typical Arab clothes, while shoppers were more often dressed in Western garb. The Libyan economy seemed to be booming in spite of the two decades the United States had maintained a tight, economic squeeze on the country.

The most important commodity in the modern Libyan economy is oil. In an oil-hungry world it is impossible to relegate Libya, with its prodigious oil resources, to the fringes of the world economy. According to a recent report

175

of the Kuwait-based Arab Petroleum Exporting Countries (OAPEC), the combined gross domestic product (GDP) of this organization stood at 402 billion U.S. dollars in real terms in 1993, compared with 392 billion dollars in 1992, an increase of 2.6 percent. Saudi Arabia, the world's leading oil producer and exporter, accounted for some 130 billion dollars. It was followed by Algeria, with 80 billion, Egypt with 75 billion, The United Arab Emirates with 35 billion and Libya with 25 billion dollars.

The UN embargo has not prevented Western countries from purchasing Libyan oil. Most developed countries are less concerned about Qadhafi's revolutionary programs than they are about their need for oil. Having an abundant supply of oil guarantees Libya's economic survival in at least the near future.

Qadhafi has used this oil wealth to endear himself to the Libyan people time and again. On September 5, 1994, he announced a second oil revenue grant whereby one million Libyans from large, low-income families would receive a share of half a billion dollars each year from Libya's oil income. "One hundred thousand families with an average of 10 members each, will receive in their bank accounts five thousand dollars, each year starting from now," Qadhafi said in a speech broadcast on Libyan radio. He said this was a first step towards a wider distribution of oil earnings among Libya's five million people. Qadhafi promised that all Libyans would receive a direct share of the country's oil wealth.

While we were touring the shops we were told by Khaled that there was a new spirit of private sector entrepreneurship in Libya. These small shop owners represented a Western type free enterprise system that had been sweeping the country since 1988.

On the occasion of the 1988 anniversary of the Libyan Revolution, Qadhafi stated his own version of the economic liberalization that was prominent in the world. He had no intention of nationalizing all trade in Libya. Local merchants, like those we saw would be allowed to import and export without restraint, and the state's control over small-sized industrial enterprises would be reduced. Also in 1988, the Executive Authority for Partnerships and Small Industries had been established to oversee the transfer of control of small state enterprises to employees.

Today, employees can buy shares in a company or can obtain partnership loans. Additionally, employee partnerships were being formed for the first time in small commercial ventures.

In theory, it is now possible for mixed-sector ventures to be created in all commercial areas, with the exception of the oil and steel industries. One published source suggested that 292 small and medium-sized industrial ventures with total assets of $62 million had passed into employee hands in the Tripoli municipality alone. Not all Libyans like the reforms. During our visit, an article in the Libyan press, condemning consumerism and personal wealth, was headed, "Fancy villas with satellite dishes: time for the bulldozer."

We passed a mosque on a back alley and observed a young man washing his feet and hands before entering the mosque for afternoon prayers. As we approached, he called out to us, "Americans—I have been to America." I asked where he had been, and he responded, "L.A., Mickey Mouse, Disneyland. Welcome to my country, Libya. We want good relations with America. We are good people. Tell your President that we are good. O.K?"

Most people were very gracious to us as we poked around in the various little shops. They would smile politely, and give a little bow as we approached or departed.

177

We didn't see, or feel, a single hostile act toward us and, much to my surprise, I felt quite comfortable moving among the crowds of shoppers.

After an hour in the marketplace, we returned to the El Mahari Hotel to rest and wait for a call from Col. Qadhafi. We were escorted to the same rooms we had occupied the previous night. As before, the rooms had been catered with trays of lovely fruits, cheeses and pastries. I desperately wanted to call Virginia, knowing that by now she had tried unsuccessfully to contact me at the Noga Hilton in Geneva. I decided that it would be too great a risk to have a record of my telephone call from Libya to America on some NSA spy satellite. If my friendly CIA agent Mr. "Dupont" from Delaware didn't know where I was by now, a communication to the States would most likely pinpoint my room in the El Mahari Hotel.

Chapter Twenty-One

Meeting the Accused "Terrorists"

I had just stretched out on my bed when there was a soft knock on my door. It was Khaled. He asked that I go with him right away. I said that I wanted to clean up a bit first but he insisted that we move quickly so that the others in my party wouldn't know that I was leaving the hotel. He was very serious in his manner and tone. He explained that Youssef had promised me a special meeting before I left Tripoli and everything had been arranged. He was very careful not to mention where we were going, or whom we would be meeting. I felt a surge of adrenalin as I realized that I was about to meet the two men accused of committing the most heinous crime ever against Western civilians, a crime which launched the greatest international counter-terrorist investigation ever conducted—spanning four continents and nearly forty countries.

I grabbed my coat and a banana. I quickly followed Khaled to a waiting service elevator located at the far end of the hall. As we approached the elevator I had a glancing recollection of that marvelous, and at the same time, horrible, December day in Vail, Colorado when I first heard the news of the Lockerbie disaster.

The elevator door was being held open by two JOS agents. Youssef and two more agents were waiting in the elevator. Youssef greeted me with a very stern face. As the elevator door closed behind me I was instructed not to talk until we were safely in the cars waiting for us at the back door of the hotel. The lighthearted atmosphere that had prevailed just an hour before in the marketplace had abruptly changed to serious business.

179

We exited the elevator into a hall just behind the kitchen. It was a strange scene. The hall was empty of hotel employees. Well-dressed JOS agents were posted at all possible entrances to the hallway, indicating that the hall had been emptied so that I would not be seen leaving the hotel.

"I hope you don't mind if my men search you before we leave," Youssef said very matter of factly. This really caught me off guard but I calmly granted his request.

I was asked to stand with my arms extended to my sides as a JOS agent gave me a thorough body search. I determined that they were not looking for weapons. Rather they were looking for hidden recording or homing devices or cameras that I might have concealed on my person. One agent took my coat and carefully inspected every little seam and pocket for hidden wires or bugs. My watch and glasses were give special attention, as were my belt and shoes that they asked me to remove. My *Mont Blanc* mechanical pencil was inspected with great care and then confiscated by one of the agents who handed it to Youssef. Youssef said the pencil would be returned later and that he would explain the need for these precautions when we got in the car.

Agents began to scurry about. Hand held radios were alive with excitement as we approached the plain, windowless steel back door. We hesitated long enough for one agent to help me slide into a rather long and ugly, tan trench coat and a wide brimmed, 1940's style fedora hat that would have been better suited for Humphrey Bogart than me. The hat's brim easily covered my face from view. Youssef pulled the coat's collar up to a point where it touched the back of the hat brim. I would have felt foolish if the intensity of the moment hadn't been so great. After he gave the front brim of the hat one final downward tug, I was ready to leave the hotel.

"Please wait here for a moment while we make a final check outside," Youssef requested. A few of his men went ahead and quickly signaled us to follow. As we exited the hotel, I noticed that the streets surrounding the hotel had been blocked with barricades by the JOS. There were no people visible on the streets as I was rushed into the black Mercedes parked at curbside with window curtains drawn tightly shut.

Youssef and one agent got in the back seat with me as we sped away from the hotel with sirens blaring. The black curtain separating us from the driver had also been closed and, although I couldn't see him, I recognized Khaled's voice coming from the right front seat. I couldn't see out of the windows and no one could see us inside. I judged from the noise of the sirens that there was one police car in front of ours and at least two behind.

I removed my newly acquired hat and unbuttoned the front of the trench coat as Youssef began his explanation. "We are going to meet with the two guys I promised this morning, Chazzy. We will meet in a special place, but I can't let you know where it is or how we get there. We don't want anybody knowing that we took you there, understand? This information would be very useful to your government and some people would pay big money to know their whereabouts. We had to be sure that you weren't wearing a wire or that you had a concealed homing device. After all, Chazzy, I have only known you a short while and you could be a CIA agent or some other secret agent for the United States. I like you a lot, Chazzy, but I can't be too careful with the lives of these men.

"If anything happens to these guys, the responsibility will be on my shoulders. If your government knew where we were going we could expect another raid or there would be some attempt to get them out of Libya or to have them killed. Remember what President Bush did in 1989 to arrest President Manuel Noriega of Panama and move him to the United States? He didn't get Congressional approval for the invasion of Panama, which was a direct violation of your own constitution not to mention international law. He would do anything to get his hands on these two men. I hope you understand Chazzy. No matter what happens, we will always deny that I brought you here and that you met with these guys. This is between us, Chazzy."

I understood what he meant about U.S. violations of international law. Actually, the 1989 invasion of Panama was a violation of many international treaties: the Charter of the Organization of American States (OAS), the Rio Treaty (Inter-American Treaty of Reciprocal Assistance of 1947), the Declaration of Montevideo (1933) and the Panama Canal Treaties (1977-78). The U.S. invasion violated a dozen articles of the OAS Charter, most notably, Articles 18-21. Article 18, for example, forbids intervention by any "State or group of States...for any reason whatever, in the internal or external affairs of any other State." The Rio Treaty and the Panama Canal treaties contain similar prohibitions. In any event, all such treaties are subordinate to the UN Charter, with Article 2(4) prohibiting "the threat or use of force against the territorial integrity or the political independence of any state."

I checked my watch as we came to a rather abrupt halt exactly thirteen minutes after leaving the hotel. "We won't have much time with these guys," Youssef noted. "I don't want your friends to find out that you are not in your room. They may call you for some reason, so I have had your phone fixed to give only a busy signal. Your Congressman Hubbard may get suspicious after a while and try to find you."

I was instructed to cover my face again with the hat as we prepared to leave the car. I could hear people milling

about outside the car door. Youssef gave specific instructions of what to do when I left the car. I was to keep my
head down with my eyes fixed on the ground in front of
me. I was to move as quickly as possible and do exactly
what Khaled told me to do. I was instructed to walk between two agents. They would have the responsibility of
seeing that I didn't bump into anything. Once inside, I could
ask whatever questions I wanted but Youssef had taken
my pencil so that I couldn't take notes of the conversation.

*Over the years I have had to develop a strong memory
for details. The Members of Congress don't want to talk as
freely as I need them to if I am taking notes during our
conversations. I was going to have to rely heavily on that
skill, and my heightened adrenalin, to remember enough
of the meeting long enough to make notes afterwards. Later
I reviewed a variety of sources to refresh my memory so
that I could more accurately fill in the facts for my report
of this clandestine meeting.*

I was rushed out of the car into a large, single house
that appeared to be situated in a quiet residential neighborhood. I could see just below the brim of my hat that there
appeared to be a great deal of security around the house. I
was first led into a large reception area and, without stop-
ping, into what appeared to be the dining room of the house.
And just like that, I was eye to eye with Abdel Basset Ali
Mohammed al-Megrahi and Lamen Khalifa Fhimah, two
of the most wanted and hated mass murderers in the world.

These were truly billion-dollar men! As a result of the
international sanctions imposed for not turning these two
men over to the West, $958.1 million in Libyan assets re-
mained frozen in banks around the world and unavailable
for Libyan use. Libya had also run out of critical medi-
cines and medical supplies which had taken a major toll
on the Libyan people. Libya's oil industry had been af-

fected by a shortage of spare parts and a lack of maintenance because of financial austerity imposed by Qadhafi as a result of the UN sanctions. It was easy to understand the need for all this secrecy.

Fhimah and Megrahi, along with their lawyer, who I think was Ibraham B. Legwell, politely stood as I entered the room. Each vigorously shook my hand. Fhimah said something in Arabic and a young female translator said, "Good afternoon, and welcome to Libya." I thanked them and took a seat at the dining table directly across from the two accused Libyan bombers. Youssef sat to my right and the translator sat at the head of the table. I was offered coffee or tea. A plate of small cakes and cookies was situated in the center of the table between us.

I very carefully studied the two men and tried my best to memorize their individual features. They were both dressed in double breasted, designer business suits and each wore colorful neckties. Fhimah was on the heavy side and had a prominent mustache. His olive-colored skin seemed soft and smooth and shone in the light of an overhead lamp. He had a most pleasant smile and seemed genuinely happy to meet me.

Megrahi was thin, with curly jet-black hair. He wore tinted aviator style glasses, which obscured my view of his eyes. I felt no warmth from Megrahi. He avoided eye contact. My first impression was that he seemed to be rather sneaky. He sat quietly and focused his eyes on a writing pad in from of him on the table.

Remembering Youssef's time constraints, I went right to the heart of the matter. I asked each man directly if he had prepared the explosives used to blow up the Pan Am jet and then smuggled them aboard the plane through a connecting flight from Malta. In turn, each man looked me in the eye and denied any responsibility for the bombing of Pan Am 103. I looked for signs that they might be lying to me. They both seemed very calm and matter-of-fact in their response. There was no obvious fidgeting or beads of perspiration forming on their brows.

I asked each man to respond to my second question individually. Did they know who was responsible for the Lockerbie disaster? Fhimah said, "Authorities in the United States and Britain know who did it. They have had the evidence since early 1989, but have failed to act on it."

Megrahi sounded in by adding that the answer was to be found in Syria and Iran, not in Libya. Megrahi said, "We have been a convenient scapegoat for the United States. The evidence against us is circumstantial and would never stand up in court, even if we could get a fair trial in some neutral country."

Fhimah suggested that I review a February, 1992, eighty page report from the Palestine Liberation Organization (PLO) which provided fresh evidence of Iranian involvement in the Lockerbie bombing. The report went right to the controversy of why the Scottish police and the American FBI changed their minds after claiming for months that the bombing was committed by members of Ahmed Jibril's group, the Popular Front for the Liberation of Palestine-General Command (PFLP-GC) under the umbrella of Iran and Syria. Fhimah said that, "The report includes the most specific evidence yet of Iran's role in the bombing."

In the report, Bassam Abu Sharif, the political adviser to PLO chairman Yassir Arafat and, coincidently, my new "friend" from the olive tree luncheon in *Cap Antibes*, claimed that the PLO had "gathered very accurate and sensitive information related to the Lockerbie affair," and that this information "points clearly to the involvement of Middle East parties, not Libya, in this crime." The report details meetings between Ahmed Jibril, Ali Akbar Mohtashami, the former Iranian Interior Minister, and other

Iranians to discuss the planned attack. (Mohtashami surfaces later as a prominent player in this drama.)

The PLO itself was somewhat put out by the seeming lack of interest on the part of the Lockerbie investigators to talk to them in their new role as a mainstream political entity. Not surprisingly, the PLO pinned the blame for Lockerbie on an old enemy, Ahmed Jibril, who broke away from the PLO in 1986. The report said Jibril's group made and planted the bomb on Flight 103 and they were paid $12 million for their trouble by Iran. The PLO went further, stating that the money was handed over to the PFLP-GC in Libya, drawing Colonel Qadhafi into the scenario.

The Libyan lawyer for the accused terrorists' gave me a powerful editorial to review that appeared in London's *The Sunday Times* on November 24, 1991. He said that the U.S. motivation for accusing Libya was well documented. He had underlined the following paragraph in red: (Upon my return home I acquired a copy of the article.)

> Maybe it has been necessary to be nice to Iran and Syria to secure the release of the remaining hostages in Beirut. It must be more than coincidence that both countries were officially cleared of any Lockerbie involvement just a few days before Terry Waite and Thomas Sutherland were at last released. Our joy at their freedom should be tempered by the shame of the cost: the relatives of the victims of the Lockerbie bomb must now come to terms with the fact that most of those behind the murder of their loved ones are going to get away with it. The cause of justice is being sacrificed on the altar of diplomatic convenience. We will live to regret it.

Fhimah explained that the West knew full well that Libya would not turn them over to the United States or

Britain for trial. This standoff served the United States well.
"The U.S. doesn't have to account for its action in our
indictments. This could go on for years, and the U.S. has
escaped the immense political pressure that was building
against them before our indictments. The U.S. has no more
right to extradite us to your country, than we do to extradite one of your citizens to ours."

This theme was highlighted in a lead article in the
International Herald-Tribune on January 17, 1992 by UN
correspondent Ian Williams, in which he commented:

> One can imagine the reaction of the White
> House if Nicaragua had tried to extradite Ol-
> iver North for his admitted terrorist actions
> against the Sandinista Government. It is not
> necessary to be an admirer of the Qadhafi re-
> gime to suspect that double standards are rap-
> idly becoming the accepted reserve currency
> of the New World Order.

My tired mind was being bombarded with conflicting
information. Was I the victim of Libyan propaganda or
was there some truth to what I was hearing? Could it be
that these two men were innocent? After all, the Lockerbie
investigation had been conducted in seventy countries. No
less that 16,000 statements had been taken and more than
20,000 names had been recorded on computers. The investigation had cost an estimated $22 million. Could the
investigators have been wrong? Or was there, as Fhimah
suggested, an international political conspiracy to cover-
up important evidence which would shift the blame for the
bombing to Libya?

A discussion followed in which Fhimah, Megrahi, their
lawyer and Youssef contributed detailed information about
the Lockerbie investigation, and how it eventually led to
the indictment of the Libyans. I later researched this information and added relevant data.

Chapter Twenty-Two

The Accused "Terrorists" Talk

This is their story, as best I was able to remember it. Over the past couple of years I have attempted to verify—or discredit—what I was told with extensive research. I have been able to obtain documentary proof to back up their testimony. I now totally believe that this is what would come out in a properly conducted court trial.

The book, The Fall of Pan Am 103, *by Steven Emerson and Brian Duffy, gives a remarkable accounting of the investigation and was most helpful to me in reporting the following events. I also found the book,* Their Darkest Day, *by Matthew Cox and Tom Foster, helpful in describing the Lockerbie investigation and verifying the information given to me during my meetings in Libya.*

On October 26, 1988, fifty-six days before the Lockerbie bombing, four men were arrested at gun point by West German Federal Police Agency (Bundeskriminalamt, BKA) as they rode in their car near the industrial town of Neuss, Germany. At the same time, in a carefully coordinated operation across West Germany, code named *Operation Autumn Leaves,* a number of apartments were being raided and known Palestinian sympathizers were being detained. The BKA raided an unoccupied apartment in Neuss while other law enforcement officials broke into an apartment in Frankfurt. The raids were the result of a major surveillance operation conducted by the BKA over an extended period of time.

One of the men detained near Neuss was Hafez Kassan Dalkamoni, age 47. Dalkamoni was suspected by the

West German federal authorities of being the ringleader of a cell of the Popular Front for the Liberation of Palestine-General Command (PFLP-GC). This organization is a PLO splinter group headed by a Palestinian, Ahmed Jibril, one of the world's most dreaded terrorists. The PFLP-GC had been active in the Middle East for many years.

Jibril and other Palestinians were in conflict with the Israelis because both claimed the same area in the Middle East as their homeland. Jibril and his organization were extremists who believed they must completely destroy the state of Israel to reclaim Palestine. They committed acts of violence against Israel and its supporters, including the United States.

Intelligence reports caused Israeli intelligence officers to warn the BKA that Jibril's followers or another extremist group might attempt to bomb an American airliner departing from the Frankfurt airport. The Israelis believed that the terrorists might strike late in 1988.

Dalkamoni had been seen visiting Frankfurt and Neuss. Items found in his car and in the apartments in Neuss and Frankfurt convinced the BKA that an attack on an aircraft was in the final stages of planning. In the car they found a radio cassette recorder, a Toshiba BomBeat 453, that was primed with a small charge of Semtex explosive. (Vaclav Havel, President of Czechoslovakia, where the explosive is made, said that the world's terrorist community had enough of the explosive to make bombs for the next 150 years.) The electronics of the cassette recorder had been replaced with a timing device connected to a barometric fuse.

In the apartment in Neuss a second Toshiba radio cassette recorder was found with other electrical equipment. This one had not been modified in any way, but the BKA believed it was awaiting the expert work to be done on it to make a second barometric bomb, a device that is designed to explode in an aircraft when it reaches a predetermined altitude. The lowering of atmospheric pressure with increasing altitude triggers the explosion.

At the Frankfurt apartment located at number 28 Sandweg, where Dalkamoni and one of the other men detained with him, Abdel Fatteh Ghadanfar, had been frequent visitors, the police uncovered an arsenal of explosives and equipment. They found a Beretta pistol with nine hundred rounds of ammunition and six Kalashnikov automatic rifles with nineteen magazines and three silencers. In addition, police found five kilos of Semtex, 5.87 kilos of another plastic explosive, three kilos of TNT, and eighty-nine detonators.

The four PFLP-GC captives were taken to Frankfurt for questioning, along with ten other people detained in raids elsewhere. The ten were released quickly for, despite the deep suspicion of the BKA, there was no evidence to link them with the weapons. Two men taken from the car were also released later for lack of evidence, leaving only Hafez Kassan Dalkamoni and Abdel Fetteh Ghadanfar in custody.

The two released car passengers owned the flat in Neuss along with Jordanian-born Marwan Khreesat. The BKA believed that Kreesat was the technician who made the bomb found in the car and that he was constructing the other devices found in Neuss. He was freed on appeal to a Frankfurt judge due to lack of evidence. The West Germans believe he immediately fled to Syria.

It has since been claimed by Western intelligence that Khreesat was a double agent working for West German security. Although this is strongly denied by the West Germans, it is clear that they did have a mole inside the PFLP-GC structure in the Federal Republic.

Dalkamoni, who led the PFLP-GC's European network, admitted being a member of the group. He claimed that he was simply the finance officer of the terrorist group and, despite the materials recovered from his car, not involved in military operations. Ghadanfar claimed only to have been Dalkamoni's assistant. However, the BKA, armed with intelligence from security agencies outside West Germany, placed Jordanian Dalkamoni at a much more central position within the PFLP-GC structure. They suspected that he was the mastermind behind the terrorist activities being planned from the Frankfurt apartment.

Two conclusions were drawn by the BKA. First, it was clear that they had interrupted a plot to blow up an aircraft in mid-flight. The barometric fuse on the radio cassette recorder meant that it was designed solely for this purpose. If a hijacking was being considered by the PFLP-GC, they would not have gone to the trouble of constructing the barometric device that would trigger itself, once primed on the ground, without the need for a suicidal terrorist to be on the target aircraft.

The second and perhaps most important conclusion was that other members of the PFLP-GC cell had either slipped through the net for lack of evidence against them, or had not been picked up in the raids of October 26th.

Police kept the seized weapons, which included the makings of deadly terrorist bombs. Soon after the raids they displayed them at a press conference in Frankfurt where they announced they had prevented a major terrorist attack. What they did not know was that they had failed to confiscate all the bombs.

Three weeks after the raid the Federal Aviation Administration released a security alert informing all airlines of a cassette-tape player bomb. The bulletin described the Toshiba cassette bomb in detail, warning that it was "nearly impossible to detect through normal inspection procedures." But a Pan Am worker at Frankfurt Airport whose job it was to post security bulletins never received the warning. This meant that baggage-inspection employees never heard they were supposed to be on the lookout for a cassette-player bomb.

I was amazed with all Megrahi and Fhimah knew about the case. I guess if you are under house arrest you would have plenty of time to study all the evidence—especially if your life depended upon it.

Late in the morning of December 5, 1988, the American Embassy in Helsinki, Finland, received a phone call from a man with a thick Arab accent and a threatening message. Sometime in the next few weeks, he said, a terrorist organization would try to smuggle a bomb onto a Pan Am flight from Frankfurt to the United States. The caller would not give his name or say where he got his information. When the embassy employee taking the call pressed him for details, the caller hung up.

The embassy informed Pan Am of the call, and the airline immediately began an investigation in Helsinki. There, Finnish intelligence officials told investigators that the call had been a hoax. Finnish officials investigated the caller, whom they knew, and found he had no connection to terrorist groups.

Just to be safe, investigators wrote a confidential memo to Pan Am officials to place "special emphasis on the handling of interline baggage at Frankfurt." But the chief of security at Frankfurt, Ulrich Weber failed to distribute the memo to his staff. Though the call was dismissed as a hoax, the threat was taken seriously enough to prompt officials at the American Embassy in Moscow to post the threat publicly so employees could change their flight plans if they wished.

When they boarded Flight 103 on the evening of December 21, passengers had no inkling of the threats to their safety. They were unaware that just a week before a man had called the American Embassy in Finland about a bomb threat for a Pan Am flight to America sometime in December.

Finally, passengers did not know that throughout November and December, the FAA had sent a number of security bulletins warning air carriers and airports to step up security measures because of increasing terrorist threats. These warnings had not made it to the security staff at the Frankfurt airport.

The passengers on Flight 103 remained blissfully unaware of any of the events that would soon conspire to change their destinies. They were simply eager to get home. They had no idea they would never get there.

Within seventy-two hours of the crash, Western intelligence sources said that the downing of Pan Am 103 was positively linked to the Frankfurt PFLP-GC cell. This was not just because of the obvious similarities in the bomb used, but also because of intelligence reports passed to the CIA by the Israeli secret service, Mossad, which claimed to have infiltrated every Palestinian terrorist organization in existence. In addition, the Israeli government's antiterrorist adviser, Yigal Carmon, had already tipped off the West German authorities that Mossad had also uncovered evidence of a planned bomb attempt on an airliner out of Frankfurt.

During the months following the crash, Scottish, British and American investigators pursued every lead and piece of evidence in their efforts to find the person or group responsible for this horrible disaster.

In November 1989, claiming access to inside information, *The Sunday Times* of London proudly published the "full story" of the Lockerbie plot. This account of the plot, was based on information pieced together by Western intelligence and security sources.

The report declared that it was:

>...now known that seven key conspirators, all members of the Popular Front for the Liberation of Palestine-General Command (PFLP-GC), are likely to be named in a Scottish police report to Lord Fraser of Carmyllie, the Scottish Lord Advocate.
>
>Western intelligence is convinced that Iran paid millions of dollars to Ahmed Jibril, the Damascus-based leader of the Palestinian faction, to carry out the bombing...Jibril is thought to have ordered Hafez Kassem Dalkamoni, the leader of the PFLP-GC's European terror network, to set up the bombing team...Dalkamoni then recruited Marwan Khreesat, a 44 year-old Jordanian terrorist to make the bomb.

The detailed report described how suspicion first began to focus on Ali Akbar Mohtashami, an Iranian hardliner thought to have paid $2 million to the PFLP-GC to carry out the bombing. A photograph of Mohtashami included in the report was entitled "Mastermind." The article called Ahmed Jabril, "The man, who, for $2 million ordered the bombing."

To back up this revelation, the article noted that, at a 1988 press conference in Libya following the shooting down of IR 655, Jabril made an ominous pronouncement: "There will be no safety for any traveler on an Israeli or U.S. airline."

In addition, the article hinted at the possibility that terrorists might have used a CIA-protected drug channel to smuggle the bomb onto Pan Am 103.

A Pan Am report leaked to my friend Congressman James Traficant, Jr. of Ohio, claimed that, "the bomb was put on board Pan Am 103 in Frankfurt with the unwitting compliance of CIA agents who were running a secret drug-for-hostages operation."

According to the *Sunday Times* story, the investigators from Lockerbie further believed that the Jordanian terrorist Marwan Khreesat had made five Semtex bombs, "...including the one that blew up Flight 103, and that he and the PFLP-GC had intended to bomb five Western aircraft as part of the Iranian-sponsored revenge attacks."

Some of the investigators believed that there could have been six bombs constructed—and that the sixth was still in terrorist hands.

Bomb number one was found in the back seat of Dalkamoni's Ford Taurus. The second bomb was found in the stereo tuner that exploded killing Has Uurgen Sonntag. The two other bombs, one in the tuner and one in the Sanyo television monitor, had been defused safely. The fifth bomb blew up in baggage carrier 14L at 7:03 P.M. on December 21, 1988, in the belly of the *Maid of the Seas* over Lockerbie.

Khreesat's bomb, according to the Lockerbie investigators, was smuggled out of the Frankfurt flat by the known PFLP-GC terrorist Ramzi Diab. He carried the bomb in a radio cassette player to Vienna, and then smuggled it into Malta for subsequent handling by a PFLP-GC cell operating in a bakery there. The *London Times* article identified the man who traveled to Malta to purchase the clothes put in the bomb suitcase as, Mohammed Abu Talb, a Palestinian terrorist now incarcerated in a Swedish jail for another bombing.

West German intelligence established that Talb and Dalkamoni had gone to Malta to instruct the cell to place the bomb on board an Air Malta flight. Baggage lists later showed that a bag had been transferred to Pan Am 103 at the Frankfurt airport from an Air Malta flight. An unaccompanied bag, originating in Malta, was in the cargo hold of Pan Am 103 when it exploded over Lockerbie.

Other media sources reported that fresh evidence had emerged linking two Palestinian terrorists, Abu Talb, a member of the PFLP-GC, and Marten Imandi, to a plot devised in Malta to plant a bomb on Pan Am 103. Talb, a known terrorist, was in Malta at the right time and surveillance records showed that he owned a brown Samsonite suitcase of the same type that contained the bomb. He also visited houses in Frankfurt where the bomb was almost certainly made. It was reported that the Scottish police believed that a PFLP-GC member smuggled the bomb from West Germany to Malta where it was placed in a suitcase and so conveyed onto Pan Am 103. Imandi, like Talb, was linked to the bomb apartment in Frankfurt.

In December, two detectives from Lockerbie flew to Belgrade to question friends and relatives of Mobdi Goben, a Palestinian with alleged bomb-making expertise and a known member of the PFLP-GC. Goben was believed to have supplied material for the Lockerbie bomb to Hafez Dalkamoni.

On December 17, 1989, *The Sunday Times* reported that the Lockerbie police were closing in "on the Lockerbie killers." Officers leading the investigation had informed their counterparts abroad that under Scottish law "charges are now possible against certain persons." At the same time, it was emphasized that because of extradition difficulties, some of the suspects would have to be tried abroad.

Again the familiar list of suspects was released. The Palestinian Abu Talb was a key suspect. The Jordanian, Marwan Khreesat was thought to have made the bomb. The Iranian Interior Minister Mohtashami was alleged to have paid a vast sum, $10 million for the bombing, and there was no doubt about the involvement of the PFLP-GC.

In the article, photographs of Khreesat, Dalkamoni, Jibril and Mohtashami were shown. A detailed examination of the PFLP-GC cell in Germany and its links to a cell in Malta and the suspected Palestinian terrorists in Sweden led the Scottish police to believe that the conspirators would be found among those individuals and organizations.

Thus, within a year after the Lockerbie disaster, there was virtually no disagreement among the investigators or intelligence officials involved in the investigation that Ahmed Jibril's organization was responsible for the bomb that blew up Flight 103.

The volume of detailed information in The *Sunday Times* articles could not have been accumulated without assistance from the Scottish police or from Western intelligence sources. This suggested that Western governments had an interest in giving publicity to the then current findings of the Lockerbie inquiry. These findings implicated a group of extremist Palestinians and the governments of two acknowledged "terrorist states," namely Iran and Syria.

Also, by the end of 1989 there was no discussion about U.S. incompetence in failing to alert the public to a bomb threat. Conclusive evidence showed that, in early December of 1988, before the Lockerbie bombing, the U.S. had been warned of a bomb threat to the Pan American airline. One warning clearly specified that the terrorist plot would involve a flight in December 1988, to the United States from Frankfurt, where the doomed Pan Am Flight 103 originated. Both warnings were phoned to U.S. embassies in Europe. American authorities at those embassies claimed that they told all the necessary security organizations. However, officials at Heathrow and Frankfurt denied that they were ever told, and no warnings were given to the public.

At the same time, in the United States, the National Security Agency's exhaustive analysis of intercepts in connection with the Lockerbie inquiry conceded that despite the tens of thousands of man-hours spent, the evidence linking Jibril and Dalkamoni to the hardline elements in Teheran was voluminous but inconclusive. From other sources, however, U.S. intelligence officials documented chapter and verse about Jibril's ties to Iran. They said that the information clearly bolstered the evidence discovered by police in West Germany, Sweden, Yugoslavia and Malta linking the PFLP-GC conclusively to the Pan Am bombing.

The question remained: If so much was known, why were there no arrests? In light of the demands being made on Libya today, one might ask why was there no pressure, possibly via the U.N. Security Council, for Iran and Syria to extradite the named terrorists for trial in Scotland or the United States? One possible answer emerged in the January 11, 1990, *Washington Post*, where it was revealed that Margaret Thatcher and George Bush, speaking on the telephone in Mid-March 1989, had agreed to downplay the Lockerbie disaster even though their intelligence services had established the Jibril/Nidal/Talb responsibility for the Lockerbie attack.

Another probable reason for this low-key approach was that the CIA, long connected with drug trafficking, had organized a drug run through the Frankfurt Airport in exchange for an Iranian commitment to free hostages, a deal similar to the "Irangate" arms-for-hostages agreement. Unfortunately it appears that this alleged drug run coincided with the plan to bomb Pan Am 103. In fact, it has been charged by investigators that the CIA may have inadvertently caused the Pan Am Crash.

It is also possible that the West had an eye on the shifting political scene in the Middle East. It would not be long before a pliant Syria and a quiescent Iran would be useful to Washington in its war on Iraq. Few independent observers doubt that Syria and Iran had been eased out of the

Lockerbie picture because of their acquiescence in the 1991 Gulf war.

It was only late in 1990 that reports began to surface implicating Libya in the Lockerbie attack. Many relatives of the Flight 103 passengers viewed this turn of events with deep skepticism. They feared the investigation was being forced in a direction that better suited the Bush administration's foreign policy goals.

Details implicating Libya were emerging at a time when the President was building a coalition against Iraq prior to the war in the Persian Gulf. A cornerstone of the alliance was Syria, home of Ahmed Jibril and headquarters of his PFLP-GC. Many parents and reporters felt it was too convenient that the U.S. progress in the investigation was taking the heat off the PFLP-GC and Iran. One of the relatives, John Root said, "It's absolutely disgusting that the President of the United States and Secretary of State are playing politics with the bodies of our dead ones."

By 1991 the relatives' concerns grew as they began getting signals that the investigation was continuing to move further away from Syria and the PFLP-GC. Shortly before the bombing's third anniversary, the families learned that indictments were imminent.

Fearing that U.S. and Scottish prosecutors might continue their pattern of secrecy by seeking sealed indictments, five relatives traveled to Great Britain to urge authorities there to make the police findings public. "The public has the absolute right to know the names of those responsible for this heinous crime," one of the family members, Bert Ammerman, said. "We will not allow government officials to quietly dispose of the results of their three-year investigation all for the political expediency of the Middle East peace conference."

On Thursday, November 14, 1991, the U.S. and Scottish prosecutors released a twenty-nine page indictment charging two Libyan men with carrying out the attack. Named were Lamen Khalifa Fhimah, thirty-nine, and Abdel Basset Ali al-Megrahi, fifty-five. Prosecutors accused Fhimah of using his job as an airline employee to store Semtex at the Malta airport. Megrahi, was allegedly identified by a shopkeeper in Malta as the man who bought an assortment of clothing at Mary's House, clothing found in the suitcase carrying the bomb. The indictment stated that both were agents of the Libyan intelligence service, the JSO.

Investigators concluded that both men used the Libyan Arab Airlines at Malta's Luqa Airport as a front. Their job was to make sure the suitcase containing the bomb was placed with luggage bound for the United States. Lamen Fhimah was a station manager and representative for Libyan Arab Airlines in Malta, a position which gave him access to Air Malta luggage tags. Abdel Basset Megrahi was the chief of JSO's airline security section giving him access to the Malta airport.

About two weeks before the Pan Am 103 bombing, Megrahi traveled from Libya to Malta. He checked into the Holiday Inn about 300 yards away from Mary's House. Investigators claimed that, on December 7, 1988, Megrahi bought the clothes that were eventually packed with the bomb and that he left Malta two days later.

The indictment alleged that on December 15th, the week before the Pan Am bombing, Lamen Fhimah made three entries in his diary to remind himself to obtain airline baggage tags from Air Malta. "Abdel Basset Megrahi is coming...take tags from Air Malta," one note said. "Bring tags from the airport," said another. In a third entry Fhimah had written "OK" adjacent to one of his earlier notes.

On December 18, the indictment states that, Lamen Fhimah traveled to Tripoli, Libya, for a meeting with Abdel Basset Megrahi. Two days later, on December 20, the two men went back to Malta, where Megrahi registered at the same Holiday Inn, this time using a pseudonym.

The following morning the two men made certain a hard-sided Samsonite suitcase with a stolen Air Malta luggage tag, was placed among luggage being loaded on Air Malta Flight KM180 to Frankfurt. The suitcase contained the bomb, concealed inside a Toshiba radio-cassette player. About twelve hours later, after the Samsonite bag had been transferred to Flight 103, the bomb exploded over Lockerbie.

The indictment stated that Megrahi left Malta the same day, boarding Libyan Arab Airlines Flight LN147 to Tripoli. Fhimah remained in Malta, although he, too, eventually returned to Libya.

Chapter Twenty-Three

The Evidence Against Libya

The possibility of Libyan involvement in the Locker-bie case had been under consideration for some time, but it wasn't until 1991 that Libyan complicity was taken seriously. According to the indictment, two pieces of evidence led to the 1991 indictments of Fhimah and Megrahi.

First, clothing packed in the copper-colored Samsonite suitcase containing the bomb, was traced to a boutique in the resort village of Sliema, Malta. This pleasant, family-run shop on Tower Road was called Mary's House. Although a year had passed, the owner, Anthony Gauci, told investigators he was certain he remembered the man who had purchased the clothing. The man was described by Gauci as being muscular and clean shaven, with dark eyes and neatly trimmed hair. He appeared to be in his middle to late thirties and spoke with a Libyan accent.

None of the reports of Gauci's recollections indicated that in Malta the generic and vernacular description of all Arab persons is that of "Libyan." Investigators also confused "passport du Liban" (a Lebanese passport) with a passport of Libya.

This was an astonishing piece of luck. According to sources in Lockerbie at the time, detectives waited anxiously by a fax machine for a police sketch of the customer who purchased the clothing from Mary's House. When the fax finally came through, a detective groaned, "It looks like Qadhafi."

While indeed the description fit Qadhafi, more importantly, it also resembled Abu Talb, the Palestinian terrorist and member of the PFLP-GC, whom investigators already suspected as being involved in the Pan Am 103 bombing. Talb was muscular and clean-shaven. He was in his mid-thirties and spoke with an accent that could easily have been mistaken for Libyan. Coincidently, Talb was under investigation in Sweden for a 1985 terrorist bombing that had happened in Copenhagen.

Initially the investigators were unable to tie Talb in with purchasing the clothes in Malta during November. Talb's passport indicated that he had been in Malta from October 3,1988 to October 26, 1988. This didn't fit with Gauci's recollection of November 23rd as the date when the clothes were purchased.

A break in the case came when Swedish police raided Talb's apartment in Stockholm on May 18, 1989. Investigators recovered a plane ticket from Malta to Stockholm via Rome. Police documents showed that Abu Talb had used the ticket to return to Stockholm on November 26, 1988. That meant that Abu Talb had made not one trip to Malta, but two. November 26 was just three days after Gauci had sold the array of clothes that wound up in the Samsonite suitcase on Pan Am 103.

Additionally, Talb's ex-wife, Jamilla Mougrabi, said that Talb had traveled to Malta in November of 1988 to recover from a knife wound. While he was there he visited a friend who owned a bakery and his brother, Salam, who owned a clothing business where Abu Talb bought some clothes.

Police in Sweden said they had a recording of a telephone call between Talb's ex-wife and some unidentified friends. The call was placed soon after Talb's arrest in Sweden on May 18th 1989. During the conversation Jamilla told her friends to "get rid of the clothes."

Finally, there was Abu Talb's own calendar. It contained a bit of circumstantial evidence that is more eerie than anything else. On his 1988 calendar, Abu Talb had circled the date December 21st!

On December 21, 1989—exactly one year to the date of the Pan Am 103 crash— Mohammed Abu Talb stood in front of a Stockholm courtroom. This was the last day of his trial for the 1985 bombing in Copenhagen. In his final statement to the court Talb said, "If being a lifelong combatant for Palestine is terrorism, then I am one of the world's biggest terrorists." Talb was found guilty and is presently serving a life sentence in a Swedish prison.

Thus it was rather shocking that, given the evidence against Talb and the articles in the London *Sunday Times* linking Talb and the PFLP-GC to the Pan Am bombing, all of a sudden, in 1991, investigators eliminated Talb and the PFLP-GC from the suspect list and began linking Libya with the bombing.

It is important to note that Mr. Gauci never personally identified either Abdel Basset Megrahi or Lamen Fhimah as the customer in his store. The identification came from a suspect book used by the FBI and Scotland Yard. Gauci had merely described the buyer as a "Libyan" and a man who had a "Libyan accent."

It may also be significant that the Libyan People's Bureau (embassy) was situated just a few hundred yards from Gauci's boutique, leading him to assume that the customer was Libyan. Neither Megrahi nor Fhimah were provided the benefit of a standard police "line up" nor were they ever conclusively identified by Gauci.

The second item of evidence leading to the indictment of Fhimah and Megrahi was a tiny portion of the circuit board used in the Lockerbie bomb's timer. It was found after exhaustive searches of the Scottish countryside around the crash scene. This tiny green fragment of a circuit board was no larger than a fingernail. It was fused into the remains of the copper-colored Samsonite suitcase. The bomb consisted of one pound of Semtex explosive concealed in a Toshiba radio cassette player. It had been wrapped in a bundle of clothes allegedly bought at Mary's House in Malta.

Although someone had tried to scratch out the manufacturer's initials, forensic workers were able to make out the letters: MEBO. The tiny piece of circuit board led police to Edwin Bollier, Managing Director of a small electronics firm, MEBO (Meister et Bollier, Ltd., Telecommunications), in Zurich, Switzerland.

Although the following information was not released to the public until November 1991, Edwin Bollier was questioned in January, 1990, approximately two weeks after the Pan Am crash.

The Swiss businessman found himself a reluctant witness after the police told him the timer that had triggered the Pan Am bomb had been made by his firm. At first Bollier found the story hard to believe. Then he recognized the charred remains of one of his "Zero Series Model MST-13" timers in a picture produced by detectives. According to information released in 1991, Bollier said in 1990 that he was certain that the Pan Am 103 timer was among a batch of twenty that he had manufactured in a special order for the Libyan military in 1985. He allegedly stated that he was positive that he had not sold the timers to any other country.

With Gauci's identification of Megrahi as the customer who bought the clothes found in the bomb's suitcase and Bollier's statement that all the MEBO timers had been sold to Libya, British, Scottish and American investigators felt they had the case sewn up. On Thursday, November 14, 1991, the United States indicted Abdel Basset Megrahi and Lamen Fhimah for the bombing murder of the 270 passengers and Lockerbie residents killed by Pan Am 103.

In announcing the indictment, U.S. prosecutors said that despite the activities of the PFLP-GC cell in West Germany and intelligence intercepts discovered in the attack's aftermath, there was no evidence of Syrian or Iranian involvement.

President Bush told reporters that day, "A lot of people thought it was the Syrians. The Syrians took a bum rap on this."

A spokesman for the Administration said, "This was a Libyan operation from start to finish."

Douglas Hurd, the British Foreign Secretary, told the House of Commons that there was "no evidence" linking any government but Libya's to the atrocity.

Nevertheless, many investigators and police who had been involved in gathering the evidence, and many families of the victims and reporters who had followed the story for two years, were not as easily convinced. More than a few wondered why Britain and the United States were so willing to let Iran and Syria completely off the hook.

Were their suspicions justified? Was it purely coincidence that, just a few days after the indictments came out against the Libyans, unequivocally clearing Iran and Syria of involvement in the PanAm 103 bombing, hostages Terry Waite from England and Thomas Sutherland, an American, were released in Beirut? Was it coincidental that a month later President George Bush met Hafez al-Assad, the Syrian leader, to discuss joint participation in the multinational task force confronting Saddam Hussein in the Gulf?

Bollier's claim was a stunning breakthrough. After interviewing 16,000 people in 70 countries the Scots had finally uncovered a strand of forensic evidence running from Scotland to Libya. It was a case prosecutors in Edinburgh thought they could make stick.

Despite the suspicion and doubts, the complex case was still held together by a single strand of apparently incontrovertable evidence—Bollier's claim that all his timers, including the timer found at Lockerbie, had been sold to Libya.

Chapter Twenty-Four

Off To Meet "The Leader"

I could hear a telephone ring in an adjoining room and, as Fhimah and Megrahi were concluding their stories, Khaled summoned Youssef to the telephone. In less than a minute he returned and announced, "My leader wants to see you now." He shouted instructions to the JSO agents. After a handshake and a thank you to Fhimah and Megrahi, I was once again in my trench coat and wide-brimmed hat being escorted quickly out of the front door of the house and into the waiting limo.

This time the sirens were blaring as we sped away from the house enroute to the El Mahari Hotel. Youssef explained that his men at the hotel had notified Gerrit and the Hubbards to be ready when we arrived. He would put them in another car so they wouldn't notice that I had been out of the hotel. We had to hurry because his Leader was going to be leaving shortly and we had some distance to travel. We pulled into the hotel drive in exactly eight minutes. Neither Gerrit nor the Hubbards were anywhere to be seen.

One JSO agent reported to Youssef that Mrs. Hubbard was not quite ready but would be down shortly. We waited an additional few minutes. Youssef became quite upset. "My Leader is waiting. Don't they understand?" Youssef asked angrily. The car phones and hand-held radios were blaring the entire time we were waiting. Gerrit arrived and it was obvious from his eyes that he had been awakened from a sound sleep. He asked, "What have you been doing? Your phone has been busy for hours!" I told him I took the phone off the hook in order to get a little uninterrupted sleep. He seemed satisfied. He wouldn't know about my visit with Fhimah and Megrahi for almost two years.

The Hubbards exited the hotel and apologized for their tardiness. They had also been asleep when the call had come. Gerrit got in the car with Youssef and me. The Hubbards rode in the car behind us. We wasted no time leaving the hotel. We were on our way to meet Col. Muammar al-Qadhafi.

Youssef said that we would be meeting Qadhafi at his tent located just outside of town. I had heard so much about his tent. It was hard to believe that I was about to see it for myself, and actually meet the man so hated by the Western world. The trip out of town was much like the one we took into town the night before, noisy and confusing. There was a sense of excitement in the air as we sped through Tripoli to rendezvous with Col. Qadhafi.

It was almost dark as we left the city and from the back seat of the car it was very difficult to see which direction we were taking. Our speed increased as we moved further away from the city, once again reaching 100 M.P.H. on a dark highway about ten minutes from the hotel. The siren noise was deafening and it was very difficult to hear Youssef as he tried to explain the reason for our speed. He said that Col. Qadhafi moved his tent frequently to avoid another surprise raid by U.S. planes, similar to the one in 1986. The location of the tent was highly secret and he wanted to keep it that way.

Youssef explained that Qadhafi was a Bedouin ("dwellers in the desert") belonging to a small tribe, the Gaddafa (literally "those who spit out vomit"). The Bedouins have retained their nomadic and pastoral way of life. Like most nomads, Qadhafi was very much accustomed to moving frequently from one place to another. He is very comfortable living and working in a tent, although he often spends time at his home in Tripoli. As a matter of fact, he was planning on leaving the tent that very night for the city. It was imperative that we get to him before he moved. Thanks to Mrs. Hubbard, we were already a half-hour late for our meeting.

Almost as quickly as we had started, we came to an abrupt stop on the side of the highway. All of a sudden it was very quiet. The sirens stopped and the head lights of the cars in our caravan were turned off. We sat quietly as we waited for our accompanying police cars to block the cars approaching us from the front and the rear. When all traffic was stopped, Youssef gave instructions on the car radio. Our tires squealed as we made a sharp left turn across the four lane highway and onto a dirt road. Our head lights remained out as we felt our way along the winding, dusty road with only the benefit of the low beams on the lead car. I couldn't imagine how our drivers were able to see where they were going. I did understand the need to keep the tent's location secret, but was it worth our lives—I wondered?

I estimated our drive time down the deserted road to be about five minutes. We had made a few fast turns along the way. There was no chance that any of us could have ever retraced our path.

We came to a stop at a large chain-linked gate guarded by two casually dressed Libyan guards carrying Russian-made Kalashnikov rifles. The only light came from a small lamp located in a guard shack just inside the chain linked fence with rolled consertina barbed wire along the top. Youssef left the car and approached the gate guards. The news he received was not good. It was obvious from his body language that he was very upset. At one point he kicked the ground with his foot as his voice got louder and louder.

From my vantage point in the back of the car, I could just make out what I suspected to be Qadhafi's tent situated behind the fence and a few bushes. The typical Bedouin tent is made from strips of cloth woven from goat or camel hair and vegetable fibers, sewn together and dyed black. Qadhafi's tent was not black but more of a brown color. It was very large and I was told that it served as both Qadhafi's office and home. He used it to entertain heads of state as well as average Libyan citizens. Khaled said that part of Qadhafi's appeal to the Libyan people was his commitment to traditional Arab values, mores and the Muslim religion.

It is estimated that there are approximately one million Bedouins who follow the traditional life-style of nomadic herders in the deserts of the Middle East. Almost all of them are Muslims and speak some form of the Arabic language. The Bedouins who follow their traditional way of life travel the deserts seeking fresh water and pastureland for their camels, goats, and sheep. They live in tents and wear clothing made from the skin and hair of their animals. The Bedouins eat mostly dairy products, dates and rice. They trade meat and dairy products from their livestock to people in nearby villages for knives, pots, and other manufactured goods. They are proud and extremely independent. They live by a moral code that emphasizes such values as courage, generosity, and tribal loyalty. Insults to their pride sometimes lead to bloody feuds between tribes.

It became increasingly clear from the discussion taking place at the gate that Qadhafi was gone. How disappointing! I could see my chance of visiting the tent slipping away, and our meeting with Qadhafi seriously in doubt. I began to wonder if we had delayed our departure for Geneva for naught.

I watched and waited as Debri threw up his arms and returned to the car. "We missed him by ten minutes," Youssef said as he got in the car. "These people make me crazy, Chazzy," he continued. "We will go back to Tripoli

212

and meet my Leader at the Al Jamahiriyah Barracks where he is staying tonight."

Once again we were speeding down the dark dirt road with lights out and radios blaring. The dust seemed to be worse going out to the highway than it was coming in. Once we hit the hard-surfaced road the sirens started again. We followed our police escort cars that were waiting for us at the end of the dirt road, although hidden from sight behind some shrubs. I once again took a firm grip on the handle strap on the back door of the car and tensed my body for the race back to Tripoli. The ride took about twelve minutes during most of which Col. Debri talked in Arabic on the car radio.

I didn't ask too many questions, but prayed my favorite prayer from the Twenty-Third Psalm, which always gives me great comfort when I am fearful: "Yea, though I walk through the valley of the shadow of death, I will fear no evil; for Thou are with me; Thy rod and Thy staff, they comfort me."

Our cars slowed down as we entered the city. Once again the sirens halted. We entered a residential neighborhood and after a few zigs and zags, we were waved through the front gates of a military establishment by two sharply dressed Libyan soldiers. Our drivers knew just where to go and we came to a halt in front of a very military looking building, not much different from those I remembered from my days at Camp LeJeune, North Carolina.

As we exited our cars, I had a chance to talk with Congressman and Mrs. Hubbard and Gerrit. They had been in the limo just behind ours on this incredible night ride around Libya. I was surprised to hear that neither their driver nor bodyguard spoke English, which left them completely confused about where they had been and what they were doing now at the Al Jamahiriyah Barracks.

Carroll's first words to me were, "What the hell is going on? That was the scariest ride I have ever taken. What are we doing here?" I explained the situation and Carroll's fear was replaced with anxious anticipation of our visit with Qadhafi. Mrs. Hubbard asked if I thought it would be safe to meet him. I assured her that it was, and that there was nothing to fear.

We walked up the front steps of the barracks and were warmly greeted at the top by a Libyan man named Ahmed, dressed in casual pants and a leather jacket. He introduced himself as a graduate of the University of Michigan, and said that he would be serving as our interpreter during our meeting with Col. Qadhafi. He escorted us down a long hallway and into a beautiful reception room.

We were joined by two lovely Arab women dressed to kill in the finest Western fashion. They wore spiked high heeled shoes and tight fitting dresses. They were introduced to us by Ahmed as Col. Qadhafi's bodyguards. I remembered reading that he had used female bodyguards for many years.

We were invited to sit and wait in the reception room for our audience with Qadhafi. During the thirty minute wait, I was given a brief lesson on women's rights by one of the female Libyan bodyguards named Adel. She was responding to Carroll's obvious surprise at meeting a woman Libyan bodyguard. Mrs. Hubbard was very interested in the discussion and asked a variety of questions about the role of women in Libya.

Adel was an army officer. She was a graduate of the first military academy for girls in the world, located right there in Libya. The Women's Military Academy was founded in 1978. In his speech at the first graduation in 1981, Qadhafi declared that the officers produced by the Academy would have duties spanning the full range of military activities. Polygamy is banned in Libya—against Islamic tradition—and women are active in the various political committees and in such unlikely arenas as the armed forces. The women would not merely serve as a corps of auxiliaries as they do in the American armed forces but have similar responsibilities as the men.

It is a source of particular pride that the Academy is graduating officers into the Jamahiriya. Qadhafi further stated in the graduation speech that, "We in the Jamahiriya and the great revolution affirm respect for women and raising their flag. We have resolved to totally liberate women in Libya, thus removing them from the world of oppression and subjugation, so that they may be masters of their own fate in a democratic milieu where they have equal opportunities with all other members of society. In this context the Women's Military Academy will serve as a cornerstone for the liberation of women in Libya, the rest of the Arab world, and beyond. A central task will be to liberate the 'oppressed and paralyzed' female half of the Arab nations."

It was clear that Qadhafi, contrary to popular belief, had long toyed with a degree of female emancipation that would have been totally at odds with the traditional Islamic practices of pre-revolutionary Libya and the modern societies of Kuwait, the United Arab Emirates and Saudi Arabia.

In 1975 Qadhafi had created the Libyan General Women's Federation to remove the worst features of social oppression, and by 1979 there were some twenty local branches. The Federation offered support in traditional female areas, helping with hygiene and baby care, running nurseries and kindergartens, but also expanding female horizons by combating illiteracy and by helping girls to enter school and the university. Health centers had been established to improve the welfare of women and their

215

children. Family planning facilities were offered, as was medical support for pregnancy, birth and lactation. These centers worked in conjunction with the Social Care and Enlightenment Centers specializing in social work and community health, institutions that were unheard of in pre-revolutionary Libya. In addition, a Center for the Protection of Women was created in Tripoli to help with the rehabilitation of women in cases of divorce, prostitution, and women abandoned by their families.

Under Qadhafi, women witnessed for the first time a proliferation of educational opportunities. The People's Committee for Education and the Ministry of Education were prohibited from discriminating on grounds of sex when granting stipends to students. Since the fall of the monarchy, the number of females in the educational system had risen at all levels.

In 1970, immediately after Qadhafi's seizure of power, there was legislation (Law no. 58) to affirm the equal status of men and women, and to establish wage parity for male and female workers in the same occupation.

As a good feminist Democrat, Carol Hubbard was enjoying what she heard. This could have been taken directly out of the 1982 Democrat platform.

Adel continued by saying that many unprecedented measures were put in place during the 1970's but women still had to contend with age-old Islamic attitudes. The inevitable tensions between tradition and emancipation could easily be detected in Libya today. Qadhafi, on the one hand, applauded the familiar domestic role for women but, on the other, he urged a revolutionary liberation of women throughout the Arab world and beyond.

Carol and I agreed that there could be no doubt that the position of Libyan women had massively improved under Qadhafi.

216

Adel and her counterpart asked Carol to join them at the other end of the large room. This seemed a bit odd to us, but what wasn't that day? The ladies sat and talked together as Carroll, Gerrit and I nervously awaited our meeting with Qadhafi. Youssef had not entered the reception room with us. We passed the time by talking about the American elections with Ahmed. He was glad to get some news from the States. He thanked us for our patience and explained that Col. Qadhafi had just arrived and that it should only be a few more minutes before we would meet him.

Youssef entered and asked that we follow him to our meeting. Anxiety and anticipation filled my body as I realized that we were about to meet the man some considered the "most hated and feared man in the world." Carol Hubbard and Adel joined us as we left the reception room and started our walk down the long hall to Qadhafi's office.

Carol was extremely nervous and couldn't wait to tell us something. In a very quiet voice she said to her husband, "He wants to talk with me alone after the meeting." Congressman Hubbard had a look of shock on his face and couldn't find words to respond. She went on, "Adel said that Qadhafi had something to say to me in private."

I tried to ease the tension with a bit of levity. I told the Hubbards that this was part of an old Libyan tradition. The first time an important guest meets a Libyan Leader, he is expected to share his wife with him. My small joke did evoke a smile, but did little to ease their obvious anxiety they were feeling. "Let's wait and see what happens during our meeting before we get too upset," I suggested. "The last thing in the world Qadhafi wants is to create an international incident over a Congressman's wife."

217

Chapter Twenty-Five

Meeting "The Leader"

As we approached a wide door at the end of the hall, a well dressed Libyan man in his 40's greeted and escorted us into Qadhafi's office. I expected that we would sit and wait a few minutes for Qadhafi to arrive, so I was surprised to find myself face to face with the Libyan Leader as I entered the room. He had been sitting on an ornate, off-white couch at the far end of the large room. He politely stood as we entered. A photographer, already in place, started snapping pictures of our arrival. This seriously upset Congressman Hubbard. His first words to Qadhafi were, "I prefer that you not take pictures of our visit." Qadhafi was quite surprised and seemed disturbed by Hubbard's request. He said a few words in Arabic to Ahmed. Ahmed instructed the photographer to leave the room.

I was embarrassed by Hubbard's initial behavior. I could understand that he didn't want a record of our meeting with the Libyan Leader, but there was no need to be rude to our host, no matter who he was. I hoped that this incident wouldn't set a negative tone for the balance of our meeting.

Col. Qadhafi graciously greeted each of us as we approached. Youssef, in turn, introduced us to his Leader and we each shook hands and exchanged pleasantries. I was the last to meet Qadhafi and deliberately delayed my handshake as I tried to make eye contact with him. He firmly shook my hand but avoided looking directly at me. He was much shorter than I had expected. Bedouins are usually under medium height and I guessed him to be about five-feet-ten inches tall. I knew that Qadhafi spoke English as well as I but he responded to me only in Arabic and through Ahmed. He extended his arm and invited me to join my colleagues already sitting on couches arranged directly in front of his.

I studied Qadhafi very carefully. I looked at every detail of his person for characteristics that I would remember in the future. I reflected on how I used to do this when I sat next to Ronald Reagan during the 1980 Presidential campaign. Qadhafi's face seemed almost puffy with aquiline features and a swarthy complexion. My eyes were fixed on the black mole located just below his left nostril. He had dark penetrating eyes that seemed to look right through me. Only strands of his black-kinky hair on the top and sides of his head were visible from under his tan, loose-fitting headscarf called a kaffiyeh.

He wore a full length brown robe which was tied over his left shoulder and was somehow draped over his right shoulder. The robe covered an aqua colored Nehru type jacket with a gold embroidered high collar and trim that ran down the front of the jacket, disappearing beneath the robe at mid-chest level. He wore a plain gold wedding band on his left hand.

Because of the hot climate of most Arab lands, both men and women have traditionally worn loose-fitting garments that cover most of the body and head, shielding them from the sun. This is especially important in Libya where the world's highest temperature of 136 degrees F was recorded at El Asisia, Libya, on September 13, 1922.

Seeing Qadhafi in his costume, I couldn't help but remember again a remark President Ronald Reagan had made in an August 14, 1986 meeting with George Schultz, Casper Weinberger, Bill Casey, John Poindexter and Admiral William Crowe. They were celebrating their successful bombing raid on Tripoli and Bengazi, and considering a fresh disinformation campaign against Qadhafi. Reagan quipped, "Why not invite Qadhafi to San Francisco, he likes to dress up so much." Schultz retorted, "Why don't we give him AIDS." The others laughed.

The Libyan Leader began our discussion by thanking each of us by name for having the courage to visit Libya. He spoke very quietly. His deliberate speaking manner was accentuated by the time delay necessary for Ahmed to translate his remarks into English. Qadhafi said that he hoped that our visit would open a new era of positive relationships between our two countries. He stared straight ahead and made no attempt to engage our eyes or to observe our reactions to his comments. I remember thinking at the time that this guy was one "cold turkey."

As he spoke I tried to take mental pictures of his office. The room was stark and completely void of color. The deep carpet was white, as was most of his furniture. The room was rigidly conforming in its style and decoration. Qadhafi's off-white couch was positioned in front of a white folding wall, opened halfway, that separated this formal reception room from the more functional working office, located just behind the wall. The office was harsh and totally void of ornaments, paintings or personal items that would give me some clue to the basic nature of this man for which it was designed.

A small, cloth-draped coffee table separated Qadhafi from us. He had a stack of papers and a small box containing a colorful array of pencils and pens situated in the center of the table. A copy of Qadhafi's *Green Book*, which outlines the sociopolitical model for Libya, was prominently displayed on the table directly in front of him. This philosophical model was first outlined in 1973 at a symposium in Paris and further developed into three published installments comprising the Green Book. Part one of the *Green Book* heralded the start of the era of the Jamahiriya (state of the masses). Part two inaugurated an international, economic revolution, which does away with the old economic structures of society. Part three launches Qadhafi's social revolution.

The *Green Book* is the philosophy of Muammar Qadhafi. On the back cover of the Book, which I later read, Qadhafi wrote the following brief summary:

It presents the genuine interpretation of history, the solution of man's struggle in life, and the unsolved problems of man and woman. Equally it tackles the problem of minorities and of blacks in order to lay down the sound principles of social life for all mankind. The living philosophy is inseparable from life itself and erupts from its essence.

Congressman Hubbard thanked Qadhafi for his hospitality and time. He realized that he had been rude to our host earlier about the photographer and apologized profusely. Just when he seemed to be making some points with our host, he once again insulted Qadhafi in an attempt at trying to be funny, "I don't want a picture of us appearing together in the Mayfield, Kentucky newspaper." It got worse when he asked Qadhafi if it would be O.K. if his wife used her camera to take some pictures after our meeting. He would then be able to control the destiny of his own pictures, which would not include the front page of the Mayfield Messenger. Without comment, Qadhafi resumed his remarks.

Qadhafi expressed his delight in the election of President-elect Bill Clinton just one week before. "The people of Libya were celebrating in the streets as the election news started arriving here. I think there is a great opportunity for us to reestablish a cooperative relationship between the United States and Libya under Mr. Clinton's administration. We suspect that Mr. Clinton will deal with us honestly, and do all in his power to get to the bottom of the Pan Am 103 disaster. Qadhafi repeated Omar's story that President-elect Clinton told Pan Am 103 families on September 17, 1992, he would make sure that all questions regarding Syrian and Iranian involvement in the tragedy were addressed and fully answered."

Qadhafi was referring to a letter sent by Clinton to Daniel and Susan Cohen of Port Jervis, N.Y. Clinton wrote, "If elected, I will do what is right and necessary to send a message that individuals who engage in, and countries which lend support for, terrorist activities will pay a high price for doing so." The Cohen's 19-year-old daughter, Theodora, was one of the 270 victims of the midair explosion that destroyed Pan Am 103.

Qadhafi continued, "This leads me to believe that the investigation will be reopened and those responsible for the bombing will be indicted and brought to justice." He said that he was looking for our help in getting the President-elect to consider a new dialogue with the people of Libya. "I thank you Dr. Chasey for bringing Congressman and Mrs. Hubbard to Libya to help us get to the bottom of this case. Youssef Debri and The Committee to Resolve the Lockerbie Dispute have been trying in vain to get an elected official from the United States to discuss the issue with us for over a year now. In every case our outreach has been rejected. I want you to know how much I and the people of my country appreciate all you have done.

"Congressman Hubbard, you have the opportunity to tell Mr. Clinton what you have heard and seen here during your visit. As you know, two of our countrymen have been accused by your country in the 1988 bombing of Pan AM 103. I can assure you that these two men are innocent and are ready to stand trial but only in a neutral country. We don't believe they would receive a fair trial in your country.

"The UN Security Council voted to impose a ban on air travel and arms sales to us unless I surrender the two suspects to your country. This ban on air travel has been very hurtful to my fellow countrymen. I am asking you to relate the results of our meeting to your new President, Mr. Clinton upon your return to the United States. I am also requesting that you and Dr. Chasey relate my country's foreign policy philosophy to the Members of the United States Congress. This U.S. election is a time of renewal for us."

Qadhafi continued his remarks by stating that, "No nation can afford to ignore the momentous changes that have occurred in the world in recent years. The foreign policy of every country today must reflect the following new realities (I took notes and later filled in the facts from some of Qadhafi's speeches):

- that the Cold War is over and the tensions of the great powers have evaporated completely.

- that the Soviet Empire has collapsed into a complex of newly independent states which face momentous difficulties as they try to construct participatory structures of government, protecting the rights of all their peoples and creating modern, competitive economies on the ruins of a failed Socialism;

- that ethnic conflicts are now rising up throughout the band of states from Middle Europe through Central Asia in a considerable number of points in Africa;

- that the industrialized nations of Europe, Japan and preeminently the United States, though now beyond challenge in their traditional sense of national security, are suddenly afflicted

224

with grave economic difficulties of slow growth, and structural rigidities and social conflicts;

- but, that as a broad global trend, the community of nations is moving, fitfully and perhaps not entirely smoothly, toward more open, democratic processes of self government, and at the same time toward a broader embrace of market economies."

He went on, "My country is both affected by these radical changes, and a part of them. It is a fact, of which little notice has been taken in the West, that Libya has quite recently inaugurated a new assembly of elected representatives of each of the tribal groups of the nation. This assembly has just met for the first time earlier in the month. It was a time of historic change. The assembly was established in order to insure a full and fair opportunity for expression to each of the identifiable interest groups of the state. It is to insure that the government is effectively representative, and is an expression of the popular will of the people. In this first meeting, the assembly fully justified its purpose. After considerable debate, marked by full freedom of expression, it elected, in an exercise of unfettered collegiate expression, each of the members of the new Cabinet of the nation.

"You had the opportunity of meeting Minister Omar Mustafa al-Muntassir this morning. He was selected to preside over the Ministry of Foreign Relations, and in the process to give voice and definition to the international position and views of our country.

"I want you, Mr. Hubbard and Dr. Chasey, to be the first to understand our foreign policy views so that you can express them to your colleagues in the White House and in your Congress. My country's foreign policy may be said to express five fundamental principles.

"First, we utterly and without qualification renounce terrorism as an instrument of state policy. I will not attempt to review and rebut the record of unfounded and unjustified allegations which have been leveled against my country in this regard in the past, beyond stating that the public record is replete with myths and legends as to our responsibility for acts of political terrorism which are untrue. I focus on the future. As to that, I am prepared to affirm with all the solemnity I can muster, that terrorism has no role in our relations with other nations, and that we do not and will not countenance, support or tolerate the use of force against innocent persons for political purposes as an instrument of state.

"Indeed, we go further and match deeds to our words. We are ready to give evidence of our conviction and commitment in this respect. We have in recent months offered to share information as to known terrorists groups with the antiterrorist authorities of other nations. We will intensify this exchange of intelligence and take such other measures as are appropriate to support and participate in the international struggle against this intolerable behavior."

Qadhafi didn't change position and his eyes were fixed on the wall at the far end of the room. Ahmed was able to translate rather quickly and was never more than a few words behind his Leader. We were transfixed with the dialogue and continued to listen without interruption.

"The second element of our foreign policy is cooperation against proliferation of weapons of mass destruction. We are not interested in accumulating biological, nuclear or chemical weaponry, or the means to manufacture, store and deliver them. We are, accordingly, prepared to open our facilities, on a reciprocal basis, to full appropriate international inspection, to give the world assurances that our country is not a repository of such weapons.

226

"The third element I should like to address relates to the Lockerbie incident, and the charge that two Libyans are implicated in that affair. The Security Council has seen fit to impose burdensome economic sanctions on our nation on that account, and these sanctions are to be reviewed further at a meeting of the UN Security Council in mid-December.

"I would like the position of my country to be absolutely clear. We do not oppose, and are prepared to facilitate, the trial of the two accused men. We interpose no restriction whatsoever to the judicial determination of these charges anywhere in the civilized world where the accused may receive a fair trial. We have made this official position known to the two accused. We are advised by them that it is their intention, in these circumstances, to present themselves to the authorities of a neutral country for the adjudication of the charges against them, following the accustomed procedures of criminal justice in that country.

"The arrangements for this are entirely in the hands of the two individuals. My government will play no role in the definition of the terms of their decision, nor in the arrangements their lawyers will make for them, to place themselves at the disposition of the law enforcement authorities of whatever country they shall choose. It is not the place of my government to interfere in these decisions.

"The fourth element of our foreign policy relates to the special conflicts and tensions of the Middle East. The entire world has an interest in the resolution of these conflicts, for the world has in the past been brought close to nuclear destruction on account of those conflicts.

"It is our view that it is now time to redouble our collective efforts toward peaceful resolution. We welcome the Middle East Peace Talks. We have attempted to play a constructive role in them. We call on all parties to those talks, not least the United States, to use every effort to bring

227

those talks to a successful conclusion as quickly as feasible, one which fully respects the just aspirations of all the affected peoples.

"The fifth and final element of our foreign policy is the most general and the broadest in its scope and implication. It is to express our aspiration for peaceful and mutually beneficial relations with all nations. It is no secret that our relations with certain countries have not been happy in recent years. Indeed, we have been the subject of armed attack resulting in the deaths of innocent men, women and children.

"We have been declared off-limits for the travel of the citizens of the United States. And Americans have been banned from doing any trade with our country, or engaging in any fruitful economic relations.

"It is not my purpose to debate the international legality of these measures, or their justification, beyond stating that these measures cannot be based on hostility on our part and are not explainable by any need to reciprocate for attacks against the United States or our side.

"Indeed, any fair examination of the public record will demonstrate that Libya, in recent years, has been singularly careful to avoid giving offense to any nation, most particularly the United States, in the public statements of its policies and attitudes. We have honored the rights of the many Americans who have continued to live in Libya and insured them against all harassment.

"We have been careful to maintain an attitude of respect toward President Bush throughout his term and, I am pleased to say that, as that term approaches its end, we have continued to entertain the most cordial attitude toward him personally. The hostility has been entirely in the other direction in recent years.

"We want to bring this hostility to an end and we believe it is timely to do so now with President-elect Clinton taking office in January. We assert that there is no ground for the continued refusal to extend diplomatic recognition, to permit diplomatic interchange or to allow travel and trade exchange between our countries. We are prepared, as I have said, to give proof of our commitment against terrorism, of our refusal to seek nuclear, biological and chemical weapons, of our willingness to open the door to the trial of the Lockerbie accused.

"We pledge our support for an early and just determination of the issues in the Middle East. In doing so, we extend the hand of permanent friendship and mutual respect, and we stand prepared to do all in our power to return our relationship with the United States to a normal and mature status."

Carroll Hubbard was almost speechless. For a professional politician this had to be a brand new feeling. He stammered a bit as he expressed his appreciation for Qadhafi's remarks. He noted that what he had just heard didn't gel with the public's perception of him around the world. Hubbard offered to help relate Qadhafi's story when he returned to the U.S. Congress. He said, "President-elect Clinton would be very interested in hearing this story." Carroll told Qadhafi about his close friendship with the new Chairman of the House Foreign Affairs Committee, Lee Hamilton. He would schedule a meeting with Hamilton as soon as he could upon his return.

My reaction was quite different from that of the Congressman. I was more puzzled as to why the United States government would not listen to Qadhafi, or at least be receptive to opening some form of diplomatic interchange. Was Libya to be another Cuba? We have had sanctions against Castro since 1959, and what good have they done? What did we have to show for this political standoff with this island-nation just ninety miles off our Florida coast? Castro had outlasted eight U.S. Presidents and we had never offered him the olive branch. Would this be the case with Libya over the two suspected Libyans? Would this stand-off last for another thirty-three years? I was sure of one thing. There was more involved in this West-Libyan con-frontation than I had first thought, and the evidence I had heard during the past twenty-four hours couldn't have all been fabricated.

Qadhafi may have been the world's greatest con-man, and his foreign policy could have been orchestrated by a clever public relations team. The other possibility, as so many had suggested over the years, was that Qadhafi was crazy and a mad man. It was obvious to me that he wasn't crazy. Were my biases based on a very cleverly contrived U.S. disinformation campaign directed against Libya by the past three administrations? If Qadhafi was just putting on a show for our benefit, he deserved the Academy Award for best actor.

Geoff Simons' book, Libya: The Struggle For Survival, *provided a very comprehensive background on Libya and Muammar Qadhafi and was extremely helpful in preparing this chapter.*

I was mesmerized by Col. Qadhafi. Although we were the same age, this was where the similarities ended. We were both born in 1940, but for some reason he didn't know his actual birth date. Qadhafi's parents, Mohammed Abdul Salam bin Hamed bin Mohammed al-Qadhafi (known as Abu Meniar, "father of the knife") and Aissha al-Qadhafi produced two daughters and a son, all born in a tent, twenty miles south of the coastal town of Sirte. His father belonged to a small tribe, the Gaddafa, a basically Bedouin group that showed strains of many other peoples, including Berbers, Circassians, Turks, Jews and others who had inhabited Libya over the years. His parents were

230

poor and illiterate but they told stories in the tradition of the Bedouin about their tribe and its history, about ancient battles and foreign enemies. Aissha died in 1978, and Abu Meniar, well over ninety, died in 1985.

The Gaddafa, though a small and humble tribe, knew the value of education, and so Muammar's parents pooled their meager savings to send their son first, to a Koranic elementary school and later, to high school at Sebba in Fessan. At around the time of independence, Qadhafi enrolled at the primary school in Sirte and so became the first member of his family to read and write. At school during the day, he slept in a mosque at night. He trekked home through the desert every Thursday, at the start of the Muslim weekend, and returned late on Friday. He was the oldest boy in his class and, as a rural Bedouin, viewed by his classmates as something of a country bumpkin. His father saw him as a serious and pious student. When Qadhafi was fourteen, his family moved to Sebba where he enrolled at the local secondary school. He attracted a group of friends who remained with him until he took power over Libya in 1969.

The early 1960's were exciting times in Libya. The country was newly independent, and the weak King Sayyid Muhammed al-Idris was unable to suppress the growing political agitation in his country. Young students were stimulated by new ideas and foreign examples of political initiative and nationalist success. Students read and listened to the radio, particularly to the powerful rhetoric of the Egyptian leader, Gamal Abdul Nasser. Nasser's Philosophy of the Revolution, *describing how he formed an "army officers' club" and overthrew the Egyptian monarchy in 1952, was one of the most important books that Qadhafi encountered during that period. He saw it as an example and model for the forthcoming Libyan revolution.*

231

Qadhafi was always a charismatic figure and attracted followers during his school years. It is said that his friends carried a stool around so that he could use it when he wanted to make a speech. His overt political activity led him to be expelled from the Sebba school and, for all intents and purposes, he became unable to attend any school in Libya. This ruling by school officials has been judged to have alienated Qadhafi from the sociopolitical system in Libya and to have further fueled his revolutionary ambitions. Using a false birth certificate, he enrolled and continued his revolutionary activities at another secondary school in Mistrata. He soon became famous and attracted more followers. Qadhafi laid down his own rules for his followers. They could not drink, play card games or interact with women. Further, they should pray and study. Lastly, they were always required to attend his political meetings.

In 1963, Qadhafi enrolled in the Royal Libyan Military Academy in Benghazi. Since he was well known by the police at the time, some wonder how he was ever accepted at the Academy. He was known as one of the "most backward" cadets, and was one of the 2% of the cadets who failed their examinations. Part of his problem was that he wouldn't learn English. He was also extremely rude to the officers and men. The Academy head, a British Colonel named Ted Lough, said that Qadhafi was "inherently cruel." There was some evidence that he was involved in the killing of a homosexual man during his academy years, but not enough evidence was presented to charge him with the crime. Qadhafi was known as a major security risk in Libya five years before he launched his successful coup.

Qadhafi applied for a four-month military training mission to the United States. Herman Eilts, the deputy head of mission at the U.S. embassy in Tripoli, interviewed Qadhafi. Although impressed with his leadership qualities, Qadhafi was not accepted for the program. As dis-

cussed earlier in this book, Qadhafi was accused of planning an unsuccessful assassination attempt on Eilts in Cairo.

Qadhafi did, however, manage to win a place in a four-month training course in Britain. One teacher commented, "I can't understand it. He must have slipped through the net." He went to Beaconsfield to study English, military signaling, automotive maintenance and armored vehicle gunnery. Qadhafi did not like his tour of duty in England. He was offended by racism and other endemic features of English society. He offended some Englishmen by always wearing his traditional Bedouin robes in London.

By the time he returned to Libya, in 1969, it was clear that a weak King Idris would not be able to retain power for very long. The country was up for grabs. There were signs that Idris wanted to abdicate. There is still a debate about the extent to which the British and Americans knew that a coup was imminent. Some observers have even suggested that the Americans helped Qadhafi into power. It is known that Western intelligence had a dossier on Qadhafi as early as 1966.

Qadhafi benefited from his British signal corps training, which was to stand him in such good stead with his fellow officers. The British instructors had been happy to tell him that, he who has control of communications is also in control of the power. As soon as he returned to Libya he used radio and simple cryptosystems to keep in touch with the various cells he had established within the country. His plans had been made over many years. Qadhafi, with some helpful training by British technicians and officers, was the best-placed revolutionary leader to take advantage of the increased political instability in the country. The coup was ready to begin.

The date of the coup *was changed over the course of six months. It was first planned for March 12th, then March 24th, and finally September 1, 1969. The coup, named "Operation Jerusalem," required that specified military and governmental installations in Benghazi and Tripoli be taken over simultaneously. The plan had been refined over the six months despite, or because of, the many delays and interruptions to the schedule.*

The coup *went off smoothly. In less than two hours from the 2:30 A.M. onset of operations, most of the key installations in Tripoli and Benghazi had been secured. There were some gun battles but these were short-lived. In Tripoli the plan was ahead of schedule. Considering the scale of the social and political upheaval, there was little bloodshed. For example, in one of the most important battles of the night, the Cyrenaica Defense Force in Gurnada only suffered one fatality and fifteen wounded.*

Qadhafi arrived at the Benghazi radio station at 6:00 A.M. to martial music playing in the background on the radio from Tripoli. Libya had effectively changed hands. At 6:30 A.M. Qadhafi went on the air to deliver "Communique One," partly ad-libbed and partly based on hurriedly scribbled notes. For security reasons, his first broadcast of the new regime was anonymous.

Now Libya was to be a free, self-governing republic, the Libyan Arab Republic. It was not until September 8, 1969, that Qadhafi was promoted to the rank of Colonel and made commander-in-chief of the armed forces. It was then, and only then, that it became clear who the main coup *leader was, when twenty-nine-year-old Col. Muammar Qadhafi took power.*

I had remained quiet long enough. It was time for me to question the basic tenets of Qadhafi's foreign policy presentation. I was certainly bright enough to see through his

2

rhetoric and get to the truth. He was, after all, making broad accusations about my country, and I couldn't imagine the most powerful nation in the world beating up on this little upstart of a nation without reason.

After thanking the Libyan Leader for his hospitality, I went right for the jugular. I asked how his statement of today related to reported incidents of Libyan terrorism around the world. I asked if I could be specific about a few of the reported terrorist activities. He didn't wait for Ahmed's translation and began nodding his head positively.

There was little doubt that Qadhafi had supported a wide range of terrorist organizations throughout the world. His past is unambiguous. His support for terrorism throughout the world was well established.

I also knew that Qadhafi's support for the Irish Republican Army (IRA) had begun more than two decades earlier. In a 1970 meeting with Nasser, Qadhafi declared that he had decided to help the IRA in order to fight British colonialism. In 1986, a large cache of Libyan arms was found in the Republic of Ireland and, in 1988, the French Navy intercepted a Panamanian ship, the *Eksund*, carrying a cargo of 150 tons of Libyan arms for the IRA. This cargo included surface-to-air missiles, Kalashnikov rifles and large quantities of explosives.

"I would like to know if you trained or in any way supported the terrorist activities of the Irish Republican Army?" I asked politely.

He responded: "We did help the IRA, but we no longer do so. They were committing acts of terrorism, which we completely reject. We do not want a war between the Protestants and Catholics. We do not support nor condone the terrorist activities of the IRA."

In March of 1986, Qadhafi had told the General People's Congress in Tripoli that "any relationship with

235

the IRA must be severed. The Provisional IRA had been supported only because of the Western bombing raids on Tripoli and Benghazi."

In May of 1992, the Libyan news agency, Jana, stated that links with terrorist groups were being terminated and that any UN committee was free to visit Libya to ascertain that there were no terrorist camps on Libyan territory. In June, Libyan officials provided information to the British authorities about earlier Libyan support for IRA terrorists. Such developments failed to impress Washington. This being so, the British government carefully refrained from applauding Libya's obvious efforts to improve relations.

I asked Qadhafi if it was true that in 1986, before the U.S. bombing, he was supporting some fifty terrorist organizations and subversive groups, in addition to more than forty radical governments in Africa, Asia, Europe, and America. Did he give help to almost all the terrorist groups of the Middle East, such as George Habash's PFLP, Ahmed Jibril's PFLP-GC, Naif Hawatmeh's Democratic Front, the Saiqa, the Popular Struggle Front and the Abu Nidal Organization?

Qadhafi's answer was, "Yes, but no longer."

I pressed further to include terrorist groups working against what he thought to be the reactionary regimes of the Arab world. Did he maintain close and sympathetic links with such groups as ETA in Spain, Action Directed in France, and the SIM group in Sardinia?

Once again the answer was "Yes," but no longer."

Name almost any terrorist or revolutionary group and you will find Qadhafi's fingers in the pie. He had supported the Tupamaros in Uruguay, the revolutionary groups in El

Salvador and the onetime Sandinista government in Nica-
ragua. In such countries as Chad, Senegal, Zaire and Tu-
nisia, help had been offered by Qadhafi to groups trying
to destabilize pro-Western or reactionary governments. An
Israeli report claimed that, in 1986, some 7,000 terrorists
were being trained by Syrians, Cubans, Russians and East
Germans in camps across Libya.

It should be emphasized that the various Israeli intel-
ligence organizations have different opinions and make
different factual claims about Libyan funding of world ter-
rorism. In the 1980's, Israeli intelligence analysts consis-
tently down-played the risk posed by Libya, saying that if
there was a mastermind behind international terror, it was
President Assad of Syria. This is an important consider-
ation in view of current Western claims that Libya has sole
responsibility for the Lockerbie attack. Nevertheless, there
is no doubt that Qadhafi's revolutionary ambitions had
their effect, albeit usually minimal, in dozens of countries
throughout the world.

Many countries, among them Egypt, Sudan, Tunisia,
Algeria, Senegal, Nigeria, Lebanon, Gambia, Mauritania,
Mali, Malaysia, Indonesia, Thailand and the Philippines,
have at one time or another accused Qadhafi of support-
ing dissident or subversive groups in their countries.

"Dr. Chasey," Qadhafi said, "I am not about to account for every activity we supported over the years. I am,
however, going to say that that was then, and this is now.
We no longer support international terrorism. We are a different people today than we were yesterday. Most of what
you cited in your questions relate to situations in which we
found ourselves before 1986."

I recently came across a quote by Muammar al-
Qadhafi in 1992 that summarizes his point of view as ex-
plained to us that day:

237

By the passage of time, everyone changes, through experience. In the 1970's we supported liberal movements without knowing which were terrorists and which were not. In the 1980's we began to differentiate between terrorists and those with legitimate political aspirations.

I could tell that Qadhafi was getting a little testy responding to my comments and questions. I was glad when Carroll Hubbard interrupted our interchange. He once again asked how he could best disseminate Qadhafi's message. As before, Col. Qadhafi asked if Hubbard would talk directly to President-elect Clinton. Hubbard said that he would have the opportunity in a few days to meet with Clinton and would use that opportunity to do so.

Col. Qadhafi turned his attention to the events of April 1986, when the United States bombed Libya under *Operation EL Dorado Canyon*. It was obvious to me during my stay in Libya that this Operation was never far below the surface. I remembered how Youssef's children had reacted and how the fear of future bombings remained. I could tell that there were obvious changes in the political philosophy and policies of Qadhafi that seemed to have emanated from the 1986 attack.

Qadhafi started by saying that the Libyan people never sleep soundly at night, knowing that there could be another surprise bombing by the United States. He felt much more secure now that Bill Clinton would become President of the United States but his people had suffered great emotional harm during the administrations of Reagan and Bush.

He asked, "Do you know what it is like sleeping with one eye open? I have been the target of assassination by your country for many years. I keep moving, but I worry about my family and my children. President Reagan had planned to circumvent your Ford ban of the assassination of foreign leaders in 1986. He said that his men shouldn't

238

worry about the assassination prohibition and that he would personally take the heat on that if I were killed."

"Youssef tells me that you have a young daughter. Her name is Katie, is that right?" I was caught completely off guard as he began speaking directly to me in English. As he spoke, he made eye contact with me for the first time in our conversation, which had been continuous for almost an hour. I was nervous knowing that Youssef El Debri, Intelligence Chief and the head of Libyan National Security, was discussing my family with one of the world's most hated and feared terrorists. Ahmed seemed to relax as he was relieved of his translation responsibilities, now that Qadhafi switched from speaking Arabic to English.

"Yes, my Katie is ten-years-old," I responded. "She is the joy of my life."

His eyes seemed to fill as once again he deliberately lost eye contact with me and the others in the room. His voice was hushed as he almost whispered, "My daughter, Hanna, would almost be eight-years-old—that is, if she had survived the American bombing of my home in 1986. Have you ever lost a child, Dr. Chasey?"

Much to my surprise, and contrary to my basic instincts, I began to feel a compassion for this man. His question pierced my shield of distrust for Libyans generally and for Qadhafi specifically. The American disinformation programs that centered on Libya and Qadhafi, had been most effective in molding my anti-Libyan biases. Were Qadhafi's tears real, or were they part of an act designed to impress his first American visitors, as well as his first U.S. Government official in many years? I wasn't sure.

"I understand that you and Congressman and Mrs. Hubbard went to visit the remains of my home today. You saw the results of your bombs, the results of *Operation El Dorado Canyon.* I left the structure just the way it was after the American bombs fell early that morning. My family was asleep when the attacks came. The entire country was asleep when the bombs fell. Who kills innocent civilians in their sleep?

"Who kills little children in their beds? The world will always remember this cowardly act. You saw Hanna's little bed? Her toys in her room? I left her things just as they were when she died, so they could be a reminder to the world of exactly what happened during those early morning hours. She was only sixteen months old when she died. Can you imagine the terror she must have felt when she heard the F-11s and A-6s scream out of the sky and release a 2,000 lb. bomb on her home? You Americans have no idea what it is like to feel the wrath of your Government's ire—your Air Force and Navy bombers.

"You were a Marine Corps Officer Dr. Chasey, an organization for which we in Libya have a history of respect. You know the sounds of an air attack; you must have felt the concussion of bombs. Some in your country have justified the killing of my Hanna by saying that she was only my adopted daughter. Can you imagine? I couldn't have loved her more if she were my natural child. My wife Safia and I wanted a daughter very badly. We have two natural sons, Saef al-Islan and Khamees, but we have no daughter. She is gone. I hope you think about Hanna and what I have told you, when you see Katie sleeping in her bed at night."

I did just that upon my return to the United States.

Congressman Hubbard, his wife, Carol, Gerrit P. Van de Bovenkamp, Youssef El Debri and I sat silently as Col. Qadhafi continued his emotional discourse (which I later found supported in Geoff Simons' book, *Libya: The Struggle for Survival*), "Your President Reagan claimed that 'he was not out to kill anybody' during the April 15th attack. In a press conference just six days earlier, he called me the 'Mad Dog of the Middle East.' Your own government has admitted that the first wave of the two-wave attack had targeted the Aziziya Barracks and was intended to kill me. This violates American law as well as international law. Officials of Reagan's own National Security Council had actually drafted a pre-attack statement describing my death as 'fortuitous.' One of your top White House officials, who was intimately involved in planning the bombing raids, admitted that, 'We hope to get him,' meaning me. Your Secretary of State, George Schultz, thought that if I survived the raids, the Libyan people would start a coup to oust me from power.

"Well, they didn't kill me and there was no coup. What they did do was murder a hundred innocent people, and wound another hundred, as they slept in their homes. My wife, Safia and my three children were all victims of the attack. They were hospitalized in intensive care for many days, suffering from pressure shock of the bomb that landed directly on our home. Hanna died a few hours after the attack from severe brain damage. You saw the damage today, Dr. Chasey. We didn't make this up! It is very sad, because there was no reason for the raid. The international community has long since cleared Libya of any complicity in the La Belle discotheque bombing that killed one of your countrymen. We were attacked without provocation. There was no evidence connecting us to the bombing, only evidence your government manufactured to justify killing me."

I had studied the details of the attack but never questioned our motivation in initiating it. Qadhafi was our enemy and that was enough to give impetus to the raids. They say that once a Marine, always a Marine. I guess I am no exception. I had a real interest in the military strategy used in Operation El Dorado Canyon. *I remembered our visit to the site earlier that day. We had seen first hand*

241

the damage that I had been shown on television in 1986. We saw many homes and public buildings with extensive damage. It was obvious to our party that most of the destroyed homes were in residential neighborhoods. The French, Austrian and Finnish embassies were also bombed in the raid.

Qadhafi's voice became stronger as he eased forward on his couch. He put his elbows on his knees and stared directly at me, and then Congressman Hubbard. "President Reagan said that he had 'irrefutable proof' that we ordered the bombing of the La Belle Discotheque. It was obvious to the whole world that Reagan's 'irrefutable evidence' was no such thing. Please keep this in mind, as we now discuss the claims of the Bush administration in 1991 and 1992, that there was 'irrefutable evidence' of our responsibility for the bombing of Pan Am 103 over Lockerbie, Scotland.

"I want to be very clear that we are willing to cooperate with the Lockerbie investigation," Qadhafi remarked. "Our two citizens have agreed to turn themselves over to a neutral court for trial. This is their choice and we don't interfere with their legal decisions. I can't see any situation in which they will turn themselves over to the United States or the United Kingdom. They could not expect a fair trial in either country, as they have already been judged guilty by the media and government authorities.

"Moreover, the guilt of the two men, and for that matter myself, has been assumed and frequently proclaimed in the western media. For example, a British newspaper said of me, 'Clearly he played a role in the Lockerbie bombing'—rendering any trial of the men in Britain or the U.S. a travesty of justice. What good would it do anyway since the U.S. State Department declared on April 16, 1992 that the U.S. would not end sanctions, even if the two men were surrendered for trial?"

Qadhafi said that the U.S. was taking steps to circum-vent the inconvenient terms of extradition law. He added sarcastically, "How insolent of weaker nations, in the absence of an extradition treaty, to refuse to surrender people whom Washington may wish to bring to court. Why not abolish extradition controls all together? On June 15, 1992, the Supreme Court in Washington ruled that U.S. agents were legally entitled to kidnap foreign nationals abroad and return them to the United States for prosecution.

"The Supreme Court decision was no surprise. The policy of the U.S. on Libya, if nothing else, has provided ample evidence of Washington's contempt for international law when it is perceived to threaten U.S. interests."

In April, 1992, Professor Francis A. Boyle, Professor of International Law at the University of Illinois, Urbana-Champaign, prepared a Memorandum of Law on the U.S./Libyan dispute over the Lockerbie bombing allegations. He examined Libya's liabilities under the terms of the 1971 Montreal Convention, the pertinent legal framework for confronting terrorist acts against civil aircraft. I quote briefly:

> *...Libya has fully discharged its obligations...there is no obligation whatever for Libya to extradite its two nationals to either the United States or the United Kingdom...both the United States and the United Kingdom have effectively violated most of the provisions of the Montreal Convention. ...the United States government has admitted that it will pay no attention whatsoever to its obligations mandating the peaceful resolution of international disputes as required by UN Charter articles 2(3) and 33. ...the United States government has purposely and illegally made it impossible for there to be a pacific settlement of this dispute...*

243

On the other side of the ocean, Marc Weller, Research Fellow in International Law at St. Catharine's College, Cambridge, England, has written a detailed analysis of the U.S./Libyan dispute. He concludes that at the levels of both Libyan state responsibility and the responsibility of two individuals, Libya has responded "in accordance with international legal requirements." To secure the UN resolutions, the United States "had to expend considerable political capital and goodwill in the Security Council, bullying fellow members to obtain the necessary votes, and enraging many nonmembers of the Council who keenly observed this spectacle..." The U.S. and UK governments "may well have contributed to, or brought about, an abuse of rights by the Security Council."

In Weller's judgement it may now be necessary for the International Court to seek a judicial review of the Security Council decisions "if the constitutional system of the UN Charter is to recover from the blow it has suffered in this episode."

Just a month before our meeting, Col. Qadhafi appealed to the United States to begin direct talks to resolve their differences. Washington made no response. I thought about my meetings with Senators Kerry, Brown and Pressler and the letters from Debri I had delivered to them the previous month. There had been no response from them.

On October 15th—just a few weeks before my meeting with Qadhafi—Douglas Hurd, addressing the Council for the Advancement of Arab-British Understanding in London, declared that unless the Libyan government agreed to hand over the suspects, "there is nothing really to talk about." The sanctions would remain in place.

At the same time as Hurd's statement, the German public prosecutor, Volker Rath, announced in a press release that received little publicity, that Germany would be suspending its legal proceedings against the two Libyan suspects as there was insufficient evidence of their involvement.

244

"The contrived case against my two countrymen comes down to two items of evidence," Qadhafi continued. "The first, and weakest element, is the testimony of Mr. Gauci, the owner of Mary's House in Malta. This evidence could never stand up in court. It is factually unreliable and completely circumstantial.

"Mr. Gauci initially gave authorities a description of the person who purchased the clothing supposedly placed in the luggage containing the bomb that blew up Pan Am 103. The police artist drew a picture from his description and distributed it around the world. This picture looked nothing like our people.

"As a matter of fact, most people who saw it thought that it looked a lot like me," he said with his first smile of the meeting. "I can assure you that I did not purchase anything from Mary's House." Again, he smiled as if he had told a very funny joke, and of course we politely laughed at his attempt. He continued, "the description given by Gauci would match thousands of individuals from all over the Middle East. I don't want to accuse my Arab brothers but the description given matched one of the leading suspects under investigation for the bombing at the time Mr. Gauci made his identification. (Abu Talb)

"The fact of the matter is, Gauci never identified Mr. Megrahi directly as the man who bought the assortment of clothing at Mary's House. He was simply presented a single picture of Megrahi by the police and asked to make an identification. This procedure is contrary to the rules of evidence in most civilized countries. Witnesses are asked to identify a suspect from a series of pictures or to select a subject from what you Americans call a "lineup." Without immense political pressure from your government, there would have never been an indictment of Megrahi and Fhimah based on this flimsy evidence.

"Gauci's testimony was considered so important that he was provided around-the-clock protection by investigators.

"The second item of evidence presented in the indictments involves a small portion of microchip recovered from the wreckage of the Pan Am jet. Forensic specialists claimed that they traced the microchip to a consignment of timers produced by the Swiss firm, MEBO, for our government. The entire case against Fhimah and Megrahi by the West amounts to whether any of these timers provided to us were also sold to other persons or countries.

"We admit that MEBO sold us five of the timers in 1985. We also have evidence that some of the timers were sold to the Stasi Secret Police in East Germany. The Stasi Secret Police were working very closely with the terrorist group PFLP-GC at the time of the Lockerbie incident.

"Once this evidence is presented, the entire case against Libya will be moot. The most troubling part of this nasty situation is that we know that the Americans and the British have had knowledge of this same evidence since 1990, but for political reasons have covered it up all these years, and laid the blame on us.

"How convenient it is for these two superpowers to deflect their ineptitude in solving this case to a small country like Libya. It is a perfect plan. First, indict two people you know didn't commit the crime and then bring sanctions against their country. Next, stop all communications and cut this country off from the rest of the world. The Americans were very smart, demanding that we hand over the two suspects for trial in your country, knowing full well we will never do so.

"The standoff continues as we speak. We have done all in our power to get an honest hearing on this matter. We are willing to have a neutral court hear the case. We are confident that a neutral body will get to the bottom of the case.

"The solution to the Lockerbie case is in the hands of two men, Mr. Edwin Bollier and Mr. Ulrich Lumpert of the MEBO Corporation in Zurich, Switzerland. They have the answers to the microchip situation. If they tell the truth, the investigators will have their answers, and they won't include Libya. The UN sanctions will be lifted."

We had been talking for over two hours and I could see that Col. Qadhafi was getting tired. It was well into the evening and I suspected that our audience was about to come to an end. Col. Qadhafi thanked us again for coming to Libya and appealed to us to use our political contacts to tell the Libyan story. He looked directly at Mrs. Hubbard and asked if she would remain behind for a few minutes. She nervously nodded her head in the affirmative.

We stood and Ahmed handed the Libyan Leader four copies of *The Green Book* which Col. Qadhafi signed and distributed to each of us. He also said that he wanted us to have a Libyan carpet as his gift to us. He was very gentle, and lingered with us for some time discussing his family and the state of U.S. politics. Carol Hubbard broke out her camera and began shooting pictures of the festivities. She asked Ahmed if he would take some pictures of her and Col. Qadhafi, and her and Carroll with Col. Qadhafi.

While Qadhafi was signing my copy of the *Green Book*, he asked if I would be able to get a Congressional delegation to come to Libya. He thought that it was extremely important that Members of Congress saw for themselves what was happening in Libya today. He wanted them to see how the UN air embargo was affecting the people of Libya. I told him that all I could do was promise to try. He thanked me and we all left the room, with the exception of Qadhafi and Mrs. Carol Hubbard.

We waited in the hallway outside of Qadhafi's office for Carol. We discussed our meeting, but it was obvious that Congressman Hubbard was extremely nervous about his wife. Youssef could sense the tension in the air and tried to comfort Carroll. I tried my best to assure him that all was well and not to worry.

After ten minutes, Mrs. Hubbard walked out of Qadhafi's office with tears in her eyes. In their first display of public affection on the trip, the Congressman took his wife in his arms and tried to comfort her while at the same time he tried to find out what had transpired.

We all automatically walked down the hall away from Qadhafi's office as she explained that he had appealed to her in a most emotional way to use her feminine, motherly instincts to approach Mrs. Hillary Clinton on his behalf. He had said that only a woman could really understand what is was like to have a child killed. He wanted her to know that he was a good and honest man who could be trusted. His hope was that Mrs. Clinton would have some influence on her husband and that normalized relations with the United States could resume under his administration.

As we left the barracks, Youssef once again thanked us for coming and listening. He asked again for our help back in America and said good-bye. Immediately, we were back in our six car caravan enroute to Jerba, Tunisia, and our flight back to Geneva.

Some fifty miles outside Tripoli, we ran into ground fog. Our three-hour drive turned into six hours. Our speeds ranged from one-hundred M.P.H. to walking speed. There were actually times when one of our JOS agents served as a ground guide walking in front of our car to be sure we didn't go off the road. I passed my time reviewing our past thirty-six hours in Libya with Gerrit and joking with Carroll Hubbard in the other car, using the JSO car radio.

I hope that the National Security Agency (NSA) has a recording of our radio conversations so that some day I might be able to laugh as hard as I did that night on the highway between Tripoli and Jerba. I called Hubbard on the radio and identified myself as the editor of the *Mayfield Messenger*, the local paper of the first district of Kentucky. I was given this number to call by the Capitol operator. My readers were wondering what in the world Hubbard was doing on a lonely foggy road in the Libyan desert. We, back home in Kentucky, had sent Hubbard to Washington not Libya. Well, Carroll got a big kick out of the interchange and played along with me as we passed the time. We all got a great laugh out of the encounter.

At a rest stop on the highway, Carroll asked if I saw any opportunity for him to do additional work with Libya once he left Congress. He explained that he was going to start job hunting in a few weeks and had thought about opening his own consulting/lobbying company. He said he would love to work for Libya. He admitted he knew very little about foreign affairs, or lobbying for that matter, but he was very anxious to give it a try.

We arrived at the Jerba Airport simultaneously with the flight crew at 3:00 A.M. The airport was closed and a janitor had to be convinced to open the front door and let us in. We were airborne at 4:00 A.M. with an ETA in Geneva at 6:30 A.M. The flight attendants were still a bit sleepy, but that didn't stop them from preparing a scrumptious breakfast at forty-two thousand feet over the Mediterranean Sea.

Chapter Twenty-Six

Government Bureaucracy At Its Worst

We arrived at the Noga Hilton by 7:00 A.M. and agreed to delay our travel plans to leave for Washington until the next day. We decided to spend the day resting and shopping in Geneva before departing for home. It was raining hard so I decided to forego shopping and spent the day in my room making calls and catching up on a little sleep.

My first call was to Virginia. She was glad to hear from me and had guessed that I had gone to "the home country." She didn't like me traveling in Libya, but after all these years she knew that life with me meant a risk now and again. Just in case the NSA was listening, I used a great deal of discretion during my phone call. I didn't talk about the trip other than to say that I had met with "Charlie."

Gerrit decided to remain in Geneva for a few days to complete some business and make arrangements to wire a portion of the money he owed me to my California account. We met and discussed the next steps to be taken in completing our project for Libya. For the first time, we both approached the Libyan situation with renewed interest. We were impressed by the information we had received from our meeting with Col. Qadhafi and felt a new enthusiasm for our mission.

We had a final dinner with the Hubbards in Geneva. The following morning we were on our way back to Washington, via London and then the Concord to New York. It didn't go unnoticed that our departure route from London's

251

Heathrow Airport took us over a small, quiet, Scottish town called Lockerbie.

I had checked the rug given to me by Qadhafi as luggage from Geneva to Washington. I wondered if I would run into any difficulty with it clearing customs in New York. I had no idea what the rug was worth and I certainly didn't want to declare that I got it in Libya. I was most anxious to avoid any questions about the rug which came from our host, Col. Qadhafi.

As I entered the customs area of New York's JFK airport, my heart started to pound. I heard my name paged. "Arriving London-Concord passenger Dr. Chasey please report to the British Airways luggage desk." My anxiety level was off the scale. I reported as directed. I knew there was going to be a fuss about the rug and I would be forced to reveal where I had gotten it.

To my delight and relief, the rug wasn't transferred from the Geneva flight to the Concord flight and didn't arrive in New York with the rest of the luggage. The British Air people were very apologetic for any inconvenience and promised to forward the rug to me in Washington on the next flight. Since I was only going to be in Washington for two days, I requested, and they agreed, to send the rug to my home in California. Virginia reported that the rug arrived at our front door by taxi the following day.

Thank you British Airways.

We transferred to an American Eagle flight to Washington's National Airport.

As we approached Washington, I detected an air of discomfort on the part of both Hubbards. They began asking strange questions about the trip. Carroll was concerned about how he was to report the trip on his financial disclosure papers that were required by all traveling Members of the U.S. House of Representatives. He wanted to know who had paid for the trip and what the purpose was for his visit to Europe. He wondered if he should say anything about Libya. Would the CIA know that he had gone to Libya?

Carol was even more nervous and uncomfortable. She expressed her concern that they would find themselves in a lot of trouble back home. No less than three times she asked Carroll to check on the rules governing travel to Libya.

It was clear at this point that there could be a real problem with the Hubbards now that the excitement of Concord travel, private jets and fancy restaurants were behind them and the skyline of Washington was becoming visible in the distance.

I tried to assure them that all expenses had been paid by Gerrit's company, ICM. I explained again. There should be no problem because ICM was a U.S. Corporation. I also explained that Mohammed's Committee to Resolve Lockerbie, also a U.S. Corporation, was contributing to the expenses of the trip.

Both Hubbards were very concerned that they had not met Mohammed as I had promised. They had no paperwork from Mohammed to submit with Carroll's travel report to Congress. Hubbard asked me to get him a back-dated letter from Mohammed requesting that the Hubbards take the trip and outlining the financial arrangements for paying for the trip. I promised to do so upon my return to Washington. We parted ways after arriving at Washington's National Airport.

I was becoming uneasy that the Hubbards might respond irrationally and do something stupid. I wondered what I could do to alleviate their anxiety.

I received a desperate phone call first thing the following morning, November 12th, from Carroll Hubbard. Once again he expressed his concern over the trip. He and

253

Carol had spent a restless night talking about the potential problems that could result from the trip to Libya. The tone of his voice was one of panic and I knew he was scared. I told the Congressman to relax until I had an opportunity to check on the legality of traveling to Libya. I promised to call him back within twenty-four hours. I had appointments all day in the Capitol and decided to do my checking later in the afternoon.

I received a second call from Carroll shortly thereafter. He had talked to our mutual friend, Congressman Mervyn Dymally, Democrat of the Thirty-First District of California, who had traveled to Libya a few years before. I had been a friend of Dymally's for many years. He was one of the most interesting and controversial Members of the Congress.

Dymally is part Afro-American and part Asian Indian. He was born and raised in Trinidad where he is still treated like a king. Dymally served as Lieutenant Governor of California prior to being elected to the U.S. House of Representatives. I traveled with Dymally to Trinidad in 1990 where he helped me negotiate a Master of Business Administration Degree for my client, City University of Seattle in Trinidad. After spending a few days there with Merv, I realized that whatever Dymally wants, Dymally gets on that small Caribbean Island.

Dymally had advised Hubbard to call the Justice Department to find out what he should do. Carroll did just that. The cat was out of the bag! The Justice Department had referred him to the United States Office of Foreign Assets Control (OFAC), a part of the U.S. Department of the Treasury. This is the agency with control over sanctioned countries such as Libya. Carroll was informed by the OFAC that he had violated Federal regulations by traveling to Libya. The OFAC had some very serious questions to ask him. They actually threatened to take his case before the Federal Grand Jury in Washington.

Hubbard panicked! He now felt that he had to try to cover himself. He began to spin a long, involved web of actions in which he tried to save his own neck. Unfortunately, Hubbard got tangled in his own web with no easy way to escape the long arm of the Federal Judicial System.

Carroll asked me for written documents that would prove that he was a "victim" of some kind of setup or conspiracy. I said, "No." A back-dated letter from Mohammed became a significant item for his web. I told him that I was to meet with Mohammed the evening of November 24th and would request a letter of invitation asking Hubbard to meet with Youssef. Hubbard was a nervous wreck. I knew that I was going to have my hands full with him.

I spent a good part of my time on my plane trip home the next day, November 13th, trying to decide just how I should deal with the Carroll Hubbard situation. Now that the OFAC knew about the trip to Libya from Hubbard it would be prudent for me to make contact with them. It was my plan to find out just what the travel policy was for a Foreign Agent. There had to be special travel exceptions to the OFAC travel policies for Agents like me. How else could I meet with clients who didn't have a U.S. Visa to enable them to come to the United States? There had to be a section of the regulations that would permit me to meet and represent my client's interests in the United States.

I called the OFAC on Tuesday, November 17, 1992, to explore my situation and options. I identified myself and requested information concerning travel to Libya. Mr. Charles Bishop was the OFAC agent who answered the telephone. He quickly recognized my name and asked that I hold for a moment while he got my file. He came back on the line and telephonically introduced me to Special

Agent Hal Harmon, who was working on my case. "Working on my case," I asked. "What was this all about?"

Mr. Harmon began by stating that I was in serious trouble with the United States Treasury for unauthorized travel to a sanctioned country, Libya. He further stated that he had been reviewing my file and was just about to call me. He had my file from the Criminal Division of the Justice Department in front of him. He acknowledged that he was aware that I was registered with Justice on behalf of ICM and its client, the Government of Libya.

Mr. Harmon went on to indicate that I had violated Libyan Sanctions Regulations, 31 C.F.R. Part 550 under the authority of the International Emergency Economic Powers Act, 50 U.S.C. 1701 et seq. The Regulations prohibit virtually all financial transactions by U.S. persons in which the Government of Libya has an interest unless authorized by general license or specific license, issued by the Office of Foreign Assets Control.

He continued, "Section 550.207 of the Regulations prohibits all unauthorized travel-related transactions by U.S. persons with respect to Libya." Harmon wanted me to know that these actions were punishable with civil penalties and/or the case could be turned over the United States Attorney for criminal prosecution. His voice was very official sounding and he warned me not to take this situation lightly.

Harmon never read me my Miranda rights, but gave me an oral Cease and Desist order that he said would be followed by a written order. It was clear from Harmon that I should perform no further lobbying activities on behalf of ICM and its client, the Government of Libya. I pointed out to Mr. Harmon that I had filed my Justice Department registration on October 8, 1992. Now, here he was, some six weeks later, telling me that I couldn't represent my client and that my activities were against the law.

Government Bureaucracy At Its Worst

This Cease and Desist Order is an example of how an unelected second-tier official treats a citizen who is conducting lawful business.

DEPARTMENT OF THE TREASURY
WASHINGTON

DEC 3 1992

<u>ORDER TO CEASE AND DESIST AND REQUIREMENT TO FURNISH INFORMATION</u>

FAC No. 131589

Dear Dr. Chasey:

This letter is further to your telephone inquiry to the U.S. Treasury's Office of Foreign Assets Control ("FAC") on November 17, 1992, during which you spoke with FAC Licensing Officer Charles Bishop about restrictions on travel to Libya. You also spoke with FAC Special Investigator Hal Harmon who instructed you to cease from providing any services on behalf of your employer, International Communications Marketing Incorporated ("ICM") and its client the Government of Libya ("GOL"), unless authorized by FAC. You stated your intention to apply for a specific license to perform those services and your request by letter dated November 17, 1992, was received at FAC on November 20, 1992.

FAC administers a comprehensive economic sanctions program against the Government of Libya ("GOL") as promulgated by the Libyan Sanctions Regulations, 31 C.F.R. Part 550 (the "Regulations"), under authority of the International Emergency Economic Powers Act, 50 U.S.C. 1701 <u>et seq.</u> The Regulations prohibit virtually all financial transactions by U.S. persons in which the GOL has an interest unless authorized by general license or specific license issued by FAC.

We have obtained a copy of your U.S. Department of Justice ("DOJ") Foreign Agents Registration Act ("FARA") filing mentioned in your November 17 letter which indicates that The William Chasey Organization ("TWCO") has been employed by ICM on behalf of its client, the GOL, to provide relationships with key members of the United States Congress to assist in the development of normalized relations between the United States and Libya. Your Agreement with ICM, dated October 8, 1992, called for TWCO to receive $120,000 at various periods during the term of the Agreement.

Section 550.202 of the Regulations prohibits the exportation to Libya from the U.S. of goods, technology or services. The exportation of a service includes the performance of a service in the U.S., the benefit of which is received in Libya. Any funds received for unauthorized services rendered on behalf of the GOL are subject to blocking. Section 550.209 prohibits U.S. persons from dealing in property (defined in section 550.314 to include contracts) in which the GOL has an interest.

The only service-related activities which may be performed on behalf of the GOL without specific authorization from FAC are those involving certain legal services, to wit: (1) the provision of legal advice and counselling on the requirements of and compliance with U.S. law; (2) defense of the GOL when named as a defendant in domestic U.S. litigation or administrative proceedings; or

257

- 2 -

(3) prosecution of such proceedings in defense of the GOL's U.S.
property or property interests in existence prior to the imposition
of sanctions against dealings in such property and interests on
January 8, 1986. In light of the prohibitions in sections 550.202
and 550.209 of the Regulations, the provision by U.S. persons of
services outside this scope requires specific authorization from
FAC. Authorization would only be granted if the activities were
found consistent with and supportive of the purposes of the
existing embargo and assets freeze on Libya. As previously stated,
your written request for a license was not received at FAC until
November 20, 1992.

Specific authorization is also required for the receipt of payment
for the provision of any service outside the limited scope noted
above -- whether from blocked or unblocked sources. Thus, receipt
of funds from the GOL, directly or indirectly, by you, your firm,
its employees or associates for any goods or services requires
specific authorization from FAC, effective immediately.
Applications for specific licenses to receive such funds may be
filed as set forth in section 550.801 of the Regulations. The sole
exception to this requirement relates to receipt of payment for the
direct costs of purchasing and physically exporting to Libya
publications exported pursuant to the exception in section 550.202.

You are hereby ordered to cease and desist from all activities on
behalf of the GOL, to include all such activities described in your
FARA filing, not within the scope of permissible services set forth
above. Activities beyond this scope for the benefit of the GOL
constitute the unauthorized exportation of services to Libya, in
violation of section 550.202 of the Regulations, as well as the
unauthorized dealing in property (which includes services and
service contracts) in which the GOL has an interest, in violation
of section 550.209 of the Regulations.

This letter also serves to advise that FAC has been made aware that
you may have engaged in unlicensed travel to Libya.

Section 550.207 of the Regulations prohibits all unauthorized
travel-related transactions by U.S. persons with respect to Libya.
Travel-related transactions may be authorized only through general
or specific licensing action or formal interpretation by FAC.

Sections 550.207 and 550.560 of the Regulations authorize, under
general license, certain travel-related transactions ordinarily
incident to travel to, from and within Libya by the following U.S.
persons:

> a) Persons traveling to engage in journalistic
> activities, who are regularly employed in such capacity
> by a newsgathering organization; and

> b) Transactions related to travel and residence within
> Libya by U.S. citizens and permanent resident aliens who
> are immediate family members of Libyan nationals.

- 3 -

The general license for travel by family members is available only
to those U.S. citizens and permanent resident aliens who **register
their eligibility** in writing with either the Embassy of Belgium in
Tripoli, Libya, or with the Office of Foreign Assets Control in
Washington, D.C. This registration requirement is not applicable
to journalists. All other U.S. persons wishing to engage in
transactions relating to travel to or within Libya must first apply
for and obtain a specific Treasury license from FAC.

**Accordingly, you are hereby warned to refrain from engaging in any
unlicensed travel-related transactions with respect to Libya, or to
perform any work in Libya without FAC authorization. Violations on
your part may be referred to our civil penalties division or to the
U.S. Department of Justice for criminal prosecution. Penalties for
individuals violating the Regulations range up to $10,000 per civil
violation, and up to $250,000 and/or 10 years in prison for each
criminal violation.**

Pursuant to the authorities granted in 50 U.S.C. 1702 (a) (2) and
section 550.602 of the Regulations, you are hereby required to
provide this office with a written report, under oath, which must
include the following information and records:

    o A copy of all contracts, agreements, and or letters of
understanding or intent into which you may have entered with the
GOL, ICM, or other third parties, involving services to be provided
on behalf of the GOL, or in which the GOL has an interest.

    o A detailed summary of any and all services which you may
have rendered on behalf of the GOL since February 1, 1986. This
summary must include a description of services rendered, dates of
service and the identity of the GOL entity for whom service was
rendered or purported to be rendered.

    o A record of all money payments or other forms of payment
received <u>directly or indirectly</u> from the GOL or from third parties
for services rendered on behalf of the GOL since February 1, 1986.
Fully describe the method of payment, to include the identity of
GOL entities, amounts and dates of payment, names and addresses of
all financial institutions involved and corresponding account
numbers.

    o Number of trips taken to Libya since February 1, 1986.

    o Date(s) of travel.

    o Reason for travel. If you traveled more than once, please
list the reason for each trip.

    o Method of travel from the U.S. to and within Libya for each
trip. Please furnish the names of all airline, rail or bus
carriers, and or ocean passenger vessels, along with copies of

- 4 -

passenger receipts for each mode of transportation utilized.
Identify all stopover locations.

o Where were passenger tickets for travel to and within Libya
obtained? How were tickets paid for and by whom?

o Identify the name and location of all places of lodging in
Libya. How was payment for lodging made and by whom?

o Describe any other Libyan travel-related transactions in
which you engaged, such as payments for meals, taxis, travel agent
fees, etc.

o If you were reimbursed for any expenses related to travel
to and within Libya, specify amounts received, reason for
reimbursement and the party which provided reimbursement. How and
through what financial institution(s) or business organization(s)
was reimbursement paid?

**You are required to provide responses to the above within ten (10)
business days of receipt of this letter.** If you believe you have
engaged in travel to Libya that was authorized by an FAC specific
or general license or an FAC interpretation of the Regulations,
please provide that information with your response. You should be
aware that supplemental information concerning your travel-related
transaction(s) may be requested.

Your attention is directed to Title 18, U.S.C., section 1001, which
provides: "Whoever, in any matter within the jurisdiction of any
department or agency of the United States knowingly and willfully
falsifies, conceals or covers up by any trick, scheme, or device a
material fact, or makes any false, fictitious or fraudulent
statements or representations, or makes or uses any false writing
or document knowing the same to contain any false, fictitious or
fraudulent statement or entry, shall be fined not more than $10,000
or imprisoned not more than five years, or both." **You are also
reminded that, as noted above, violation of the Regulations may
constitute a criminal offense.**

Your response should be addressed as follows:

U.S. Department of the Treasury
Office of Foreign Assets Control
1500 Pennsylvania Avenue, N.W.
Washington, D.C. 20220.

- 5 -

In the interim, if you have any questions concerning this letter, you may contact FAC Chief of Enforcement William Wasley or Hal Harmon of his staff at (202) 622-2430.

Sincerely,

R. Richard Newcomb
Director
Office of Foreign Assets Control

The William Chasey Organization
Attn: Dr. William C. Chasey
The Flour Mill of Georgetown
1015 33rd Street, N.W., suite 509
Washington, D.C. 20007

Some serious questions came to mind: What took the OFAC so long to contact me? Why didn't the Justice Department deny my registration when they received it six weeks before? Why didn't the Federal Government try to prevent this situation before it occurred?

Harmon also told me that in order to travel to Libya in the future I would need a license from the OFAC. I asked how I could obtain such a license. He answered that I should send a letter to him and my request would be considered.

Mr. Harmon and I agreed that I would not perform further on my ICM contract, until I received a letter from his office explaining what I could and could not do. I actually felt that he was pleased with my willingness to cooperate with him and his office. I felt that Harmon and I had established a rather friendly relationship. I felt secure from my discussion with Harmon that, once I received his official letter, the situation would go away with no further ramifications.

As our conversation continued, Harmon seemed especially interested in ICM and Gerrit P. Van de Bovenkamp. He asked a number of questions about him. It occurred to me that if he actually had my Justice Department Registration Form in front of him, as he claimed, he would have known that I had been hired to represent ICM and its client, the Government of Libya. He wanted to know how he could contact Gerrit and Brendan Kelly. I gave Harmon all the information he wanted. I had been up front with my involvement in this case and I felt that I had nothing to hide. After all, I had officially done what I was required to do—register with the Justice Department. To be perfectly honest, I knew nothing about the activities or requirements of the OFAC until that very morning.

Virginia and I had a long conversation about the situation over breakfast at the La Jolla Beach and Tennis Club. Although we were concerned about my conversation with Special Agent Harmon we both felt, as we still do, that I did everything I could to comply with my responsibilities as a Foreign Agent, i.e., registered with the Justice Department. I had registered the day I signed the contract with ICM. I had submitted all of the required forms, including a copy of the ICM contract and the contract addendum between myself and Gerrit and Mohammed. I felt exonerated. The question of illegal travel to Libya was a matter of debate.

Since returning from Libya and finding myself a victim of the OFAC, I have followed very closely the action of our government in relation to citizens, businessmen and Congressmen who travel to sanctioned countries. What I have found is that the "law" against such travel is applied inconsistently, at best, and enforced indiscriminately, at the least. Travel to Cuba is the best example.

Despite all of our bravado over trade sanctions, embargoes and problems with Fidel Castro, U.S. citizens have been traveling to Cuba for some thirty-two years. Former Senator George McGovern has been traveling to Cuba for more than twenty years. He has publicly acknowledged that he met with Castro as recently as September, 1994. Lee Iacocca jets to Havana via Canada and Mexico on a regular basis to dine with Castro and hold investment talks with Cuban leaders.

On Tuesday December 27, 1994, USA Today reported that sixty-nine American companies have signed secret letters of intent to do business in Cuba. Yet, prior to 1993, as noted on my passport, the only country to which travel was prohibited was Cuba. In November 1993, one year after my trip to Libya and two years after the indictments of Megrahi and Fhimah were issued, Libya and Iraq were added to Cuba as countries where travel was prohibited.

In addition, the U.S. Treasury Department spells out on a passport the countries with whom trade is restricted or prohibited. Prior to 1993 the list included Cuba, North Korea, Vietnam and Cambodia. Libya was not on the list. However, in November of 1993, the following countries were added: Libya, Iraq, Yugoslavia, Haiti and Iran.

We also know that Americans have been traveling to Vietnam—both North and South—for years to search for American soldiers and to revisit war locations. Businessmen have been traveling to North Vietnam to open trade and commerce between our two countries.

I had grown up believing that American citizens were able to travel the world freely without U.S. government interference. I also knew that as a U.S. citizen, I was free to enter any country I chose, but at my own risk. I knew that there were some countries in the world in which I couldn't count on the U.S. for help if I got into a jam. These are countries that have no diplomatic relationships with the U.S.

In December, 1994, Congressman Bill Richardson, Democrat of New Mexico, traveled to North Korea on his own—not part of an official delegation—to this restricted country. Ironically, no one would have known it if North Korea had not shot down an American helicopter, killing one pilot and capturing the other. Despite this outrageous act on the part of North Korea, one month later, with the return of the captured pilot by the North Koreans, the U.S. Government removed trade sanctions against North Korea.

The one event that made this whole scenario of action against me by the Treasury Department so ridiculous was the U.S. policy toward Yassir Arafat and the PLO. On Friday, September 10, 1993, Yassir Arafat was high on the U.S. list of known terrorists and unable to secure an entrance visa to the United States. Three days later, on Monday September 13th, I joined millions of television viewers around the world as we watched Arafat embracing

President Bill Clinton on the White House lawn during the signing ceremony for an Israeli-Palestinian Peace Agreement with Yitzak Rabin. I remember wondering how long it might be before we watched similar embraces with the likes of Fidel Castro, Saddam Hussein and even Muammar Qadhafi.

Finally, to set the record straight, a little known fact is that thousands of U.S. citizens live in Libya. Thousands more, like Mohammed Bukhres, travel in and out of Libya to the United States on business and/or to visit relatives every year. Mohammed had explained to me how he, a U.S. citizen, traveled to Libya several times a year to do business, meet with "Charlie" and with Youssef and his own family. This travel is done without the benefit of a license from the United States Government. Scores of U.S. citizens can be found on the ferry boats that carry them daily from Malta to Tripoli and back.

As far as I can tell, none of these travelers from the Mohammeds to the Iacoccas have requested, or been granted, a license from the OFAC to travel or conduct business in these sanctioned countries.

It seemed to me that my situation was being singled out. The U.S. Government was pulling out all stops to make sure I did not return to Libya or do any business with Libya or its representatives here in the United States. Furthermore, through threats and cease and desist orders, it was obvious that the Government was willing to use fear, intimidation of me and my family and even put me out of business, if it felt it necessary. One thing for sure, the U.S. Government was trying to stop me from investigating the Pan Am 103 bombing more thoroughly.

Why? What was the United States Government—or perhaps the shadowy, out of control unelected second-tier officials—afraid of?

Chapter Twenty-Seven

Back To Washington

On Tuesday, November 24th, 1992, I arrived at Mohammed's suite on the fifth floor of the Park Hyatt Hotel in Washington, D.C. at exactly 6:00 P.M. I could hear quite a few voices through the door as I waited for someone to respond to the door bell. Mohammed opened the door and invited me in. As I entered, I was shocked to see a once famous Capitol Hill face, former United States Senator Harrison Williams of New Jersey. Williams had been convicted a few years before for his involvement in an FBI sting operation called ABSCAM. I couldn't believe that Williams was here. I felt a sinking feeling in my stomach as Mohammed introduced me to Williams. I had met the Senator some 12 years before but it was obvious that he didn't remember me.

Williams was just finishing his business with Mohammed and was about to leave. Mohammed said that Williams had been employed by Libya to try to get some help from Williams' old friend and colleague, Senator Claiborne Pell, Chairman of the Senate Foreign Relations Committee. I remember thinking that I was quite capable of dealing with Pell without the help of this convicted felon who was persona non grata in the U.S. Capitol.

Mohammed gave me a copy of a letter from Senator Pell to former Senator Williams dated May 4, 1992. In the letter, Pell responded to Williams' suggestion of a meeting between Secretary of State James Baker and Youseff Debri. He also discussed Debri's inability to secure a U.S. visa. I was sure that Harrison Williams was involved in representing Libya in some form or fashion. I wondered if

FOREIGN AGENT 4221: The Lockerbie Cover-up

Williams had registered with the Justice Department or if he was licensed by the United States Treasury.

TEL: May 14,92 11:27 No.002 P.02

United States Senate
COMMITTEE ON FOREIGN RELATIONS
WASHINGTON, DC 20510-6225

May 4, 1992

The Honorable Harrison A. Williams, Jr.
P. O. Box 02
Bedminster, New Jersey 07921

Dear Pete:

Thank you for your letter of April 29 expressing your thoughtful concerns regarding the charges against two nationals of Libya for the bombing of Pan Am Flight 103.

I note your suggestion that the delivery of the two defendants to the jurisdiction of the United States might be facilitated through the good offices of the Libyan National Security Advisor, Yousef Debri if Secretary Baker were able to meet with Mr. Debri to discuss both that issue and possible exculpatory evidence on the issue of Libyan involvement in the Pan Am 103 bombing. Such a meeting has not taken place, you understand, because the approval of Mr. Debri's visa has been delayed at our Embassy in Berne for some 28 days.

Although there may be concerns we are not aware of which account for the delay in approving Mr. Debri's visa, I would think that there might be a number of ways for Secretary Baker or his representative, to communicate with Mr. Debri on this matter. If a meeting is not possible in the United States, perhaps some other mutually agreeable location would be available to discuss the suggestions Mr. Debri may wish to present regarding this important matter.

I am certain you will not object to my forwarding a copy of my reply to Secretary Baker today, in the event he is not aware of Mr. Debri's desire for such a meeting.

With every good wish.

Ever sincerely,

Claiborne Pell

268

I next met a most cheerful gentleman by the name of Robert Flynn. Flynn was the attorney for Lamen Khalifa Fhimah, one of the two indicted Libyans. Flynn, and his partner on the case, Paul Riley—who represented the other indicted Libyan, Abdel Basset Ali al-Megrahi—were hired by Libya to defend the two suspected bombers. They were the official U.S. lawyers of record for the two accused men. Riley was unable to attend our dinner meeting but Flynn was very pleased to meet me and to know that I had been so successful in taking a U.S. Congressman to meet with "Charlie."

Bob Flynn impressed me with his in depth knowledge of the Lockerbie case. He and Riley had been to Libya to meet with their clients. They had been licensed by the OFAC to represent the two Libyans and to receive payments from the Libyan Government for their services.

I asked Flynn and Mohammed to be my guests for dinner at the Jockey Club.

The Jockey Club is located in the Embassy Row section of Massachusetts Avenue in Northwest Washington. At the time it was one of the most powerful places to eat in Washington. The Jockey Club was the only place in Washington where Ronald Reagan ever went for dinner outside of the White House during his tour as President. He showed up one night while I was there with his old friends from California, Charlie and MaryJane Wick. The Washington Post carried a story the next day on how shocked the President was to pay twenty-dollars for a piece of swordfish. It was obvious to all that he had lost touch with the average man during his confinement in the White House.

As we entered the Jockey Club, we paused long enough for me to introduce Mohammed and Bob Flynn to Senator and Mrs. Lloyd Bentsen from Texas and to Democratic stalwart Bob Strauss and his wife. They were frequent guests at this Washington landmark and I had seen them in the club many times before.

Bentsen's first senatorial campaign in 1970 was also my first political campaign. He ended up beating another Texan who later gained some political fame, George Bush. I had also gotten to know "Mr. Democrat," Bob Strauss during my political days as a faculty member at the University of Texas at Austin. Strauss and I met in May of 1972, the night Lt. Governor Ben Barnes lost his bid for the Democratic Nomination for the Governorship of Texas. Barnes, the leading vote getter in Texas just four years before, got caught up in an anti-incumbent mood brought on by the Sharpstown State Bank Scandal and ended up not even carrying his home district, Comanche County. I worked hard on Barnes' campaign and, even though we lost, I got to know some of the leading political figures of the Texas past and future, including John Connally. (I worked closely with the former Texas Governor in his 1980 bid for the Republican Presidential nomination.)

I traveled on the campaign trail with Frank Erwin, Chairman of the Board of Regents of the University of Texas. I was a lowly Assistant Professor at the University but ended up spending a good part of my time campaigning with this powerful Board Chairman. One night, Erwin and I flew in a University plane to Brownwood, Texas, to attend the "Kick Off" for the Barnes for Governor Campaign, only to be greeted upon our arrival, on a dark airstrip, by a photographer and reporter from The Daily Texan, *the University newspaper. Our pictures were prominently displayed the next day on the front page of the school paper and my notoriety in the College of Education grew rapidly.*

270

Erwin was a "shoot from the hip" kind of guy with a penchant for making headlines. One such incident occurred when a bunch of "hippies" climbed a tree to stop bulldozers from knocking it down to make way for a new gymnasium building on the campus. Frustrated with his inability to negotiate with the long haired students, Frank took the controls of the bulldozer and knocked down the tree, students and all. The incident made Time Magazine.

While Barnes lost the nomination for Governor, Bentsen won the Senate seat which he held until he gave it up in 1992 to become Secretary of the Treasury under President Bill Clinton. He resigned the position on December 22, 1994, to return to private business. During the same time, Strauss served in a variety of high visibility jobs from United States Trade Representative to U.S. Ambassador to the Soviet Union. He always managed to return to his law practice in between political appointments and massed a small fortune brokering his powerful Washington connections into big financial deals.

Virginia and I often see a lot of both Strauss and Bentsen at the Turf Club of the Del Mar Race Track during the six week racing season every August. The track is just a few miles from our new home in Rancho Santa Fe, California. Bentsen built a retirement home in Rancho Santa Fe. Strauss spends the six week summer racing season at track side. Strauss was asked one day by a reporter if he would take another ambassadorship after he completed his assignment in the Soviet Union. He responded that he would only consider one other ambassadorship—Ambassador to Del Mar!

The conversation between Mohammed, Bob Flynn and myself seemed to flow freely that evening. I recounted my adventures in Libya and my unprecedented meeting with Col. Qadhafi. Although Flynn had been to Libya to meet

271

his clients, he had never met "Charlie." Mohammed said that he and Charlie were best of friends and that he was frequently called by the Libyan leader to give him advice on world issues. I learned to believe only a fraction of what came out of Mohammed's mouth.

Flynn gave me some free counsel about my unfortunate situation with the OFAC. He believed that the OFAC was an Agency without teeth and that I shouldn't worry about future problems coming from them. He expressed an interest in my helping him and Riley prepare a defense for their Libyan clients. He stressed the point that the indictments against the two Libyans were more political than legal. He admitted that he needed help on Capitol Hill to convince various Members of Congress to pressure the administration into moving the trial to a neutral country. He felt it was the only way for the two Libyans to get a fair trial.

After dinner I had Paul drive the three of us back to the Park Hyatt. Mohammed, Bob and I talked long into the night.

Suite 506 was rather small and cluttered with stacks of new and old Arabic newspapers. Mohammed lived his entire life, both personal and professional, out of the suite. He often claimed to own a home in the State of Washington and a luxurious palace on the Island of Malta. He said he ran a medical supply business in Seattle called American Medical Supply that sold medical products to Libya.

In addition to the hotel telephones in his suite, he had at least three additional telephone lines. A fax machine was situated on a small table in the corner of the room. It was seldom silent. He would walk about the suite talking with us as he monitored faxes coming off the fax machine. He had an uncanny skill of reading and talking at the same time. He made no comments about what he had read and almost unconsciously threw the faxes on a pile of papers almost two feet high on his coffee table.

I asked Mohammed and Flynn why in the world they had gotten involved with Senator Harrison Williams and how they thought he could be of service to them. Mohammed told me that he had met Williams through his personal friend, Washington Attorney William Rogers. I, of course, thought that he was referring to "The" William D. Rogers, Secretary of State under President Carter. It was almost three months later, after being asked by Mohammed to get tickets for the Clinton Inauguration for Rogers and his wife, that I found out that it wasn't the same William Rogers. Mohammed's William Rogers did serve in the State Department, but never in the lofty position of Secretary of State. Mohammed often referred to his close association with Rogers and said that he was a frequent visitor at the Rogers' home. He also gave me a copy of a contract that Rogers had prepared for his law firm, Arnold and Porter, to represent the Libyan Government. It was interesting that everyone seemed to be getting a piece of Libyan business. Arnold and Porter were not to be left out.

The next order of business with Mohammed was the $200,000 he and Gerrit P. Van de Bovenkamp owed me for taking Hubbard to meet with Youssef Debri and Col. Qadhafi. I was confronted with the first of Mohammed's many classic stalls. He said he had spoken to Gerrit and that Gerrit would be sending me the full amount due from Switzerland, very soon. I was told by Mohammed, "Not to worry. The money is a small thing in relation to the good that you are performing in resolving the Lockerbie issue." Mohammed was sure that Gerrit would pay me in full."

Upon my return to San Diego the next day I received a series of calls from Gerrit, still in Geneva. He gave me a variety of excuses why the $200,000 had not been transferred to my California account. His major theme was that he was having trouble transferring the money from his home country, Holland, to Switzerland. He could not wire my money until he had the money safely in his account in

273

Switzerland. He did agree to wire a partial payment of $50,000 to me as a good faith gesture.

Gerrit was true to his word. On October 30, 1992, $50,000 was wired to my La Jolla account from a Swiss bank. Although I was very displeased with the fact that Gerrit and Mohammed had not lived up to their side of the agreement, which called for me to be paid $200,000 within forty-eight hours of taking a Member of Congress to meet with Youssef, I was encouraged that he had at least kept his word on the partial payment. Payments are always slower after the goods are delivered.

Life returned to normal as we prepared for our upcoming Christmas open-house and our annual Christmas trip to Vail. There was little activity from Gerrit and Mohammed. I spoke to Gerrit on the telephone every couple of days and he promised to pay me the balance of my fee as soon as he received his payments from his clients. Mohammed became harder and harder to reach by telephone. Bob Flynn told me he had become quite ill and was spending a lot of time visiting various doctors in the Washington, D.C. area.

I finally reached Mohammed on December 1st. We had some rather harsh words about the money he and Gerrit owed me. He assured me that all was well and that the one-hundred-fifty-thousand dollar balance he and Gerrit owed me was "small potatoes." Right now he wanted to talk with me about my involvement with the lawyers, Flynn and Riley. He asked if I could fly to Washington to meet with him and the lawyers the next day. Apparently, Flynn and Riley wanted to hire me to help them over a one year period. They were offering to pay me a million dollars for my efforts. He said that he would pay my airfare and expenses for the trip. I agreed to the trip.

Since Virginia and I were to be the guests of hotelier and close friend, Larry Lawrence, owner of the famous Hotel Del Coronado, at a black tie dinner the following evening, I made arrangements to take the red-eye to Washington. I just made my 11:10 P.M. flight by changing from my tuxedo to my traveling clothes in the back seat of the car in the airport parking lot.

Paul delivered me to the Park Hyatt the following evening. I asked him to stay close by the hotel while I met with Mohammed and the lawyers. I was getting more and more concerned about my personal safety, not only from the Libyan standpoint but also from the standpoint of the U.S. Government. I knew a great deal about the Libyan standoff with the U.S. and I was beginning to wonder if maybe one or both countries would be happy to see me go away.

I had received a short hang-up phone call from an American man a few days before with one short message, "Stay away from Libya." I didn't take it very seriously— at the time!

I told Paul that I would call him on his portable phone every half-hour. If he didn't hear from me he was to call Mohammed's suite. If he still couldn't get in touch with me he should call my close friend, Sergeant-at-Arms of the United States House of Representatives, Jack Russ.

Among Jack's responsibilities was the supervision of a twelve hundred member Capitol Hill Police Force. Jack was a very savvy guy. He often carried a 9mm semiautomatic pistol, a perk of his lofty position as the head of the Capitol Hill police force. If Jack knew that I was in a difficult situation he could dispatch a police car to the Park Hyatt under the guise that a Congressman was in some kind of trouble.

Jack and I had been friends for many years. As a lobbyist and foreign agent, having the House Sergeant-at-Arms as a friend was important to the trappings of my business. I would have breakfast with Jack most mornings

275

in the House Member's Dinning Room. We were joined by various Congressmen, professional staff members and an array of House officers. Speaker Jim Wright would often stop by for a cup of coffee and a joke or two. He was a true man of the people and he always had time for a kind word or pat on the back. By contrast, Speaker Tom Foley, his successor, conducted an "imperial speakership" never taking the time for kind word or deed.

Speaker Wright was very helpful to me in my lobbying efforts. I had the great pleasure of representing television minister, Dr. Robert Schuller of the Crystal Cathedral, during hearings before the House Ways and Means Committee. Dr. Schuller was asked to testify in relation to the PTL Scandal and its effect on the tax deductibility of TV ministries. One day the Speaker heard that I had Dr. Schuller in the Capitol and sent me a message that he would be honored to meet the world famous preacher. Schuller and I went to the Speaker's office. Jim Wright and Bob Schuller quickly became good friends. This was a very special time for me—the three of us knelt and prayed in front of the warm fire roaring in the Speaker's ornate fireplace.

Schuller was also very impressed with Jim Wright and extended an invitation to the Speaker to be his guest on his "Hour of Power" television service. He said that he had never had a politician on the program but would make a special exception for the Speaker of the House. I was asked to arrange the appearance and, on a lovely spring Sunday morning in Garden Grove, California, the Speaker of the United States House of Representatives, Jim Wright, told millions of viewers of the "Hour of Power" about his personal walk with Jesus Christ. It was a most memorable experience for Virginia, Katie and me to be with Jim Wright and Bob Schuller that Sunday Morning.

Jim Varey of the United States Secret Service, would spend some time with us at breakfast most mornings. Jim was the lead Secret Service Agent assigned to the Capitol. He worked closely with Jack Russ and the Capitol Police in organizing visits of the President, Vice-President, Secretary of the Treasury (his boss) and all Heads of State. Jim was a great source of information for me. I always knew who and when dignitaries were coming to the Capitol.

Jack Russ first came to Capitol Hill as a young man and had spent his entire career serving the wishes of Democratic Speakers of the House, first as a Door Keeper and eventually as House Sergeant-at-Arms. The Sergeant-at-Arms is elected by the Members of the House of Representatives after first being recommended for the position by the Speaker.

Jack was a very powerful person on Capitol Hill. He was also the last Sergeant-at-Arms to wield such power as a result of his administrative control over the now infamous House Bank. Jack's activities in performing his banking duties led him into big trouble. He was fired over the House Bank Scandal by House Speaker Tom Foley, just three months short of qualifying for his full federal retirement. I watched as the various Members of the House quickly turned their backs on Jack. These were the same Members who just weeks before relied on Jack for their daily financial existence. The one exception was my friend Mervyn Dymally of California. He was the only Member with the courage to hire Jack for the three months that would make him eligible to collect his full federal pension.

Under Jack Russ's administration, I was afforded almost carte blanche access to the Capitol and to the Members of the House. I had access to all non-public areas of the Capitol. I had a special parking pass that permitted Paul to park my Lincoln Town Car directly in front of the Capitol East Front entrance, an area normally reserved

277

for the Speaker and the other members of the House Leadership.

Jack would strategically station me and, if I requested, one of my clients near the House East Front door in order to meet visiting dignitaries or Heads of State. Jack, whose job it was to be the official greeter for such individuals, would be sure to bring President Bush, Nelson Mandela, Sugar Ray Leonard, Benazir Bhutto, Lee Iacocca, Gerald Ford, Margaret Thatcher and the like to my designated spot for a brief introduction and a photo session. The pictures, compliments of the Sergeant-at-Arms' staff photographer, made great office displays for my clients back home.

If I asked, Jack would put me on the House Floor for special Joint-Sessions of Congress or for a State of the Union Speech. After a private reception for key invited guests in Jack's elegantly appointed office, I would be escorted to a seat on the House floor with all of the other dignitaries. I would often have this privilege extended to important clients of mine.

Nothing was as impressive as having Jack Russ as a friend during a Presidential Inauguration. Access to Capitol parking, when all streets around the Capitol were closed, was mind boggling to my clients. A brunch served for the Bush Inauguration in Jack's office prior to being escorted to our front row seats for the swearing-in ceremonies was most memorable for my friends and special guests, including football great, Joe Theisman and his then girl friend, actress Kathy Lee Crosby.

I often used my closeness to Jack to help some of my Capitol Police Force friends. I would discuss their gripes with Jack and served as an unofficial lobbyist for the Capitol police. I also brought a few of my friends to Jack's attention for promotions and special positions. I was responsible for moving one of my longtime friends, Bob Vitarelli, from a uniformed position at the Democratic Door, to a plainclothes position on Jack's personal staff.

Jack and I spent hours discussing his many business dealings. Although I never invested my money in his ventures, some of my clients did get involved with Jack. One in particular, Walt Taylor, invested $30,000 in Jack's flag case business. Jack's company sold American Flags folded in true military fashion by off-duty soldiers at Arlington National Cemetery and placed in a triangular wooden and glass flag case perfect for display. Jack got the idea from the Capitol flag office and he actually sold his display cases in the Members' store located in the basement of the Longworth House Office Building. Walt was one of many investors who lost their money in the deal which led to a series of indictments against Jack Russ.

Jack was in many ways a victim of circumstances. As Sergeant-at-Arms, he was expected to operate the House Bank just as his many predecessors had done. Tradition provided that the House Bank was the tool of the various Members of Congress, and it operated at their convenience. Members' paychecks were automatically deposited into their bank account once a month like clockwork. Since there was no built-in accountability in the banking function, Members and their spouses would write bad checks knowing full well that their monthly deposit would eventually cover the overdrafts. It was only a problem when overdrafts were larger than the size of the pay checks. Jack Russ would approve the overdrafts as a part of everyday business. When funds remained insufficient from month to month, Jack would have what he called a "Heart -to-Heart" discussion with the errant Member.

Mickey Leland, a black Congressman from Houston and Chairman of the African Subcommittee of the House Foreign Affairs Committee, was one of the worst violators of House Bank procedures. Mickey was a good friend of Jack's and mine. He was always happy to help out on key issues before his committee. Mickey was a resident member of my early morning breakfast sessions in the House

279

Member's Dining Room. He liked the good life. He also loved to gamble.

His gambling habit was getting the best of him and rumors of his massive gambling debts were beginning to circulate in the Capitol. Mickey would often ask to borrow money from me, but instead settled for me buying his breakfast. Jack Russ and I often discussed his predicament with Mickey. We knew that Mickey was financing his gambling debts with money advanced from his House Bank overdrafts. Jack, as the responsible House Officer, was on the line. He had to approve the overdrafts.

In 1988, Mickey Leland was on an official trip to Africa on subcommittee business when his plane crashed into the side of a mountain killing him and everyone aboard the plane. Few people know that it was actually Jack Russ who found the plane in the dense jungles of Central Africa. When Jack heard that the plane was missing, he personally joined the search party and was the first one in the rescue party to spot the wreckage.

Jack often expressed his frustration on just how he should handle the $35,000 overdraft that Mickey left unpaid at the House Bank at the time of his accidental death. Capitol reporters were starting to snoop around the workings of the House Bank and Jack was worried that there could be a major scandal. Jack had to cover the overdraft, but was very reluctant to discuss the circumstances with Mickey's widow, Jackie. Fortunately, the money was eventually repaid to the House Bank from the proceeds of a Congressional life insurance policy carried on Mickey's life. It wasn't until 1992 that the inner workings of the House Bank became public—and all hell broke loose.

Jack Russ quickly became the "fall guy" for the indiscretions of the House Bank. The practice of writing overdrafts had been a part of the day to day business of running the House Bank for over a hundred years. Every

Member knew it was the standard operating procedure and, as the record would later show, most Members enthusiastically participated in the practice. All of a sudden, people like House Speaker Tom Foley were "shocked" to find out that the practice had taken place. When confronted with the nasty situation, the Speaker pointed the finger of guilt at Jack Russ and demanded that Jack resign immediately from his post. It was all I could do to listen to all of the Members Jack had helped over the years, condemn him on the House Floor in speech after speech.

On September 29, 1993, I was questioned about the House Bank scandal for over two hours by FBI Special Agent Chuck Anderson and one of his associates. I asked the agents to meet me in the Capitol and, as usual, I ended up buying the agents breakfast in the House Members' Dining Room. From the nature of their questions it was obvious that Jack Russ was the target of their investigation. They were most interested in what I knew about the $30,000 investment my client Walt Taylor made in Jack's American Flag Case Company. They wanted to know if Jack had used his powerful position to coerce unsuspecting people into making investments in Jack's business ventures. I defended Jack and his activities. I felt sorry for Walt but the investment was his decision and his alone.

The FBI agents went beyond the Jack Russ House Bank Case. They asked me to tell all I knew about Chairman Dan Rostenkowski's alleged misdeeds with the House Post Office. They were very direct and asked if I had ever given money to "Rosti" in campaign contributions, or personal loans or gifts. Fortunately, I was able to answer no to all their questions.

I am very proud to say that Jack Russ is my friend. During the entire House Bank episode, Jack Russ never implicated a single Member of Congress in the affair. He was afforded many opportunities to plead his way out of a long prison term by simply telling the "Feds" what he knew about the financial dealings of some of the most visible Members of the United States Congress. Jack refused the offer. He was indicted and convicted on three felony charges stemming from the House Bank scandal, and his personal business dealings while serving as Sergeant-at-Arms. Under the terms of his sentence, Jack will have to make restitution to Walt Taylor and all of the other investors.

Jack Russ is now prisoner #18480-016 and is serving two years at the Federal Corrections Institution in Morgantown, West Virginia.

Chapter Twenty-Eight

A Million Dollar Contract

Both Bob Flynn and Paul Riley were with Mohammed when I arrived at the Park Hyatt the evening of December 3, 1992. I felt a bit more secure being in
Mohammed's suite with the two lawyers close by. However, it was true that in the cloak and dagger world in which
I found myself, you really never knew who the good guys
were!

Finally I had the opportunity of meeting Paul Riley.
Paul was a retired CIA agent in his early sixties. He was
very interested in my conflict with the OFAC and probed
me to tell exactly what had transpired. He and Bob Flynn
got a big laugh when I reported the details of my conversation with Special Investigator Hal Harmon. Mohammed
just sat, listened and kept shaking his head in disbelief. I
was assured by both Flynn and Riley that I had done nothing wrong in the eyes of the law, and that I shouldn't worry
about the incident with the OFAC.

Mohammed suggested that we go to dinner at the
Melrose Restaurant located on the ground floor of the Park
Hyatt. On our way down to the Melrose, I slipped away
long enough to call Paul on his portable phone and told
him that all was well, and not to worry. No need for Jack
Russ tonight!

The four of us continued our ongoing conversation
over dinner. All three of my dinner partners had the opportunity to relate their personal experiences with the OFAC.
Mohammed was convinced that the OFAC Director, Richard Newcomb, was a "Jew" who hated all Arabs. The truth
was that Mohammed hated all Jews and repeatedly blamed
them for all the ills of the world.

Mohammed said that OFAC agents had recently raided the Seattle office of his American Medical Supply Company. They reportedly searched his home and his office to no avail. Mohammed told me that his requests for export licenses for his medical supply sales to Libya, had often been turned down by Newcomb for no apparent or legal reason. Mohammed wanted me to help him secure future export licenses for his company from the OFAC. Medical supplies were exempt from the U.N. Sanctions against Libya, but a license from the OFAC was still a requirement. It was for this purpose that Mohammed had added a $50,000 addendum to the contract that was offered to me by Mohammed and Gerrit in Geneva, on October 29, 1992.

Bob Flynn had also been frequently harassed by Newcomb and his agency. The OFAC agents had come to his office to give him severe warnings and threats about his continued representation of the Libyans.

He and Riley were each awarded a license to travel to Libya to meet with their clients. They had traveled to Libya three times to work with Megrahi and Fhimah. They were convinced after their trips that the case against the Libyans had been fabricated and was politically motivated. This was the reason they needed my political expertise.

After dinner we went back to Suite 605. Bob Flynn had a draft contract he wanted me to review overnight, and give him my comments the following day. The hour was late. We briefly discussed the contents of their contract for my services. They offered me a one year contract for $1 million dollars, in return for my political advice and counsel.

Both attorneys advised me that I wouldn't need an individual license from the OFAC to perform the political activities they needed. I would be working directly under the auspices of their law firm, which was already licensed. Additionally, they explained that as the lawyers of record, they could hire anyone they needed to help in the defense of their clients. Flynn and Riley intended to hire forensic experts, detectives and other professionals in their defense preparations. I said I would study the contract and meet with them the following day for lunch.

Before I departed, Mohammed reached into his coat pocket. He handed me an envelope containing twenty-five, one-hundred dollar bills which were intended to reimburse me for my travel expenses to Washington. I had previously seen Mohammed's U.S. passport. Again I had no qualms about taking the money from a U.S. citizen.

After reviewing circumstances related to the OFAC, I made a decision that night that I really wanted to get to the bottom of the Pan Am 103 incident. There was no way the OFAC was going to let me do it as a foreign agent with ICM for Libya. It seemed the best way for me to do it was to work directly for the law firm of Flynn and Riley. I felt that this association with Flynn and Riley would take me out of direct conflict with the OFAC, and provide me with the platform I needed to help bring this case to a logical conclusion.

Later that night as I was lying in bed reading Flynn's proposed contract, I was startled by the phone ringing. It was well past midnight. I was very concerned that something was wrong at home in California.

The man on the phone didn't identify himself, but in a very thick Arab accent, he warned me not to pursue the Libyan case further. That is, if I wanted to "stay healthy." Just prior to hanging up on me, the voice said, "There are a lot of people who don't want this case reopened. If you want to stay alive, stay away from Pan Am 103."

I hung up the phone in total disbelief and shock. My thoughts ran from fear to outrage to humor. Was this for real, or was I casting myself into a James Bond movie? I spent a sleepless night after receiving the threatening telephone call. Mostly, I was glad that the condo telephone hadn't been forwarded to California as is normally the case. Virginia could have answered the telephone and heard the same death threat that I had. This would have been especially bad, since the OFAC had faxed to Virginia that same day, an Order to Cease and Desist and Requirement to Furnish Information. She didn't need another shock.

Was it a hoax, or was it a real threat? Was it a coincidence that the meeting with Flynn and Riley, the threat and the fax from the OFAC occurred the same day? I decided at that point that my future involvement in this case would be secret. I had no idea who wanted me out of the Lockerbie case more, the Arabs or the United States Government. I needed to use special care in dealing with both.

After spending the following morning, December 4th, on Capitol Hill, I met Mohammed and Bob Flynn at the Park Hyatt for lunch. We discussed the proposed contract, and the death threat I had received the previous night. Both Flynn and Mohammed didn't seem to express any particular concern over my late night phone call. They both felt that my telephones were probably bugged by the CIA, FBI or the OFAC. If the call didn't come from one of these agencies, the U.S. Government was at least now aware of the death threat. They also warned me to be aware of anyone following me or any suspicious characters lurking in the dark - as if I had to be reminded!

I thought about my personal safety. I recalled a few years back trying to get my driver Paul Williams armed in the District of Columbia. It was a futile task. In order to carry a gun in Washington, D.C., it was necessary for Paul to become a Deputy U.S. Marshall. It seemed only the bad guys were allowed to have guns in this crazy town. I realized that there was little value in trying this security approach again.

AGREEMENT

This Agreement, made this 27^{7L} day of November 1992, at Washington, D.C., by and between Flynn & Riley, 1730 K Street, N.W., Suite 304, Washington, D.C. 20006 (hereinafter "Unified Counsel") and The William Chasey Organization, 1015 33rd Street, N.W., Suite 509, Washington, D.C. 20007 (hereinafter Unified Counsel's "Consultant").

WHEREAS, Unified Counsel is desirous of obtaining the services of a consultant to assist Unified Counsel in extrajudicial efforts with respect to the indictment of Lamin Fhimah and Abdel Basset; and

WHEREAS, Consultant is willing to provide the above-desired assistance to Unified Counsel in directing such efforts.

NOW, THEREFORE, in consideration of the mutual covenants, promises, and understandings set forth below, the parties hereto agree as follows:

A. Services Provided by Consultant

Consultant agrees hereby to perform the following services:

1. Provide assistance and direction to Unified Counsel in the preparation of extrajudicial efforts as they relate to the Senate of the United

287

States, the United States House of Representatives, and the Committees and Subcommittees thereof.

2. Provide assistance and direction relating to the dissemination of printed and published material to the national and international media.

3. Assisting Unified Counsel in the preparation of extrajudicial efforts concerning international organizations, bodies and tribunals.

B. <u>Compensation to be Rendered Consultant</u>

For the above services, Consultant shall be compensated as follows:

1. Consultant shall receive compensation in the amount of $200,000 by December 1, 1992, such compensation being rendered to Consultant for the following enumerated services to be completed within the time frames set forth below:

a. During December 1992, Consultant shall arrange for the visit, either official or unofficial, of selected members of Congress to either Malta, Europe or Africa, and during such time Consultant shall engage in direct lobbying efforts in Congress.

b. During January 1993, Consultant shall arrange for further visits, either official or unofficial, of selected members of Congress, to either Malta, Europe or Africa, and during such

time period Consultant shall engage in direct
lobbying efforts in Congress.

c. During February 1993, Consultant
shall arrange for a formal fact-finding visit to
Africa, Malta or Europe, and during such time
period Consultant shall engage in direct lobbying
efforts in Congress.

d. Upon the arrival of February 15,
1993, the parties hereto shall reevaluate the
services performed and to be performed by
Consultant, and upon approval thereof, Unified
Counsel shall be obligated to make a payment of
$200,000 to Consultant and, should Unified
Counsel determine to continue to use Consultant's
services, Unified Counsel shall be obligated to
pay Consultant $200,000 at ten (10) week
intervals until the total compensation paid to
Consultant shall total $1,000,000.

WHEREBY, the Parties hereto, having read and
acknowledged the contents, mutual obligations and

- 4 -

promises contained herein have signed this Agreement at Washington, D.C. on the date set forth herein.

Flynn & Riley
(Unified Consultant)

By: _Robert J. Flynn, Jr._
     Robert J. Flynn, Jr.

The William Chasey Organization
(Consultant)

By: _William Chasey_
     William Chasey

I wanted to have a second opinion on the legality of the Flynn and Riley contract. I understood from the two lawyers that the license they held would afford me protection from the Libyan Sanctions Act, and the OFAC. If they were correct, I wouldn't need my own separate license to conduct political consultation on their behalf. If they were wrong, I would be in deep trouble with the OFAC again.

The deal they offered me sounded attractive and logical. But, I had dealt much too long with the federal establishment to take anything for granted, especially anything that sounded attractive and logical. I needed to get a second opinion to be absolutely sure. If necessary, I would apply for my own license from the OFAC.

I was leaving for Switzerland on December 7th on some personal business. I told Flynn that I would work on the license situation and our pending contract when I returned five days later. Mohammed said that he was going to be at the Noga Hilton in Geneva on December 10th, and suggested that we meet in Geneva. He said that being in Switzerland would make it easier for him to pay me $150,000—the balance due on my account.

On December 7, 1992, I flew to Zurich, Switzerland with my then business partner, Allan Bird. Our business in Switzerland related to a new product line we were introducing in the United States. I had come up with the concept of developing a line of environmentally responsible, Swiss cleaning products for sale in the United States and elsewhere. I brought Allan Bird, a wealthy California entrepreneur, into the deal as my financial partner. We were in Switzerland to meet with our Swiss chemists and to design the packaging for our new BCD International line of products.

After completing our business in Zurich, Allan and I took the train to Geneva on December 10, 1992. We only had one scheduled BCD meeting in Geneva with a Swiss marketing agency. As agreed, I tried to contact Mohammed at the Noga Hilton. Mohammed had not checked into the hotel, and there were no messages for me. Allan and I personally went to the Noga Hilton that night after dinner, to see if Mohammed could be found. Once again, Mohammed had disappeared.

We returned to San Diego on December 11th with much accomplished on our BCD business, but without making contact with the elusive Mohammed.

Chapter Twenty-Nine

A Christmas Surprise
From Uncle Sam

It was great to back home in San Diego, especially with the Christmas holiday quickly approaching. We were scheduled to leave for Vail on December 19th, just two days away. I was catching up on some final paperwork in preparation for our upcoming ski trip.

On the morning of December 17th, Virginia was in La Jolla doing a few last minute errands and giving Santa a helping hand with his upcoming visit to Katie in Colorado. She planned to stop at the bank and pick up enough cash for the trip, pay some bills and return home to complete our last minute packing. We always looked forward to our traditional Christmas trip. But this year, I especially needed the break. For ten glorious days I would be free of the OFAC, Libya, Mohammed, Congressman Carroll Hubbard and that worrisome threat on my life.

This was a morning I will never forget. Virginia called from the bank in a panic. "They froze our bank account," she blurted. "The United States Treasury has taken all of our money. They won't give me a penny at the bank. The bankers can't tell me any more than that they are sorry. Apparently the Government has every right to freeze bank accounts without notice and without giving a reason for its action. Now what are we going to do for Christmas and for money?"

I tried as best I could to calm Virginia over the telephone. I asked her to come home right away. While waiting for her to return, I immediately called the Office of Foreign Assets Control and asked to speak to Agent Hal

Harmon. Fortunately, he was in the office and took my phone call.

I asked directly, "Did you freeze my bank accounts?"

Harmon responded with haste, "Yes, we decided that the $50,000 paid to you was dirty Libyan money, and the U.S. Treasury has every right to the money."

I wondered how many companies could survive the loss of their business bank account.

With great anger, I responded that the money paid to me came from ICM, a U.S. Corporation, and OFAC had no right to do what it did. I tried in vain to tell Harmon that the U.S. Treasury had no evidence that the money came from Libya. In fact, I had plenty of evidence that it didn't. In addition, the money in the account came from a variety of clients, not just from ICM.

Harmon had betrayed me. We had agreed that I would be open and forthcoming in his investigation, and that I would cease and desist all of the activities contained in my Foreign Agent Registration. We had agreed to cooperate in all matters related to Libya. Now, without the benefit of a trial, hearing, administrative review, or even a warning, this faceless government bureaucrat took it upon himself to freeze my account just days before Christmas. Merry Christmas Mr. Harmon!

None of this seemed real. First the death threat, and now frozen assets. After a lengthy discussion, Virginia and I decided to go forward with the ski trip. We would attempt to enjoy our vacation for the sake of ten-year-old Katie and family members who had already made plans to stay with us in Vail. We would decide what action to take upon our return to La Jolla. After making some very creative financial arrangements, we were off for our Christmas "vacation" in Vail, Colorado. No matter how hard I tried, the death threat and Hal Harmon were constantly with me on the slopes of Vail.

I decided to call Mohammed while in Vail. He was not to be reached. I figured he had a lot of explaining to do about not showing up in Geneva. With my money frozen by the OFAC, the $150,000 he and Gerrit still owed me became critical. I had no concern about accepting my fee from Gerrit or from Mohammed. No matter what the OFAC said, ICM was a certified U.S. Corporation and Mohammed was a U.S. Citizen.

It was Mohammed's style to let the telephone go unanswered for long periods of time. His usual routine was to sleep until noon, and stay awake until the wee hours of the morning. He would be on the telephone to Libya late at night conducting his international business while most people in this country were sleeping.

I decided to call him late one night. As soon as Sharla, the Park Hyatt operator, connected me, I heard the familiar soft "Hello" on the line. I brought him up to date on my recent encounters with the OFAC. He expressed his sadness with Harmon's freezing of my account. He once again assured me that he would make good on the money he owed me.

Mohammed then asked that I fly to Geneva with him the first week in January so that he could pay me from one of his international bank accounts. He claimed to have better access to money in Europe and the trip would help expedite his payment. I said that I would think it over.

I was surprised to get a call back from Mohammed later that same evening. This was not at all like Mohammed. He had made arrangements for us to meet in Geneva on January 6, 1993. He thought it would be a good time to meet since Youssef El Debri would also be in Geneva at

295

that time. Youssef was anxious to meet with us. Mohammed promised to have a First Class Plane ticket waiting
for me at the San Diego Airport when I returned home.

Mohammed said that the Libyan Foreign Minister,
Omar Muntassir, wanted me to call him as soon as possible. He gave me Muntassir's home and office telephone
numbers in Libya. To avoid having my telephone call
traced, or show up on my phone bill, I decided to delay my
call until such time that I could use a pay phone in some
obscure location. We were leaving Vail in two days, and I
could use a pay phone someplace in Utah on the drive
home.

In the fall of 1992 we had purchased a new "Jeep"
Grand Cherokee, and decided to drive the 1000 miles to
Vail instead of taking our usual flight. We stopped for the
night in St. George, Utah, half way between Vail and San
Diego. This was the perfect place to telephone Omar in
Libya. I used the pay phone in the lobby of the St. George
Hilton Hotel.

I was very conscious that the National Security
Agency, (NSA) monitors all communications between the
United States and Libya. The NSA has all telephone and
fax communications between our two countries recorded
but, because of the heavy traffic, they don't have sufficient
human resources to monitor each individual conversation.
If, however, they are looking for some specific conversation, they can easily retrieve it from their computers.

An English speaking male secretary answered Omar's
office telephone. Omar was in a meeting and wanted to
know who was calling. I said to tell Omar that it was "Hollywood Bill," his nickname for me. In a matter of seconds, Omar Mustafa al-Muntassir, the Libyan Foreign
Minister, was on the line with me. He wished me a Merry
Christmas and asked about my family. He said that he was
expecting my call and that it was good to hear from me.

296

I told Omar that I was being watched very carefully by the U.S. Government. He was indignant to hear that the U.S. Treasury had frozen my bank account under the guise that the money I had received was Libyan. How could the United States do such a thing to one of its own citizens without a trial? "We could never do such a thing to one of our own people," he said. "The United States is famous for taking the moral high-ground, as it has with us over the Lockerbie situation, and then they sidestep their own legal system of due process when it comes to one of its own citizens." He was very concerned for my welfare and asked if Libya could be of financial help. I explained that the cease and desist order I was under prohibited me from accepting Libyan money. I graciously rejected his kind offer.

I told Omar that it looked as if I would be applying for a license from the OFAC to assist the law firm of Flynn and Riley in the defense of their two Libyan clients. He seemed pleased with this prospect. Omar said that he would be available to me anytime in the future to provide assistance. I told him I expected to go to Geneva the following week with Mohammed, and hoped to see Youssef during my stay. I was very clear with Omar that I felt more and more confident that there was an international conspiracy taking place to cover-up the truth about Lockerbie, and that I intended to do my best to get to the bottom of the case. He said that the U.S. Government would do all it could to keep me from pursuing my investigation.

His last words were, "You haven't seen anything yet."

Chapter Thirty

Meeting Youssef in Geneva

As Mohammed promised, a prepaid first class airline ticket to Geneva was ready for me at the San Diego, American Airlines ticket counter, early on January 4, 1993. I had planned a one day stopover in Washington to attend the Swearing-In Ceremony of the 103rd Congress, and then it was off to London the evening of January 5th.

I was only in London long enough to transfer to a 9:20 A.M. British Air Flight to Geneva. I used great care to be sure that I wasn't being followed as I changed planes. I felt confident that no one from my London flight made the same Geneva transfer that I did. If I was to be followed this trip, my tail would have to pick me up in Geneva.

I never check luggage and almost always sit in the bulkhead aisle of the first class cabin. I am usually the first one off the plane. To avoid being followed, I made a hasty exit from the plane and quickly took the first cab in the airport taxi queue. I instructed the driver to take me to the Intercontinental Hotel-Geneva. I entered the hotel lobby and waited long enough to make sure I wasn't followed.

My apprehensions satisfied, I took a second cab to the Noga Hilton. Without identifying myself, I told the hotel clerk that a room had been reserved for me by Mr. Mohammed Bukhres. The clerk informed me that Mr. Bukhres had not checked into the hotel yet. However, with no questions asked, the clerk gave me my room key. I wasn't asked my name, address or to produce a credit card, or any other form of payment. I love the Swiss!

I no sooner entered my room, than I received a telephone call from Youssef Debri. I guessed that one of his secret agents, strategically positioned in the lobby, had notified him of my arrival. He invited me to his suite for lunch at 1:00 P.M. He wanted to know if I had heard anything from Mohammed. "Are you sure he is coming Chazzy?" he inquired.

Almost laughingly I responded, "No."

Youssef and I were joined for lunch by Salah El Fituri, President of Fitex, S.A. It was good to see Salah again. The last time I saw him was at dinner at Youssef's home in Tripoli. We had a long discussion, over cow's scalp stew—again, about how best Libya could open a serious dialogue with the U.S. Government.

Youssef was aware of the deal that Mohammed and Gerrit had made with me, and that I was never paid for bringing Congressman Hubbard to meet with the Libyans. Youssef didn't trust Mohammed. He felt sure that Mohammed wouldn't show up in Geneva. "Mohammed makes me crazy," he said under his breath. Youssef generously offered to pay me the $150,000. I am sure he could have covered it with the crisp new U.S. one-hundred dollar bills strategically placed around the suite in brown shopping bags. I explained the cease and desist order I was under, and expressed my thanks to him for the offer, but grudgingly declined.

As it turned out, Youssef spent most of the afternoon, answering my questions about Pan Am 103, and the U.S./Libyan standoff. Over the past few weeks, my suspicions had grown stronger that there was much more to Lockerbie than what was publicly presented by the United States and Great Britain. Having had the opportunity to meet and discuss the disaster with many of the key players in the drama, I knew I wanted to have all the answers. I now had the opportunity to question Youssef Debri about the role Libya played, if any, in the Lockerbie disaster.

Youssef, as Chief of Libyan Intelligence, probably knew more about any Libyan involvement in the Pan Am 103 affair than anyone else. The two indicted Libyans, Megrahi and Fhimah, were both Libyan Intelligence Agents, and therefore worked for Youssef at the time of the 1988 bombing. I knew that I was being afforded a rare and special opportunity to spend this time interviewing him at such great length. I took full advantage of the opportunity. A good part of the information I gleaned from Youssef is contained in this book.

It was obvious that Mohammed was not going to show up in Geneva. Who could understand why anyone would spend the money for my plane ticket, hotel and expenses (about $7,500) if he had no intention of coming? It really didn't matter. I was satisfied that I had been able to pick Youssef's brain. The information provided by Youssef may have been more valuable than the money I had expected to collect from Mohammed.

I left Geneva on January 8, 1993 enroute to Chicago to attend the National Houseware Show. Allan Bird and I, along with our ever-increasing staff, were introducing our new BCD line of environmentally responsible Swiss cleaning products at the show. Libya was nudged to the back burner while I sold soap for the next three days at the Houseware Show.

Chapter Thirty-One

Another Bureaucratic Blunder

I continued my discussions with Bob Flynn and Paul Riley over the next few weeks. I was convinced that they were honest and committed to providing their clients with quality representation in the United States. Although both lawyers felt that I could work for them without my own separate license from the OFAC, I decided to file an application to be sure not to violate the Libyan Sanctions Act.

In addition, I sought a second opinion from Washington Lawyer, Chris Myers, of Dunnells, Duvall & Porter. He also advised me that I didn't need to file for a separate license. However, he said to be safe, I might want to apply anyway and that he would help me.

It took Myers weeks to prepare my application to OFAC to engage in extra-judicial consulting and assistance on behalf of my clients, Attorneys Paul J. Riley and Robert J. Flynn. Myers worked closely with Flynn and Riley in preparing the application. It was finally filed with the OFAC on February 23, 1993.

There was little doubt among all three attorneys involved that the OFAC would comply with my request for a specific license. What else could they do? The U.S. Constitution guarantees that every defendant, no matter how heinous the crime, is considered innocent until proven guilty. The Constitution also provides that every defendant is guaranteed the right to full and complete legal representation. An attorney must use all of the legal resources available to provide his client a quality defense. This representation very often includes private detectives, expert witnesses, forensic experts, legal scholars and political consultants.

303

DUNNELLS, DUVALL & PORTER

ATTORNEYS AT LAW

2100 PENNSYLVANIA AVENUE, N.W.

WASHINGTON, D.C. 20037-3202

(202) 861-1400

CHRISTOPHER A. MYERS
(202) 861-1085

FACSIMILE
(202) 861-1417
(202) 861-1416

February 23, 1993

VIA COURIER

Mr. R. Richard Newcomb
Director
Office of Foreign Assets Control
U.S. Department of the Treasury
1500 Pennsylvania Avenue, N.W.
Washington, D.C. 20020

Re: **The William Chasey Organization**

Dear Mr. Newcomb:

Pursuant to 31 C.F.R. §550.801(b), our client, The William Chasey Organization ("TWCO"), submits the following application for a specific license to engage in extra-judicial consulting and assistance on behalf of its clients, attorneys Paul J. Riley and Robert J. Flynn.

Messrs. Riley and Flynn represent Libyan nationals Abdel Basset Ali Al-Megrahi and Lamem Khalifa Fhimah, respectively with regard to their indictments related to the 1988 aviation incident over Lockerbie, Scotland. In connection with this representation, Messrs. Riley and Flynn have informed us that they are authorized by the Office of Foreign Assets Control to engage in transactions in connection with the provision of legal services to their clients pursuant to License Numbers L-00723a and L-00722a. In furtherance of their representation of their clients, Messrs. Riley and Flynn would like to retain the services of TWCO to assist them in resolving the current impasse between their clients and the United States government regarding resolution of the indictments.

Based on our reading of the relevant Executive Order and regulations, we are of the opinion that TWCO may be able to conduct this activity without obtaining prior approval from the Department of the Treasury. First, as more fully described below, TWCO has been asked to undertake this assignment by attorneys Riley and Flynn as part of their provision of legal services to their clients. The Office of Foreign Assets Control has already issued a license authorizing transactions related to those legal services. Since TWCO's activities will be under the direction of Riley and Flynn, and all compensation will be made through them, we believe

Another Bureaucratic Blunder

Mr. R. Richard Newcomb
February 23, 1993
Page 2

that your office has already given sufficient approval to this activity, and TWCO need not submit a complete application for a license of its own. Instead, TWCO need only be identified as an "interested party" operating under the license which has already been granted to Riley and Flynn.

Second, while not specifically referenced in the regulations concerning trade activities with Libya and Libyan entities, we note that the Office of Foreign Assets control has taken the position that a license is not needed to engage in the provision of certain legal services including "the provision of legal advice and counselling on the requirements with U.S. law," and the "defense of [Libyans] when named as a defendant in domestic U.S. litigation or administrative proceedings." Order to Cease And Desist And Request to Furnish Information, FAC No. 131589 at 1. We believe this exception should apply to TWCO's proposed activity, since it would be directly related to the provision of legal advice.

Although we are of the opinion that TWCO could engage in this activity without specific approval from the Department of Treasury without violating 31 C.F.R. Part 550, TWCO has decided to seek approval from the Office of Foreign Assets prior to accepting this assignment in order to avoid a situation similar to the misunderstanding surrounding TWCO's activities this past fall. See Order to Cease and Desist and Requirement to Furnish Information dated December 3, 1992 - FAC No. 131589. Thus, TWCO requests that the Office of Foreign Assets Control issue to TWCO a specific license to engage in transactions related to the provision of assistance and counselling to Riley and Flynn in their representation of their clients, Messrs. Al-Megrahi and Fhimah. In support of this request TWCO submits the following information as required by 31 C.F.R. §550.801(b)(2) and (3).

The Parties

The William Chasey Organization - The William Chasey Organization ("TWCO") specializes in representing the interests of its clients before national governments, primarily through direct contact with governmental officials. TWCO has offices in La Jolla, California and Washington. D.C. The principal of TWCO is Dr. William C. Chasey. Dr. Chasey has operated TWCO for 20 years. Except for certain clerical and secretarial assistance, Dr. Chasey is the only individual associated with TWCO who will work on this proposed transaction.

Riley and Flynn - Paul J. Riley and Robert J.Flynn are attorneys licensed to practice law in the District of Columbia. They have informed Dr. Chasey that they represent two Libyan nationals currently under indictment issued by a federal grand jury

FOREIGN AGENT 4221: The Lockerbie Cover-up

in the District of Columbia related to the explosion of a United States airliner over Lockerbie, Scotland in 1988. Pursuant to the District of Columbia Bar Rule of Professional Conduct 2.1, a copy of which is attached as Exhibit A, Messrs. Riley and Flynn seek to retain TWCO's services to assist them in their extra-judicial efforts on behalf of their clients.

As you know, since the indictments at issue were handed down by the grand jury, the defendants and the United States Government have not been able to reach an agreement about how the issues raised by the indictments will be resolved. In fact, the parties have not even been able to agree about the forum in which the issues will be resolved. Messrs. Riley and Flynn believe that with TWCO's assistance, some movement toward resolution of the impasse is possible, and that, therefore, it is in their clients' interest to retain his services.

Obviously, neither this law firm, nor the Office of Foreign Assets Control can predict whether, with TWCO's assistance and counsel, Riley and Flynn's efforts on behalf of their clients will be successful. We can only involve ourselves in the issue of whether TWCO may lawfully take part in those efforts. We submit that the answer can only be "Yes."

As noted above, Riley and Flynn are currently operating pursuant to licenses granted by the Office of Foreign Assets Control. These licenses allows them to receive legal fees and reimbursement for incurred expenses from unblocked accounts. As contemplated by the parties, TWCO would be retained as a consultant directly by Riley and Flynn. TWCO would work under the direction and supervision of Riley and Flynn in a manner similar to any expert consultant retained by a lawyer during the course of legal representation. Furthermore, TWCO would be paid by Riley and Flynn using funds obtained by their clients from unblocked accounts.

The Client

In the proposed representation, TWCO would perform its services as a subcontractor to Riley and Flynn. As you know, Riley and Flynn represent Abdel Basset Ali Al-Megrani and Lamem Khalifa Fhimah, the indicted Libyan nationals

The Transaction

As described above, Riley and Flynn seek TWCO's services to provide extra-judicial assistance and consulting with respect to their efforts to accomplish a political solution to the current stalemate between their clients and the United States government.

DUNNELLS, DUVALL & PORTER

Mr. R. Richard Newcomb
February 23, 1993
Page 4

It is expected that Mr. Chasey will be called upon to assist in contacts and negotiations with relevant Congressional committees and their members, Executive Branch officials and international political bodies. All of the work will be directly related to Riley and Flynn's representation of their clients.

As noted in the attached copy of Rule 2.1 of the District of Columbia Rules of Professional Conduct, in rendering legal advice a lawyer may need to "refer not only to law but to other considerations such as moral, economic, social and political factors, that may be relevant to the client's situation." In the situation in which Messrs. Riley and Flynn's clients find themselves, expert consultation with respect to political factors may be as, or more important than their courtroom representation of their clients. Just as there is no doubt that as part of their criminal representation of their clients, Riley and Flynn would be entitled, and perhaps obligated to retain the services of a forensic expert, the circumstances of the case make it necessary to retain a political consultant like Dr. Chasey.

In conclusion, we hope that this submission provides the information that the Office of Foreign Assets Control needs in order to issue a specific license forthwith. However, if you need any additional or clarifying information, please feel free to contact me directly, and we will respond to your needs as quickly as possible.

In advance, thank you for your prompt attention to this matter.

Sincerely,

Christopher A. Myers

CAM:mq

cc: William Chasey
     Paul Riley
     Robert Flynn

9632-001\t-app.pte

In addition, Rule 2.1 of the District of Columbia Rules of Professional Conduct states that in rendering legal advice a lawyer may need to "refer not only to law but to other considerations such as moral, economic, social and political factors (emphasis added), that may be relevant to the client's situation."

In this situation in which Messrs. Riley and Flynn found themselves, expert consultation with respect to political factors could have been as or more important than their courtroom representation of their clients. My application further stated that, "Just as there is no doubt that as part of their criminal representation of their clients, Riley and Flynn would be entitled, and perhaps obligated to retain the services of a forensic expert, the circumstances of the case make it necessary to retain a political consultant like Dr. Chasey."

Much to my surprise and outrage, on March 22, 1993, while I was in Zurich, the OFAC denied my application. Flynn, Riley and Myers were amazed at the blatant disregard for the legal points and authorities they had cited in my application. We all wondered how Flynn and Riley would be able to fully represent their clients without my type of political advice and expertise.

In the brief, one-page, three-paragraph letter, OFAC Director, R. Richard Newcomb, states, that:

> . . . my provision of political consulting and advisory services to the Attorneys constitutes an indirect export of services from the United States to Libya as the beneficiaries of such services would be the Defendants who are presumed to be currently located in Libya.

In addition to Newcomb's lousy English, the denial didn't respond in any way to the legal points contained in

Another Bureaucratic Blunder

DEPARTMENT OF THE TREASURY
WASHINGTON

MAR 2 2 1993

FAC No. L-133098

Dear Mr. Myers:

This is in response to your letter of February 23, 1993, to the United States Department of the Treasury's Office of Foreign Assets Control on behalf of the William Chasey Organization ("TWCO") requesting a specific license to authorize TWCO to provide political consulting and advisory services to Messrs. Paul J. Riley and Robert J. Flynn (the "Attorneys") in connection with their representation of Abdel Basset Ali Al-Megrahi and Lamen Khalifa Fhime (the "Defendants").

Pursuant to Section 550.202 of the Libyan Sanctions Regulations, the export from the United States of goods, technology or services to Libya is prohibited. TWCO's provision of political consulting and advisory services to the Attorneys constitutes an indirect export of services from the United States to Libya as the beneficiaries of such services would be the Defendants who are presumed to be currently located in Libya. It would be contrary to current U.S. Government policy to authorize the export to Libya of the kinds of services that TWCO contemplates. Furthermore, the type of activity that TWCO would engage in and the services it would provide to the Attorneys is outside the scope of the authorization pursuant to License Nos. L-00723a and L-00722a where the Attorneys are limited to providing legal services and representation to Messrs. Al-Maghrahi and Fhima. The services TWCO intends to provide consist of political lobbying and consulting

In accordance with the foregoing, the request for a license to enable TWCO to provide the services described in your letter of February 23, 1993, must be denied.

Sincerely,

R. Richard Newcomb
Director
Office of Foreign Assets Control

Christopher A. Myers, Esq.
Dunnels, Duvall and Porter
2100 Pennsylvania Avenue, N.W.
Washington, D.C. 20037-3202

my request for a license. Newcomb did what most federal bureaucrats do in similar situations. He copied a few lines from a Federal Regulation, as a boiler-plate answer, disregarding any questions or points of law. In between the lines, Newcomb was telling me that if I didn't like his decision, and had enough money to take on the Federal Government, I should file a lawsuit.

Realistically, the decision said that Megrahi and Fhimah couldn't receive a fair trial in the United States. I, of course, had heard this said directly by Qadhafi, Debri and other Libyan officials, but now for the first time I had confirmation from a Federal Agency Administrator. Was it true that the U.S. system of justice didn't apply to major international crimes? I realized that if the defendants were tried in the United States, their lawyers would be engaged in a political courtroom battle without the benefit of political advice and expertise. They wouldn't have their full complement of arrows in their quiver.

I no longer wondered why Qadhafi let this standoff continue for such a long time. He could have removed the UN sanctions imposed on his country with the flick of a finger. Just turn Megrahi and Fhimah over to UN officials, and the ordeal would be over.

Both Megrahi and Fhimah had looked me in the eye and told me that they were very anxious to have their trial go forward, but they were afraid that they couldn't get a fair trial in the United States. The pretrial publicity could never be neutralized in a U.S. courtroom. They believed strongly that the United States was directly responsible for their indictments, and any chance of a fair trial was, at best, remote. They were, however, most willing to be tried in a neutral territory such as The Hague or Switzerland.

I was confronted with a major decision. Should I spend the time and money required to appeal the OFAC decision, or should I find another way to get to the bottom of the Lockerbie situation? If I told my story publicly in a book, it would reach masses of people without the threat of the U.S. Government coming down on me anymore. But first I needed to impeach the case brought against the Libyans by the United States and Great Britain. I didn't know how I was going to do it but I felt that I should try.

The answer came after a great deal of prayer and consultation with Virginia. I decided not to appeal the decision. I would instead, begin my own personal investigation into the matter. If my investigation proved fruitful, I would take the information public in a book. I had a cause. If the federal bureaucrats were lying and if there had been a cover-up and a conspiracy, the American people had a right to know.

Chapter Thirty-Two

The FBI Sting

First, I had to pick up the pieces of my life and make a living. I continued to lobby in Washington and pursue my personal business dealings. Virginia, Katie and I had visited Hungary in 1987, and Poland in 1989. Virginia, a direct descendant of the famous Polish poet and statesman, Adam Miczkiewicz, always had a keen interest in Poland. Her enthusiasm for the former Soviet Republic quickly spread to me. The fall of the Berlin Wall, and the new transformations taking place in the Eastern Block, presented me with a new business opportunity. I began establishing U.S./Polish joint business ventures in Poland.

Six months after the OFAC denied my application for a license, on September 8, 1993, I was having lunch in the House Members' Dining Room. My client and lunch guest was David Otten, President of Celsat Corporation of Los Angeles. Carroll Hubbard unexpectedly walked up to our table and engaged us in a lighthearted conversation. He accepted my invitation to join us and the House Restaurant Manager, Scotty, brought an additional chair to our table.

It seemed that now that Carroll was out of Congress he was anxious to pump some blood into his new legal and lobbying company in Washington. He claimed that he had tried to reach me so that I could give him some inside lobbying tips, although I had no record of any such calls. I agreed to give him whatever advice I could. He suggested that we get together for dinner sometime soon, so he could pick my brain.

On October 7, 1993, Carroll called me at my La Jolla home and invited me to be his guest at dinner the follow-

313

ing week at one of Washington's "in" restaurants, Duke Zieberts. After agreeing on a time, Carroll reflected on how much he enjoyed the time he spent in my La Jolla home, and how much he appreciated having Virginia, Katie and me as friends.

Carroll and I met at Duke's at 7:00 P.M. on October 12th. The Carroll Hubbard I met that night was a new Carroll Hubbard. He was full of life and vigor. He enjoyed being recognized by the Maitre' de (Duke's son) who greeted us at the door with a, "Welcome back Congressman Hubbard." Carroll had money in his pockets for the first time that I could remember. He suggested that I order anything I liked from the menu, because the treat was on him. Carroll Hubbard was actually going to pick up a check! I liked the new Carroll.

Most of our conversation focused on Carroll's attempts to become a business consultant and lobbyist. He mentioned all of the business people back home in his former district who were anxious to have him represent them in Washington. He liked what he was doing domestically, but preferred working in the international world like me.

This brought us to the topic of Libya. He was most curious about my work on the Lockerbie disaster. He wanted to know how he could get involved with Qadhafi and make some "big bucks." He asked if I had had any more contact with the Libyans, and if I still had a good relationship with Youssef and Omar. I told him that other than a few telephone conversations with Omar and Youssef, I had had no contact with the "home country." Carroll asked if I could use my Libyan contacts to be helpful to some of his clients back home, who would love to tap into some of that Libyan oil money.

I took the time to explain the ramifications of doing business in Libya, especially as far as the OFAC was concerned. I outlined the government's policy in just a few words, "It can't be done."

314

We had a few glasses of wine and a relaxed discussion about our trip to Libya, including some of the laughs we shared during the trip. He wanted to know more about my clients. He wanted to know how I was so successful in having so much access to the Members of Congress. Carroll always had a way of probing deeper and deeper into an issue, so his interest in my business activities didn't seem very unusual to me. He asked if I would be willing to work with him representing some of his new clients. He admitted that he needed me to show him the ropes, especially in the international marketplace.

He went into detail about one of his new prospects, a gentleman who was interested in developing a foreign operation out of his home base in northern Virginia. Carroll suggested a meeting with this person in a week or so, if I were interested. I was and agreed to a meeting. With the exception of Carroll's annoying questions, the evening was rather enjoyable.

Carroll phoned me again sometime during the week of October 18th asking me to join him and his client at Duke's, on October 26th for dinner. I accepted the invitation.

I arrived early, and was sipping a glass of California Merlot when Carroll and a gentleman in his early 40's were escorted to my table by Duke Junior. Carroll introduced me to his client, Robert Vieta, President of Crystal Trading Ventures of Falls Church, Virginia. He said that Robert and I had a lot in common, both having served as Marine Corps Officers.

After a rather extended period of telling Marine Corps war stories, we got down to some serious business discussions. Carroll shocked me by handing me an envelop containing pictures of me with Col. Qadhafi, taken during our trip to Libya. Carroll had previously refused to give me the pictures because he felt they might be used against him

315

in some future political campaign. It was all I could do to keep from laughing when I first looked at them. Carroll had carefully cut himself out of all the pictures. It was curious that he would still be concerned about exposing his picture with Qadhafi, since it was very clear that the OFAC knew about his trip and our meeting with the Libyan leader. I was also surprised that Carroll didn't mind Robert Vieta seeing the pictures and hearing our discussion about the trip.

Vieta said that he was a former Marine helicopter pilot and had served a tour of duty in Vietnam. He started Crystal Trading Company when he left the Corps. His company manufactured and marketed medical supplies throughout the United States. Now that his business was doing well, he was interested in expanding into the international marketplace. Carroll kindly commented that I was the best person in Washington to ask about getting a business going internationally.

Robert used the Libyan pictures to direct our conversation toward the sale of medical supplies to Libya. He asked if it were possible to sell such supplies to a sanctioned country. Could I use my Libyan contacts to help him work a deal? I explained that he really didn't need me or my contacts to sell his products to Libya. Medical supplies were exempt from the Libyan Sanctions Regulations. All he needed to do was to apply to the OFAC for a license. As I found out later, my response was a disappointment to both Vieta and Hubbard.

I quickly changed the course of our discussion to business opportunities available in Eastern Europe. It seemed to me that Vieta lost interest in our discussion when we left the subject of Libya. After dinner, we were joined by a friend of Vieta's and his girlfriend. Robert said he accidentally ran into them in the bar on his way to the restroom. I don't remember their names. To this day, I wonder what their real relationship was to Vieta.

The dinner concluded with a promise that Vieta and I would talk again about doing business internationally. It was a very strange evening, and I had the impression that Hubbard and Vieta had some hidden agenda. However, if they did, it never surfaced that night.

Feeling uncomfortable about the dinner meeting, I called Vieta's telephone number in Virginia the next morning to see if his business was real or a front of some kind. I reached a female secretary twice who promised to have Vieta return my call. He did return my call on one occasion. After some small talk, I determined that he really had no interest in doing international business with or without my help. He said he would get back to me if he decided to get involved in Eastern Europe.

I still felt that there was something wrong about my two dinner meetings, the first with Hubbard, and the second with Hubbard and this guy Robert Vieta. It was a real puzzlement. For some reason Vieta wasn't the kind of person I felt I could trust. I reviewed the circumstances of these meetings in my mind over the next few weeks, but just couldn't find answers to my questions. I put the entire episode in the back of my mind until I opened *The Washington Post* two months later, on December 11, 1993. There on the front page was Carroll Hubbard's picture.

The article under Hubbard's picture entitled, "Ex-Representative Reveals FBI Duty," said that Former Congressman, Carroll Hubbard had turned FBI informer because he feared prosecution in an investigation that started with the House Bank scandal. I could feel my heart start to pound as I read further. The paper said that Hubbard worked for six months in 1993 wearing a recorder on his body and taping conversations and phone calls about a dozen times. He allegedly did it to stave off prosecution in an FBI investigation.

The Post article stated:

> Carroll Hubbard, whose nine terms in Congress ended after his loss in a Democratic primary last year, said he was an informer from April to October. Justice Department spokesman Carl Stern confirmed that Hubbard had worked as an informer for the FBI this year but would not elaborate.

The details of Hubbard's unusual story, according to Hubbard, his former lawyer and Justice Department sources, involved a Congressman on the way out in 1992 looking forward to a new career as a lawyer and lobbyist, who instead found himself the target of a federal investigation into his misuse of campaign funds.

Hubbard felt his only way out of the predicament was to cooperate with the FBI. He admitted that he had been used to investigate Libyans and Libyan Lobbyists. My heart stopped beating as I read further that, "Hubbard said he recorded two conversations with a lobbyist for Libya." Dear Lord, that was me! It appeared that my "good friend" Carroll Hubbard was trying to save his own neck at the expense of his old friend, Bill Chasey.

The article continued that Hubbard had been provided with a beeper, fictitious stationery, business cards and the code name "Elmer Fudd." (How appropriate!) *The Post* article went on, "In September, Hubbard said he refused to sign a plea agreement, fearing he might eventually be asked to investigate his former colleagues on the Hill." In other words, he wouldn't investigate his Hill colleagues, but he had no problem trying to entrap his old buddy, Dr. Bill Chasey.

Since Hubbard rejected the plea offer, he risked prosecution on charges of theft, mail and wire fraud, obstruction of justice and federal election law violations. The article stated that Hubbard was being investigated for improperly using his congressional aides in his wife's unsuccessful race in another Kentucky congressional district. In addition, Hubbard's lack of documentation for some expense reimbursements from his campaign could be used as evidence for fraud and election law charges.

If Hubbard were indicted and convicted of all the charges that prosecutors were reviewing, he could face a sentence of more than seven years in federal prison. This was about twice the maximum sentence that he could have received under his plea offer.

"I've been absolutely destroyed by this," said Hubbard in the article. He denied that he tried to obstruct justice and stated, "And while there may be violations of federal elections laws, they were honest mistakes."

The following day, December 12, 1993, *The New York Times* carried a similar story entitled, "Ex-House Member Aided FBI Inquiry." Much of the information was taken from the *Washington Post* story of the previous day with a few exceptions.

Dennis L. Null, a former law partner of Hubbard's, who represented him in dealing with the government said, "The Congressman was attempting to cooperate with the Government to the fullest extent, even at the risk of his own life. He was willing to risk everything in helping the U.S. Government." He further stated that, "Mr. Hubbard traveled to Libya, and met with the Libyan leader, Col. Muammar al-Qadhafi, in the course of his work as an informer"

What a fabrication! To think that Carroll Hubbard was working for the FBI when I took him to Libya. How ridiculous! It was obvious that Null was trying to put a positive spin on Hubbard's trip to Tripoli and save his neck.

The New York Times concluded by stating, "The nature of Mr. Hubbard's work for the FBI is unclear. But it is common for the Bureau to use suspects as informers to help uncover crimes. In such cases, the Government typically promises that if a suspect is convicted, Federal prosecutors will recommend a reduced sentence in return for the suspect's cooperation with law-enforcement authorities."

The reason for my dinner meetings with Hubbard was very clear now. It was obvious that Hubbard was used by the FBI to set me up. Robert Vieta was an undercover FBI Agent. The whole Crystal Trading Venture was a front for an FBI sting directed at me.

The same questions kept coming to mind. Why would the FBI go to such great lengths to entrap me? Were they short of major criminal cases at the time, or were they really afraid of what I knew, or what they thought I knew about Pan Am 103? Could it be they didn't want me to spill the "beans" to my friends on Capitol Hill?

A couple of months later, my curiosity got the best of me. I put in a phone call to one Robert Vieta of Crystal Trading Ventures in Falls Church, Virginia. Vieta took my call. He was caught totally off guard when I directly asked him one question: "Are you an FBI agent, and did you and Hubbard try to pull a sting operation on me?" Vieta talked around my question, but never gave me a yes or no answer.

If the United States was involved in an international cover-up over Pan Am 103, it would be the biggest fraud ever perpetuated on the American people, and for that matter, the entire world. It was obvious now that The United States Government didn't need or want Bill Chasey snooping around Libya and telling what he knew to his friends in high places. How would they stop me? Why not try to discredit Chasey through a sting operation?

My response to the FBI sting revelation took many forms. It ranged from fear and apprehension, to outrage

320

and anger. How dare they do this to me? What happened to freedom in America? Who do these people think they are?

I was now more convinced than ever that there was more to the Lockerbie story than the United States wanted the world to know. The various attempts to discredit me gave me renewed resolve to get to the bottom of this case. If my suspicions were found to be true, I would do all in my power to let the world know. I was about to become a Lockerbie scholar.

Chapter Thirty-Three

Why Me?

Why me? Still I wondered.

The slate of indignities directed at me seemed to be increasing daily. I was astonished by this most recent FBI sting attempt. It was obvious, even to the most naive observer, that I was the focus of a carefully crafted conspiracy to keep me from telling what I knew about the Lockerbie cover-up. The roster of Federal Agencies hell bent on getting their pound of my flesh was swelling. I could never have anticipated the fallout over the past two years emanating from me being innocently introduced to a Dutchman named Gerrit P. Van de Bovenkamp by my friend, Senator Larry Pressler. Virginia and I sat down and recounted the government's actions against me:

• I was the recipient of a Cease and Desist order from the Office of Foreign Assets Control (OFAC). The order denied me my constitutional right to fulfill my contract with an American Company, ICM, at a financial loss of $120,000 in lobbying fees.

• The OFAC prohibited me from collecting an additional $200,000 in lobbying fees due me under a legal contract with ICM, a U.S. Corporation, and Mohammed Bukhres, a U.S. citizen.

• The OFAC rejected my application for a license to represent the U.S. Law Firm of Flynn and Riley. My signed contract for $1 million in lobbying fees was illegal according to the OFAC.

• My business bank account was frozen without notice by the OFAC, and remains frozen twenty-six months later.

• My life has been threatened.

• The CIA has followed me, and tapped my business and home telephones.

• I was the victim of an FBI undercover sting operation conducted by Former Congressman Carroll Hubbard and an undercover FBI Agent, Robert Vieta.

• And most recently, May 19, 1994, the OFAC served me with a Pre-penalty Notice, FAC No. L134165, indicating their intent to fine me $50,000. The notice charged me with five violations of the Libyan Sanctions Regulations, and stated their intent to fine me the maximum amount permitted by law, $10,000 for each violation.

It is important to be very clear just what the U.S. Government has done to me, the same U.S. Government I served for nine years as an infantry officer in the United States Marine Corps.

I was never afforded the benefit, or even the courtesy, of a meeting, an interview, a hearing, trial or any similar form of due process guaranteed by the United States Constitution. Other than my written response to their inquires, I wasn't provided a mode of defending myself against the Government's charges and/or fines. I have been left to the mercy of a small, faceless band of Washington bureaucrats (the unelected second-tier), whom I have never met, to decide my fate. They sat in judgment, found me guilty, and fined me for the following opprobrious violations:

Violation #1. On October 8, 1992, Chasey entered into a written contract with ICM to lobby members of Congress to assist in the development of normalized relations between the United States Government and the Government of Libya, in return for remuneration of $120,000. Fine: $10,000.

Comment: I would be fined $10,000 for simply signing a business contract with a U.S. Corporation? It wasn't important to the OFAC if I performed on the contract, only that I had signed it. I couldn't believe it. And what did I do after I signed the contract? I immediately filed my Foreign Agent Registration papers, along with a copy of my contract, with the Criminal Division of the United States Department of Justice in Washington, D.C. The Justice Department accepted my registration without comment and assigned me Foreign Agent Registration 4221 on behalf of ICM and its client the Government of Libya. I didn't receive a penny of the $120,000.

Violation #2. On or about October 29, 1992, Chasey entered into a contract as memorialized by a written confirmation dated October 29, 1992, with Gerrit P. Van de Bovenkamp, a principal of ICM, and Mohammed Bukhres, to arrange for a U.S. Senator to meet with the Government of Libya officials Youssef El-Debri, Head of Government of Libya (GOL) National Security, and Omar Muntassir, GOL Secretary of Planning and Economics, to discuss the normalization of relations between the United States Government and the GOL, in return for remuneration of $150,000, and to procure medical export licenses, in return for remuneration of $50,000.

Comment: I was being fined for entering into a contract. The contract, which I never signed, was between me and a United States Corporation, ICM, and with a United States citizen, Mr. Mohammed Bukhres.

There is no law that prohibits me from doing business with U.S. companies and/or citizens. I was operating as a registered foreign agent, and the meetings that I arranged were outlined in my registration papers filed with the United States Department of Justice. The only payment I received,

$50,000, was frozen in my corporate bank account by the OFAC over two years ago, and the account remains frozen today.

Securing export licenses is a common practice in Washington, and many companies do as Mohammed did, hire a consultant to assist in the process. The sale of medical supplies does not constitute a violation of the Libyan sanctions regulations. These items fall under the category of humanitarian assistance, but do require an export license.

Violation #3. On or about October 30, 1991, Chasey received $50,000 from Gerrit P. Van de Bovenkamp as payment under the Agreements.

Comment: The $50,000 in question was wired to me by my client, Mr. Bovenkamp, on behalf of ICM. I was paid in U.S. dollars by a U.S. Corporation for services I performed as a Registered Foreign Agent with the Criminal Division of the United States Department of Justice. There was never any evidence presented by the OFAC that the money I received was anything but clean U.S. money. There was no evidence that I was paid from either frozen or unfrozen, blocked or unblocked Libyan accounts. In any event the OFAC froze my account containing the money.

Violation #4. Between November 8-9, 1992, Chasey traveled to Tripoli with (now former) Representative and Mrs. Carroll Hubbard, Jr. and Mr. Bovenkamp in performance of the Agreements.

Comment: The U.S. Justice Department was fully aware of my activities related to my representation of ICM. They never registered an objection concerning any of my actions. Further, I didn't enter Libya by using my U.S. Passport, nor was there a restriction against travel to Libya listed in my Passport. There was a travel restriction listed only for Cuba.

Violation # 5.   On November 27, 1992, Chasey entered into a written contract with Flynn to provide assistance and direction in the preparation of extra-judicial effort directed toward lobbying the U.S. Senate and House of Representatives in connection with international efforts related to the indictment of Lamen Fhimah and Abdel Basset al-Megrahi, Libyans charged in the bombing of Pan Am Flight # 103.

Comment: This one really took the cake. Once again I was to be fined for entering into a written contract. The only way the OFAC knew that I had signed a contract with Flynn, was because I told them in my application for a License to represent Flynn and Riley. I never performed a single function, nor was I remunerated in any way under this contract. I couldn't believe what I was reading. They had the audacity to fine me for requesting a license from their office! I had been advised by three lawyers that I didn't need to apply for a license. I did so to be sure that I wouldn't run afoul of the OFAC. This is how they rewarded my candor? They fined me $10,000.

Even the most unsophisticated student of law could see from the above violations that the OFAC had no case against me. There wasn't a single violation that would stand up in a court of law. OFAC Director, Newcomb, had to know the violations were contrived. What he and his cast of henchmen really wanted to do was to silence me about what I knew about the Lockerbie cover-up. They were afraid of what I knew. The last thing they needed was to have me share my revelations with my Congressional friends. It was their plan to neuter me by fear and intimidation which they hoped would destroy my creditability and effectiveness on Capitol Hill.

The attacks of the U.S. Government against me were aimed at keeping me out of Libya and away from Libyan officials. They couldn't let me represent the lawyers for the two indicted Libyans. They tried to strap me financially with frozen bank accounts and fines. And finally their strategy was to entrap me into an illegal business deal which would put me behind bars and out of their hair forever.

I knew that there had to be a plethora of former and present government officials from three administrations very nervous about what I might say to Congress. My disclosures could very well lead to a full Congressional investigation of a Lockerbie cover-up that would make Watergate pale by comparison.

Why were they so afraid of Congress? Because our system of checks and balances provides for the Congress to have both oversight and investigative powers over the Executive Branch. This system has proven effective in indicting the likes of John Dean, Oliver North, John Poindexter and a growing slate of Presidential advisors with each new administration. Our forefathers were perceptive in predicting the corrupting effect that power would have on mere men in positions of authority. Such power, more and more frequently, creates renegade governmental officials who, if left unchecked, could put our system of democracy in serious jeopardy.

As I reviewed the facts as I knew them, Libya was the perfect "fall guy" for the United States and Great Britain. These two superpowers could cause the indictments to be issued against the two Libyans, intimidate the United Nations into bringing sanctions against Libya, and then hope that interest in the Lockerbie case would fizzle out over a period of time. If the plan worked, there would never be a trial, and the embarrassment of a cover-up would never surface.

Why not blame this tiny pariah state, with a madman for a leader? Who cares about Libya anyway? It could never become a part of the world order as long as Qadhafi was alive. It was a perfect solution that has worked for almost five years. What better way to keep the world from knowing the real role the U.S. and Britain played in the 1988 Lockerbie bombing? Why else would the U.S. and Britain be so adamant in denying Qadhafi's attempts at solving the stand off?

Qadhafi has offered to have the two Libyans tried in a variety of international courts. Qadhafi's latest offer, supported by the Arab League, was to allow the two Libyans to be tried for the Lockerbie plane crash by Scottish judges at the International Court of Justice in the Hague. It was reported by the Reuters News Service on January 7, 1995, that Esmat Abdel-Meguid, Arab League Secretary-General and a former Egyptian foreign minister who studied international law, said the Libyan offer was "legally correct because it agrees with the principles of international law."

The next part of Abdel-Meguid's statement must have sent chills up the Justice Department's back, and explains why the U.S and Britain rejected Qadhafi's offer. Abdel-Meguid said, "That Scottish law had an 'advantage' over British law because it grants defendants the option of 'insufficient evidence' in addition to verdicts of guilty or not guilty."

It is important to note that Great Britain and Libya are signatories to the Montreal Convention for the suppression of unlawful acts against the safety of civil aviation. Article 7 of the Convention states that unless there is an extradition treaty in force, Libya "is entitled, indeed obliged, to try the offenders under her own domestic law." Since there is no extradition treaty between Britain and Libya, Article 7 of the Montreal Convention applies. Great

329

Britain has no right to demand that the two Libyans be tried in its country, and violates the Convention by doing so.

Libya, by contrast, has acted in accordance with its own domestic law and with international law by appointing a High Court Judge who is carrying out an investigation into the charges levelled against the two Libyan citizens. Although invited to do so, Great Britain has refused to permit their police officials to work with the Libyans in their investigation, as international law both permits and demands that they do. This is most important since Libyan law prohibits the handing over of the men without proper evidence. Ironically, this criminal procedure was set up for the Libyans by the British in 1973. The standoff continues.

No doubt, I was onto a major governmental cover-up, and I desperately wanted to tell my story. Unfortunately, there were two missing pieces to the Pan Am 103 puzzle:

First, the target of the Lockerbie investigation had always been Syria and Iran, until November, 1991, when a tiny piece of circuit board led to the indictment of two Libyans. If Libya was the only one with this circuit board, as claimed by investigators, I had an uphill climb.

Second, the brown Samsonite suitcase carrying the bomb was traced back to an Air Malta Flight leaving Malta's Luqa airport. The two Libyans were accused of stealing Air Malta baggage tags, and placing the bomb on the first leg of its journey which eventually ended up on Pan Am 103.

How could this be refuted? Until I had answers to these questions, I couldn't shift the blame for what the Brits call the Lockerbie "insult" or "outrage" from Libya back to Syria and Iran.

Chapter Thirty-four

The United States' Cover-up Unravels

While most people in America have accepted the official U.S. and British view that Libya was solely responsible for the destruction of Pan Am 103, investigators in Scotland and the media in England haven't been so sure. Some six years after the disaster, Lockerbie remains an open case in these countries. The British Broadcasting Corporation (BBC) and *The Sunday Times* of London have been the most diligent in their pursuit of the truth. I have devoted most of my research to finding answers in this part of the world.

A major breakthrough in my personal investigation came on Monday, December 20, 1993, just one day before the fifth anniversary of the Pan Am 103 bombing. A BBC investigation suggested that Britain and the United States may have fingered Libya in the bombing of Pan Am 103 to divert suspicion from the other possible culprits—Syria and Iran.

In the radio broadcast, called *Silence Over Lockerbie*, marking the fifth anniversary of the Lockerbie crash, the head of a Swiss electronics firm, which made the circuit board used as the bomb's timer, said he had wrongly told investigators the devices were supplied only to Libya. This was exactly what Qadhafi had told me over a year earlier. My suspicions of a cover-up were now founded on hard evidence and this new revelation refuted the key piece of evidence against Megrahi and Fhimah.

As pointed out in this book and in numerous legal and political sources over the years, the entire case against

Libya was based on the fact that the timer was manufactured for, and delivered to, only Libya. Now for the first time, there was factual information that some of the timers were sold to the East Germans, and that the United States, Britain and Switzerland had known about it for the past five years. This was just what I needed!

According to the report in *Silence Over Lockerbie*, the Swiss businessman who gave Scottish police the vital evidence they needed to blame Colonel Qadhafi had changed his story.

Originally it was reported that Edwin Bollier, Managing Director of MEBO, recognized the charred remains of one of his "Zero Series" timers from a picture produced by detectives. He was never able to see the original because it was being kept as evidence. At that time he said he was certain that it was one of only seven or eight prototype timers made in 1985 and sold to Libya.

For the first time Bollier recounted that he was initially visited by the CIA just seven days after the bombing. He was asked by the CIA to sign a statement declaring that he had sold the timers only to Libya, which he did.

It was Bollier's positive identification of the MST-13, Zero Series, timer an d his signed statement that these timers had only been sold to Libya that shifted the investigation to Libya and away from Syria and Iran leading to indictments against Fhimah and Megrahi.

As Buck Revell, Director of the FBI investigation into Lockerbie stated in the *Silence Over Lockerbie* program, "It was this forensic evidence that led us to focus on the Libyan Intelligence service, and then to be able to identify two specific individuals." Revell was asked during the program how firmly did the electronic fragment and the forensic evidence he got from it point towards Libya? He responded, "I can't discuss the evidence, but suffice it to say it was sufficient for an indictment to be returned in both the United States and in Scotland, so that obviously means we felt very confident that we had identified the right people that have now been indicted."

Now, in the November, 1993, recording of *Silence Over Lockerbie*, Bollier shocked the reporter. Bollier said for the first time in public that, in October, 1993, he had changed his story and told investigators that, while five of the prototype timers did go to Libya in 1985, two timers were delivered to the East German Government at about the same time. "I remembered that two such prototypes were delivered to the East German Army. I took them myself to East Berlin in 1985 to a representative of the purchasing department for the army and police. I know the name of this gentleman."

When asked if he would disclose the name of the purchasing agent, Bollier responded, "No. No." When pressed further by the program's commentator, Bollier said, he couldn't tell who, "Because the investigation is still in progress and I wouldn't like to prejudice the inquiries."

Mr. Bollier said that he was reminded of the delivery to East Germany by one of his staff, Ulrich Lumpert. Lumpert, an engineer, said that he remembered having to come in to work on a Saturday to get the prototype timers ready for delivery. He was quoted as stating, "The first two prototypes had to be produced quickly, and I had to get them finished quickly so Mr. Bollier could take them to East Germany. It was 1985."

Mr. Lumpert's and Bollier's recollections present reasonable doubt of the Libyan connection to the Lockerbie bombing. But more important still, is that Lumpert said that he told the investigators about the East German link when he was first questioned in late 1990, a full year before the indictment of the two Libyans. He said there were British, American and Swiss detectives present when he was interviewed. He told the interviewer, "I told the police that I remembered that the first two had gone to East Berlin."

To Vincent Cannistraro, leader of the CIA investigation into Lockerbie, this new evidence that East Germany had timers like the one that set off the Lockerbie bomb, is of "exceptional importance." Because of the well documented links in 1988 between the East German secret police, the Stasi, and the West German cell of Ahmed Jibril's PFLP-GC, Cannistraro stated, "We know that there was a very symbiotic relationship between the PFLP-GC and the Stasi. We also knew at the time, that much of the infrastructure to Ahmed Jibril's operational cells was contained in East Germany, and supported by the Stasi. There was a very clear link between the PFLP-GC and the Stasi."

When Cannistraro was asked what it would mean if MEBO had supplied these prototypes not exclusively to the Libyan army but also some to the Stasi, He answered, "That would mean that the PFLP-GC and Jibril would have had another source of supply for detonators."

When the link was first made to the Swiss firm and through them to Libya in 1990, the press was briefed by investigators that this new forensic evidence did nothing to put Iran and Syria in the clear. The piece of circuit board only identified the source of the timer, the bomb itself still pointed to Ahmed Jibril's group.

At the same time, the governments of the United States and Great Britain began to act as if Syria and Iran had been cleared of suspicion. As cited earlier in this book, President Bush broke a thirteen year embargo with Syria by holding a meeting with the Syrian President. And Douglas Hurd announced that after a four year break, Britain was resuming diplomatic links with Syria.

There was an outcry from those closest to the investigation when the pressure was taken off Syria and Iran. Some U.S. and British relatives of the victims of Pan Am 103 accused their governments of diplomatic amnesia over Lockerbie. They believed that it was easy to pin all the blame on Libya, and play down evidence suggesting the government of Iran ordered the bombing, and a Syrian terrorist group planned it. One unnamed parent was quoted on *Silence Over Lockerbie* as saying, "I think justice demands that the people who planned and perpetrated the crime need to be brought to trial. Justice becomes a joke if the truth is traded off against international political expediency."

Some of the relatives of the dead of Lockerbie, like the Reverend John Mosey, felt that they could smell a rat. Being interviewed on *Silence Over Lockerbie* he said, "It does seem strange to us that while all of the evidence was pointing towards the Syrian based terrorist group, financed from Iran, all of a sudden it was all worth nothing, and there was a switch. That has disturbed us a great deal. I think needing the help of Syria and Iran in the Middle East, and the war that was coming against Saddam Hussein, it could well be that attention was switched. We needed those people, but who needed Qadhafi?"

Reports in the press in 1990, reflected an important change in the direction of the Lockerbie investigation. Libya was not only involved in the bombing, but now was behind it. This new tone paid quick dividends for the United States. Shortly thereafter, President George Bush met Hafez al-Assad, the Syrian leader to discuss joint participation in the multinational task force confronting Saddam Hussein in the Gulf. At the beginning of 1991, Syria became a part of the military alliance that defeated Iraq, while Iran stayed neutral.

Two months later a Western diplomat was quoted as saying, "We now have adequate satisfaction that Syria has disjoined itself from terrorism. Then in mid 1991, unnamed officials were quoted as saying, "The evidence against Libya has effectively absolved Syria over Lockerbie."

When the formal indictments on Pan Am 103 were announced in mid-November, 1991, the U.S. Attorney General, William Barr, had only two names, both Libyan.

He stated, "Our job was to determine whether we could indict anybody for the bombing of Pan Am 103, and the evidence we have supports the indictment of the Libyans."

American relatives of the Lockerbie dead were briefed by the Bush Administration on the indictments. They were told by the U.S. Justice Department that it was mainly coincidental that shortly before Lockerbie, both Ahmed Jibril's agents and the Libyans were building Semtex bombs into Toshiba radios to attack American aircraft.

Dr. Jim Swire, spokesman for the British relatives of Pan Am 103, had always suspected a political cover-up. He told the *Sunday Times* on December 19, 1993 that, "The whole Lockerbie scenario is a hypocrisy created for international political convenience. It's a deliberate way of preventing the relatives from getting the truth. The only way to resolve this now is to have a full international investigation."

The relatives couldn't believe this coincidence, nor could the recently retired CIA Investigator, Vincent Cannistraro. He told the listeners of *Silence Over Lockerbie* that, "The Libyans had been a supporter of the PFLP-GC. They provided quarterly subsidies to the PFLP-GC. The PFLP-GC was represented in Tripoli. So then to turn around and indicate that by the way, the PFLP-GC were planning to destroy an American airliner, and Libyan intelligence was planning on destroying an American airliner. This was done completely independent and without coordination, I think is a rather large leap of faith."

Hidden in the small print of the U.S. State Department briefing paper on the indictments was a statement that said that it couldn't be ruled out that there was a broader conspiracy of other governments and terrorist organizations involved. But that was just what the State Department had ruled out. The Department's position was, as widely reported in the press conference, "this was a Libyan operation from start to finish."

Chapter Thirty-Five

A Closer Look at the Evidence

As noted earlier, President Bush captured the media headlines by proclaiming that, "The Syrians took a bum rap over Lockerbie." When Vincent Cannistraro, the former CIA Agent in charge of the Lockerbie investigation, read the President's "bum rap" remark about the Syrians, he was astonished. He told *Silence Over Lockerbie* listeners, "Oh, I was outraged because I didn't think that there was anything in the nature of the indictment itself that excluded a Syrian role in the operation. And it seemed to me a rush to judgment to exculpate the Syrians and let them off a possible hook."

Both George Bush and James Baker refused to be interviewed for the BBC radio program. But one of Bush's senior colleagues, former Director of both the CIA and the FBI at the time of Lockerbie, Judge William Webster, was more forthcoming. He told the BBC interviewer that President Bush was quite conscious of Syria's importance in the Gulf War, and the Middle East peace talks. He stated, "Certainly if we had to pick our demons, we would rather have Qadhafi than someone who might play a peace making role in the future." In other words, it was much more politically expedient to sacrifice a Qadhafi than an Assad.

There was no use for Qadhafi in the Gulf War or in the peace talks, but neither event could be successful without President Assad and Syria. Webster continued, "I think the two (war and peace talks) have allowed others to conclude that Syria was behind all of this. It would have been taken as a great affront. If the President had not said something, that he wasn't one of those who believed that." When asked who would have taken it as an affront, Webster answered, "Well, Assad for one." Asked further what that would have meant to the United States, Webster said, "I hope that neither of us is making too much of this, but it would have poisoned the well in an emerging but still fragile cooperative relationship with respect to peace in the Middle East."

Jerry Bremer, the U.S. Ambassador for counter-terrorism at the time of the Lockerbie bombing, was not in a government position when the State Department and President Bush directed all the blame to Libya. He told the BBC radio audience, "I am uncomfortable with that, because I find that certain of the things that happened, like the kind of bomb that was used, suggested some kind of a contact with the Jibril organization. The fact that Libya is guilty, does not prove Syria's innocence."

David Leppard, in his 1991 book *On the Trail of Terror*, said that the CIA had knowledge of Iranian complicity and that, "Libya is being used as a sole whipping boy when there was an alliance of elements from Iran, Syria and Libya."

Bremer was asked what he thought Bush meant when he said Syria took a bum rap. "You would have to ask President Bush. I mean we are not children here. We understand that there are other aspects of foreign policy than just the fight against terrorism. There cannot be a peace in the Middle east without Syria. And so I think, Secretaries of State and Presidents wisely have always had to weigh the question, how hard do you push Syria on their involvement in terrorism versus the desire to have them engaged in some way or at least not hostile to a peace process."

There were other immediate benefits to the West just three days after the State Department and British Foreign Office exonerated Syria and Iran. After 1,763 days in chains, two hostages, Terry Waite and the American, Tom Southerland were suddenly released by their pro-Iranian captors at the headquarters of Syrian Intelligence.

And then, within three weeks, all of the remaining hostages were set free. Press reports at the time made the link to Lockerbie. *The Daily Telegraph,* in November 1991, for example, told of the recent vindication of Syria and Iran, and said that without it, "Mr. Waite would still be languishing in a Beirut cellar." On November 24, 1991, *The Sunday Times* said that:

> Our joy at their freedom should be tempered by the shame of the cost: the relatives of the victims of the Lockerbie bomb must now come to terms with the fact that most of those behind the murder of their loved ones are going to get away with it. The cause of justice is being sacrificed on the altar of diplomatic convenience. We will live to regret it.

The UN correspondent, Ian Williams of the *Tribune,* on January 17, 1992, mentions speculation in the UN that "John Major and George Bush are looking to fight their 1992 election campaigns on the back of military action against Libya."

Both Washington and London were adamant that it was just a coincidence that just three days after they had made statements exonerating Syria and Iran, two of the most important hostages were released.

The head of the Iranian mission in London also felt that it was a coincidence that the hostages were released so soon after Syria and Iran were put in the clear. He was questioned on the radio program *Silence Over Lockerbie*: "So these hostages had been held in some cases for five or more years, statements that are taken to exonerate Syria and Iran are made, and within three weeks all remaining hostages are released. And that's just a coincidence?"

His response was, "Yah, of course, Maybe. You know we have done our best during these five years to release the hostages, and someday that happened. So there is no link."

339

Relatives of the Pan Am 103 victims on both sides of the Atlantic are convinced that their governments made a calculation of the greatest good for the greatest number. Nothing could be done to bring back the dead of Lockerbie. If a political spin of the investigation of their murders could produce tangible gains for the living, might that not be a price worth paying? A balance lay between freeing the hostages, the potential for peace in the Middle East, and 270 casualties.

One of the more active parents of the Lockerbie dead, Daniel Cohen, father of Theodora, summed it up like this: "We've heard them all. We can't do anything now because of the hostage crisis. We can't do anything now because of Desert Storm. There are always bigger fish to fry. It's amazing how many people have told me, well why are you doing this? You can't bring her back to life. All right, what does the word justice mean? All you have to do is commit a murder. Well they're dead. You can't bring them back, so let's not bother with this. The murderers are too powerful; the murderers are too useful."

When Bill Clinton became President of the United States there was a new carrot handed to the Lockerbie families. At the request of Dr. Robert Kupperman, of Georgetown University, Clinton sent a letter to Daniel and Susan Cohen. In the letter, the new President said, "I will assure that all questions regarding Syrian and Iranian involvement in the Pan Am 103 tragedy are addressed and fully answered. The U.S. owes it to the victims' families to see that these charges are thoroughly investigated."

Nothing has happened since, and the Cohens and the other Lockerbie relatives feel they've been let down.

Clinton's letter was seen as just another campaign promise. Daniel Cohen said in an interview for *Silence over Lockerbie* that, "Whatever Pan Am 103 may be to us, it is a very low priority to this administration. You know, we will pursue the lines of investigation that lead to Libya. We won't push too hard on the other people because Libya is easy to push. Iran is bigger and Syria is bigger. If you push them you got bigger problems, so just sort of let it go you know, maybe eventually it will all go away. It's not just an issue with them. It's an issue with them only when it embarrasses them, only when it comes up and bites them. Then they begin scurrying around a little bit, but other than that, let sleeping dogs lie."

Reluctantly, Dr. Kupperman, an expert on terrorism and advisor to the Clinton campaign, has reached the same conclusion. He's watched first the Bush Administration, and now the Clinton Administration juggling the interests of justice and pragmatism over Lockerbie. Faced now with one solid foreign policy success in the Middle East and Clinton's coziness with President Assad of Syria, he doesn't expect the new President to put his foreign policy in jeopardy with excessive zeal in the Lockerbie investigation.

Dr. Kupperman agrees with Mr. and Mrs. Cohen's charge that the campaign promise he engineered with Clinton, was worthless. He told *Silence Over Lockerbie*, "My guess is that they are right. You know were I President, a job in which I am thoroughly unqualified, I don't know that I could do better. Yet I am terribly angry over the matter. It all becomes futile. I wonder whether I am as much at fault as those in the senior most positions of government trying to avoid facing the Syrians and others, when it's not clear that Libya was acting alone."

Chapter Thirty-Six

Solving the Lockerbie Puzzle

The first missing piece of the Lockerbie puzzle had finally fallen into place thanks to Mr. Bollier's new recollections. Now for the first time there was factual information that some of the timers were sold to the East Germans and that the United States, Britain and Switzerland had known about it for the past five years. This new evidence in itself is enough to acquit the two Libyans. At the very least, it presents a solid question of reasonable doubt. But would they be acquitted by their accusers?

With the situation of the timer behind me, I needed to get to the bottom of the Maltese connection.

The accepted theory is that the bomb had been loaded into a brown Samsonite suitcase. Baggage loading lists supposedly showed that the suitcase had been shipped aboard a flight leaving Malta's Luqa International Airport. On arrival in Frankfurt the bag had been transferred on to the first leg of Pan Am Flight 103 to London, destined for New York.

By coincidence, I recently picked up a copy of the November 13, 1994 London *Sunday Telegraph* while on a layover at London's Heathrow Airport. I was heading home from Warsaw, Poland, and had two hours to kill at the American Airlines Admirals Club, when I happened to read the Sunday paper. Page four of the *Telegraph* carried an article that quickly caught my attention, "Fresh Clues Point to Lockerbie Cover-Up." Dennis Phipps, a leading aviation security expert had raised doubts about the case against the two Libyans, Megrahi and Fhimah.

Phipps, former head of security at British Airways and a former colonel in the Military Police, had conducted an

343

extensive investigation as an expert witness for Air Malta in a libel case settled in November of 1993. His investigation suggested that there was no evidence to show that an unaccompanied suitcase, containing the bomb that blew up Pan Am 103, was planted on an aircraft that left Malta on the day of the attack. Until he retired from British Airways, Phipps served on the government's National Aviation Security Committee. He examined the baggage-handling records at Malta airport for the day of the bombing and had interviewed baggage handlers on duty at Malta's Luqa airport.

The indictments issued jointly by the Scottish and American courts in 1991 accused the two Libyans of planting a suitcase with a bomb on Air Malta Flight KT180 from Luqa to Frankfurt. The two are alleged to have placed a stolen baggage tag on the suitcase and slipped it into the sorting system at Malta. Phipps was interviewed in a new television documentary on the Lockerbie bombing, *The Maltese Double Cross*, which was played before the British House of Commons on November 16, 1994.

The film claims that Hizbollah, the Lebanon-based Islamic fundamentalist group, organized the attack, and not the Libyans. It says the bombing was carried out on behalf of Iran in revenge for the shooting-down of an Iranian Airbus by the Americans in the Persian Gulf. The documentary claims that Hizbollah, working with the terrorist group PFLP-GC in Germany, duped a drug courier into carrying the suitcase bomb on to Pan Am 103 at Frankfurt. The bomb was hidden inside a Toshiba radio cassette recorder which the courier thought contained drugs.

The documentary states that, "The courier, Khaled Jafaar, was an agent working for the U.S. Drug Enforcement Agency (DEA) which was monitoring regular "controlled deliveries" of narcotics from Lebanon to the U.S. via Frankfurt. As such, he was able to pass unhindered through security controls. A double agent working for both

Hizbollah and the CIA bought Jafaar's air ticket to New York on the day of the bombing."

Drugs had been rumored to be a factor in the Pan Am 103 disaster from the very beginning. Many of the rumors stemmed from an accounting told by a Lockerbie farmer by the name of Jimmie Wilson.

On Christmas Eve day, 1988, while Wilson was inspecting his flock of sheep, which had been scattered by the falling debris of *The Maid of the Sea* some three days before, he found a burst-opened leather suitcase in his field. The bag had a red-and-white ribbon on it, indicating a searcher had already found it and marked it for collection, but it had not been picked up. Wilson summoned the police.

Wilson and an unnamed police officer, emptied the contents of the suitcase into a plastic bag. Wilson remembered all the brightly colored clothes in the bag. A label on the suitcase identified the bag as belonging to a "Robbi," but the name couldn't be matched to the passenger manifest.

Emmerson and Duffy describe the incident in their book, *The Fall of Pan Am 103* this way:

> "The most interesting thing in it," Wilson said, "was buried deep among the clothes. It was a Khaki-colored webbing belt, (money belt), about nine inches wide."
>
> "Uh oh," Wilson remembered the officer saying. "I know what we got here."
>
> "What have we got here?" Wilson asked.
>
> Wilson never got a good look at what was in the belt, but he did catch a glimpse of what looked like white powder in plastic bags in the belts top pockets. He remembered that there was also a shorthand notebook in the bag, its pages

345

smudged by rainwater. The officer never used the word "drugs" but said only that the stuff in the belt, whatever it was, was "of substantial value." Wilson tried to press for information, but the police officer refused to have it drawn out. "We know about this one," Wilson recalled him saying. But the policeman would say no more. What else could it be but drugs? Wilson wondered.

Scottish and U.S. authorities would say afterward that no drugs were found in the wreckage of Flight 103.

This statement doesn't gel with an early report prepared in September, 1989 by the security firm, Interfor Inc. The company was working for Windels, Marx, Davies & Ives, the law firm that had been hired by Pan Am's insurer, U.S. Aviation Underwriters. The twenty-seven-page report revealed a "complex and murky background to the disaster." It recounted a colorful tale of drug runners, spies, and a renegade CIA team—all woven into the fabric of the Flight 103 bombing.

According to the report, in 1987 three terrorist organizations (Interterror Group) began raising money and seeking out secure routes for smuggling weapons and drugs. The purpose was to develop ways of striking at U.S. targets in a way that would keep the attacks from being traced back to them. Eventually, the three terrorist groups: PFLP, PFLP-GC, and the Abu Nidal Organization, set up a web of drug and arms smuggling operations throughout Europe.

As part of the smuggling network, the terrorists had established a route through Frankfurt that relied upon the cooperation of at least one passenger and one baggage handler. According to the report, a frequently used drug "mule" was a young man from Detroit named Khaled Jaafar. Jaafar was known to frequently visit relatives in Beirut. This is the same Jaafar described in the new television documentary, *The Maltese Double Cross*.

The Turkish baggage handler was a seven year veteran of the job by the name of Kilins Aslan Tuzcu. Tuzcu, relying on his memory, reported that on the day of the bombing he had sent twelve interline bags through the X-ray screening before he placed them on Pan Am 103. X-ray operator Kurt Maier, who kept meticulous records, contradicted Tuzcu. Maier stated that he had screened ten suitcases, two garment bags and a cardboard carton for a total of thirteen items. Months later it would appear that this thirteenth bag was the bronze Samsonite that contained the bomb.

Pan Am gave polygraph examinations to three Frankfurt baggage handlers who worked on Flight 103. Each of the three was asked if any suitcases that hadn't belonged on the flight had been switched with one that did. The results of the polygraph test showed that two of the handlers had lied. One was Roland O'Neil and the other was our old Turkish friend, Kilins Aslan Tuzcu.

Actually the baggage handling scheme worked like this. When a terrorist wanted to make a drug run, the Turkish baggage handler would remove a suitcase checked in by the accomplice passenger, and replace it with an identical case containing the contraband. The passenger then claimed the bag at the end of the trip.

The report stated that the CIA, and the U.S. Drug Enforcement Administration knew about the drug route and kept it under surveillance. These agencies planned to increase police visibility at other smuggling points in West Germany, hoping to channel the illicit activity toward the Frankfurt airport.

The Interfor report suggested that the Frankfurt CIA team, referred to in the report as CIA-1, was a renegade unit that failed to communicate some of its activities to CIA headquarters. The Interfor report states that, "It appears that it eventually operated to some or a large extent as an internal covert operation without consistent oversight, a la Oliver North." In March 1988, CIA-1 received reports through the German secret service (BND) about meetings in Vienna between French and Iranian delegations. After the covert session, Iran received a shipment of weapons, and French hostages held in Lebanon were released.

Despite the revelations of the Iran-contra arms for hostages scandal in the United States, CIA-1 decided to strike a similar deal to free U.S. hostages, the report said. The renegade CIA team had identified Monzer al-Kassar, a Syrian whose brother-in-law was the head of Syrian Intelligence, as an intermediary in protecting the drug routes under surveillance. Now the CIA offered to protect Monzer's drug smuggling operation in return for his cooperation. According to the report, al-Kassar helped send weapons to Iran to further the release of U.S. hostages. In return CIA-1 gave him a free hand with his drug operations. "It is believed that U.S. Customs at JFK were ordered by CIA to allow certain baggage to pass un-inspected due to national security interests," Interfor stated.

By the fall of 1988, the terrorist leaders were under pressure to attack an American target largely because Iran wanted revenge for the downing of Iran Flight 655 by the USS Vincennes, the report found. It also noted that Ahmed Jibril of the PFLP-GC, aware of the success of the drug route operated by al-Kassar but unaware that it had CIA protection, met twice with al-Kassar. One meeting, in the presence of Abu Nidal, was held at a hotel in Warsaw and one meeting was held at a restaurant in Paris.

Jibril's goal was to use al-Kassar's smuggling route to plant a bomb on a commercial airliner. The PFLP-GC leader recognized the Frankfurt smuggling route as a perfect channel, especially because drug mules had not been previously associated with terrorism. Al-Kassar and Abu Nidal knew the outline of Jibril's plan, but neither was given the specific details. They suspected he would attack a plane flying out of Madrid or London.

According to the Interfor report, al-Kassar brought the bomb into Germany in a car he rented in Paris. He had picked up the explosives in France from his sister-in-law, who in turn had received them from a Syrian living in Bulgaria. The report named all the alleged bomb couriers, even listing a telephone number for the Syrian contact in Sofia, Bulgaria. Jibril initially targeted American Airlines, but a fast-paced series of events beginning in early December changed the plan and resulted in the bomb being placed on Pan Am Flight 103.

First, an agent for the Israeli Mossad tipped off his superiors that a major attack was being planned at Frankfurt against a U.S. carrier. Then Mossad warned the CIA and BKA. The CIA team in Frankfurt wanted to steer the threat to where it could be best observed, so the presence of police and security officers was visibly increased around all U.S. carriers except Pan Am, the report said.

Al-Kassar and Nidal realized that Jibril was going to use the Frankfurt airport to carry out his attack. They figured that the target might be Lufthansa, American Airlines, or Pan Am. They were anxious to protect their drug route, so on December 18th, al-Kassar and Nidal informed the BKA that a bomb would be placed on one of Pan Am's regular Frankfurt to London to New York flights. "Unwittingly, these terrorists tipped off the authorities to what proved to be the very act," said the report. The BKA informed CIA-1, and the threat was relayed to CIA headquarters in the United States. At about the same time a BKA undercover agent made a separate report to his superiors outlining the plan to bomb a Pan Am jet. Warnings were sent to various embassies, but no warning was sent to Pan Am.

The Interfor report continues that one or two days before the bombing, al-Kassar's Turkish baggage handler in Frankfurt went to the airport parking lot and picked up a suitcase that had been left inside a black Mercedes. The baggage handler carried the bag inside the airport and placed it in an employee locker area. "This was his usual practice with drugs," the report said.

The day of the bombing a BKA agent on surveillance duty noticed that the drug courier's suitcase, a brown Samsonite, was different from luggage used in past runs. The report stated: "He, like the other BKA agents on the scene, had been on extra alert due to all the bomb tips. Within an hour or so before takeoff he phoned in a report as to what he had seen, saying something was very wrong." The BKA alerted the CIA-1 team but was told to let the suitcase pass through.

The Interfor report went on to say that in Lebanon a separate CIA team led by Army Major Charles McKee was gathering information on the location of Western hostages. In the course of its investigation, the team uncovered the work of the CIA-1 team in West Germany. They believed that the team's work would jeopardize both their missions and their lives. As a result, the members of the unit in Lebanon broke off their work until they could personally report their concerns to CIA headquarters. The eight-person team decided to return home and, unsuspecting, purchased tickets for Pan Am Flight 103. Interfor identified five of the intelligence officers on board Flight 103 as Beirut CIA deputy station chief Matthew Gannon, agents Ronald Lariviere, Daniel O'Connor, William Leyrer, and McKee. The other three agents were unnamed.

The basic premise of the Interfor report was that the U.S. government had not only failed to stop the bombing, but had actively, if unwittingly, participated in it by protecting the drug courier who slipped the bomb on board. Pan Am was just an innocent bystander. To disprove the allegations, U.S. intelligence services might have had to reveal specific details of their sensitive spy operations. They were unlikely to do so. The report by Interfor turned out to be very useful in defending the airline against various lawsuits brought by the relatives of the victims.

In late June, 1992, a German Investigating Magistrate by the name of Folkratt, in Frankfurt, Germany, completed an exhaustive investigation of all facts, most notable among them the claim that the bomb which blew up Pan Am 103 had been introduced to the interline baggage from Malta Flight KM 180 in Frankfurt and thus wound up on Pan Am 103 which landed at Heathrow. The Folkratt Report exonerated Libya and the two Libyan defendants. Magistrate Folkratt indicated that he had sent a copy of his investigation to Washington. It clearly fell on deaf ears.

Support for the Interfor report was found in the clandestine activities of the CIA immediately after the crash of Pan Am 103. Agents of the CIA were among the hundreds of workers flowing into Lockerbie. It was not unusual for the CIA to participate in such an investigation when it was an American plane that had crashed.

The local Scottish police thought that the CIA was in Lockerbie to investigate the possibility of terrorist involvement in the crash. The real reason for the CIA's involvement, however, was made known only at the highest levels of the investigation. The CIA gave searchers a list of specific items of luggage to look for. Most investigators thought that the agents were searching for missing secret documents carried by their dead comrades, documents which they didn't want to fall into the wrong hands.

A Lockerbie farmer by the name of Chris Graham remembered a lot of strange things occurring on his farm in the days following the crash. He remembered a white helicopter landing in his field on Christmas Eve. An American came to him from the helicopter and asked Graham not to go up on Torbeck Hill that day. This was the only time he was ever asked to stay off his own property.

On that particular day the CIA allegedly searched for, and found, what they had been looking for on Torbeck Hill. Later investigations revealed that it was the remnants of a suitcase belonging, interestingly enough, to Major Charles Dennis McKee, leader of the CIA team in Beirut, Lebanon. This was the same CIA agent who had decided to expose the renegade activities of the CIA-1 team in Frankfurt. Having found what they wanted, the CIA disregarded all rules of evidence. They took the suitcase and its contents into the chopper and flew to an unknown destination.

Since McKee was a communications specialist, most speculation was that his suitcase contained sensitive messages and codes. Few suspected that the suitcase may have contained information showing the CIA's own complicity in a drugs and/or weapons for hostage operation, an operation that was based at the Frankfurt Airport, and which may have been responsible for the crash of Pan Am 103.

The next chain of events was most interesting. According to Lockerbie police, on Christmas day, a small group of detectives was called together for a briefing by members of the Lockerbie investigation team and two CIA agents. One CIA man outlined what was planned for the day. McKee's suitcase had to be returned to the exact position in the farmer's field from which it had been taken.

The detectives split into two groups. The party with McKee's suitcase, directed by CIA men, did not make much headway. There was a heavy mist in the air and it was hard for them to find their way around Torbeck Hill. One detective was even lost for a period of time.

The detectives were confused as to what was expected of them. It slowly dawned on them as they negotiated a path around the hill. They were, they thought, expected to accidently "find" the empty suitcase and pretend that it had never been removed. They would then be expected to sign statements to the fact.

They didn't like it. The detectives had no idea why the case was of importance to the CIA. More importantly, they feared that they might find themselves at some future court hearing having to lie about their find. Finally, the detectives refused to participate in the charade and called a halt to the operation.

McKee's suitcase was eventually relocated on the Hill by the CIA and later "found" by two British Transport police officers. In their ignorance, they were quite happy to sign statements about the case's discovery.

Chapter Thirty-Seven

Major Breaks . . . .

Two major breaks occurred in January, 1995.

The first came on January 24, 1995. A Scottish newspaper, *The Daily Record,* quoted U.S. Air Force Intelligence Agency files as saying that an Iranian diplomat paid $10 million for a guerrilla group to "blast the airliners to pieces." The article said that Britain was under pressure to say whether it was aware of U.S. Intelligence documents placing Iran, not Libya, at the center of the bombing of Pan Am 103.

Sir Teddy Taylor, a member of Parliament for the ruling Conservative Party, demanded that Foreign Secretary Douglas Hurd tell Parliament if and when Britain was made aware of the four-year old document. "If the Americans did not tell the government, something will have to be pursued with the U.S. authorities," Taylor told reporters. "And if the government was advised, it seems little more than unbelievable because at repeated meetings I was told there was no evidence of any sort to implicate any other party than the Libyans."

The Daily Record quoted the U.S. files as saying the attack was funded by Ayatollah Ali Akbar Mohtashami, a friend of guerrilla leader Abu Nidal, as revenge for the downing of an Iranian passenger jet by the American warship USS *Vincennes* in July, 1988. These files were released to a Washington law firm in November, 1994, after a four year legal battle. This law firm represents Pan Am's insurers who face massive claims from the relatives of the victims.

On Monday, January 23, 1995, (the same day *The Daily Record* story broke) the U.S. Supreme Court denied a Pan Am appeal over liability, upholding a jury's finding that the airline can be held liable for "willful misconduct." The relatives are now free to pursue their claims against Pan Am.

Questions about the Libyan connection were also raised when *The Times* of London printed details of a secret 1991 U.S. National Security Agency Report. The NSA report also said that Mohtashami paid to have the Lockerbie bombing carried out.

Mohtashami, a leading hardline cleric, was Iran's ambassador to Syria at the time of the bombing—a time when he helped organize the Lebanese militant Hizbollah party. After this assignment he returned to Iran and served as Interior Minister until 1989. The Air Force report said the diplomat Mohtashami paid $10 million in gold and cash for the bombing.

This is the same Mohtashami that the PLO had identified as a Lockerbie planner/conspirator in their February, 1992 report shown to me by Fhimah during my meeting with him and Megrahi in Tripoli over two years earlier, on November 9, 1992!

Now, in 1995, Labour Member of Parliament Robin Cook was calling for a full inquiry into the newspaper report and asked whether the U.S. had shared the information with Britain. "If so, why for the last four years has the British Government, British ministers, repeatedly denied that any other country originated the appalling attack on Lockerbie?" asked Cook.

Labour Member of Parliament Tam Dalyell, who has consistently maintained Libya's innocence, said, "It is absolutely wicked that the Libyans have been blamed."

The Daily Record accused the United States of "covering up details" and added, "It was inconceivable Britain was not aware that the Lockerbie attack was revenge for the shooting down of an Iranian Airliner."

Additionally, flaws in the evidence against the two accused Libyans were revealed in a British radio program on Tuesday, January 24, 1995. The BBC "File on Four" investigation said leaked prosecution documents showed that the only direct eyewitness evidence (by Tony Gauci of Mary's House in Malta) identifying one of the Libyan agents, Abdel Basset Ali al-Megrahi, was "weak and confused."

The second break came on January 30, 1995, when *The Independent,* a London newspaper, reported a leaked, five-page FBI report. This document casts serious doubt on the case against the two accused Libyans by challenging prosecution evidence that the bomb that blew up Pan Am 103 originated in Malta, where the Libyans worked. The leaked report also proved that the FBI had this evidence before the Libyans were indicted by the United States in 1991. The newspaper article came out as the House of Commons began debate on claims that Iran—not Libya—ordered the attack.

Computer records reportedly showed that an unaccompanied suitcase thought to contain the bomb arrived in the Frankfurt airport December 21, 1988, on Air Malta flight KM 180 and was transferred onto Pan Am 103. The *Independent* said the Frankfurt airport baggage records provide the only direct link between Malta and Germany, and therefore, between the two Libyans and the unaccompanied suitcase.

But the paper quoted the FBI document as saying that the only link with the Maltese flight is that some transfer baggage from KM 180 was unloaded at the Frankfurt airport baggage-processing point where the suitcase was first sighted.

357

It quoted the FBI document as saying:

There is no concrete indication that any
piece of luggage was unloaded from Air Malta
180, sent through the luggage routing system
at Frankfurt airport, and then loaded on board
Pan Am 103.

The *Independent* quoted the FBI paper as saying that
the baggage records were "misleading" and that the bomb
suitcase could have come from another flight or have been
simply a "rogue bag inserted into the system."

The *Independent* predicted that the FBI document
would increase pressure on investigating authorities to re-
open the case against Iran.

This new evidence, suppressed by the United States
Government, added to my resolve to get to the bottom of
the matter. I began to wonder if I would be able to break
the case first, since the story about the U.S. Air Force cover-
up of the Mohtashami affair was reported on the
NBC *Today Show* news summary on January 24, 1995.

Chapter Number Thirty-Eight

The Cover-up Continues

Today the question still remains: was Libya responsible for the bombing of Pan Am 103?

The official line from the governments in London and Washington about Bollier's timer and the Maltese connection is that we must wait for the two Libyan suspects to surrender for trial before we will know the whole truth about Lockerbie. U.S. Attorney General William Barr, who issued the indictments, doesn't expect this to happen short of the fall of Col. Qadhafi.

After my discussion with Qadhafi, I agree that there is no way that Abdel Basset al-Megrahi and Lamen Fhimah will ever be turned over to either the United States or Great Britain.

Robert Muller, who directed the U.S. criminal investigation into Lockerbie for the Justice Department, maintains that all lanes of inquiry wherever they lead are still open. He stated on the BBC *Silence Over Lockerbie* radio program that, "It would be the fervent hope of any prosecutor to pursue every lead until every last person who was involved, whether that person be Libyan, Syrian, Iranian was indicted, prosecuted, and sentenced, and jailed for involvement for that crime."

This being said, it is difficult to see how Syria could be found guilty for planting the Lockerbie bomb after President Bush announced so publicly that they had been falsely accused. If the Syrians took a bum rap, as Bush said, how could a case be built against the Iranians who were believed to have commissioned them for the attack?

359

Col. Muammar Qadhafi is still in power. His resolve to keep the two indicted Libyans out of U.S. and British hands grows stronger as new evidence surfaces almost daily shifting the blame for the bombing of Pan Am 103 away from Libya and back to Syria and Iran. He continues to generate support around the world for his position.

Abdel Basset Ali al-Megrahi and Lamen Khalifa Fhimah remain under house arrest at a secret location in Libya.

On March 23, 1995, the Clinton Administration announced a $4 million reward for the arrest of Megrahi and Fhimah. At the same time their names were added to the FBI's Ten Most Wanted list.

Abu Talb has been convicted in connection with terrorist bombings in Sweden and sentenced to life in prison.

Merwan Khreesat, the bomb maker, is serving a life sentence in Sweden for an unrelated bombing.

Hafez Kassem Dalkamoni and Abdel Fattah Ghadanfar were convicted in 1991 in Bonn, Germany, of trying to bomb two U.S. military trains in West Germany in the late 1980's. Ghadanfar was released from prison in November, 1994, after serving only six years of his twelve year sentence. Germany expelled the Palestinian bomber but denied press reports that a deal with Iran was cut to trade Ghadanfar for a German engineer sentenced to death in Iran for spying.

Ahmed Jibril is reported to be operating his terrorist activities out of Syria

Abu Nidal, the master terrorist, is reportedly living and conducting his terrorist activities out of a base in Syria.

Mohammed Bukhres has disappeared.

Life is good for me. I continue to lobby the U.S. Congress, do business in Eastern Europe and enjoy my life with Virginia and Katie. I recently completed a TV program for NBC and the BBC called "TV Nation." I was selected to lobby a congressional resolution through Congress while cameras were rolling. The program played to about 40 million people.

My hope is that the contents of this book will agitate people to action and that those responsible for the Lockerbie tragedy, and its cover-up, will be brought to justice

I do not believe Fhimah and Megrahi are guilty of the bombing of Pan Am 103. It should be obvious to the readers of this book that there is no case against the two Libyans—and yet the standoff continues. The United States Government—my government—has put a lot of time, money and pressure on me to make sure that I do not pursue the truth or justice in this case. There is a story they don't want told. I fully intend to tell it.

Life is not so good for Carroll Hubbard. The Former Congressman, reported January 5, 1995, to the Federal Corrections Facility at Maxwell Air Force Base in Alabama, to begin serving a three year sentence. Hubbard pleaded guilty to conspiracy to defraud the U.S. Government by lying to the Federal Election Commission, theft and conversion of government property, and obstruction of justice. The judge that sentenced him stated that his crimes "seriously jeopardized" confidence in government.

In April 1994, Hubbard's wife, Carol, pleaded guilty to a single misdemeanor count of using her husband's congressional staffers for her own 1992 failed House campaign. She was sentenced to five years probation.

The relatives of the Pan AM 103 victims, like Susan Cohen who lost her 20 year old daughter, believe there will be no justice for the 270 people killed on that freezing December night in 1988. The lesson learned six years after the crime, is that when dealing in international politics, the greatest good for the greatest number, always prevails.

Mrs. Cohen told the BBC radio program *Silence Over Lockerbie*, "What you have is a mass murder, and a horribly cruel injustice system. They were mostly young kids, young people on that plane. If you can say that they can just die and we'll forget it, then you start down the road of forgetting and cover-ups. You can forget and cover-up anything. No, I don't think there was any excuse for allowing this crime to happen, and being part of a cover-up."

And so, the saga continues . . . .

Index

A

B

F

Federal Bureau of Investigatdion vii, 130, 150, 185, 267, 281, 313, 317-320, 323-324, 332, 337, 357-358
Fernandez , Guido 29-30
Fernandez, Joe v
Fhimah, Lamen Khalifa 24, 129, 183-187, 193, 201-203, 205-206, 209-210, 245-246, 263, 269, 284, 301, 310, 327, 331-332, 343, 356, 359-361
Fiers, Alan v
Fituri, Sala El- 120, 300
Fitzgerald, Jennifer 36
Flake, Floyd 88
Flynn, Robert 269, 271-274, 284-286, 291, 297, 303, 308, 323, 327
Flynn and Riley 274, 285-286, 291, 297, 303, 308, 323, 327
Foley, Thomas 276-277, 281
Ford, Adrian 13
Ford, Gerald 3, 278
Ford, Kenneth 153
Fraser, Lord 195

G

Gandhi, Rajiv 84
Gauci, Anthony "Tony" 203-206, 245-246
George, Clair v
Ghadanfar, Abdel Fetteh 191-192, 360
Ghazala, Abdul Halim Abu 151
Glenn, John 4
Goben, Mobdi 197
Gray, Pat 80
Gustafson, Ramona 76

H

Habash, George 236
Habib, Phillip 36
Hagan, Betty Ruth 27
Hagan, Frank 27
Hanson, Jean v
Hamilton, Lee 91, 133, 229
Harmon, Hal 256, 262, 283, 293-295

Harrington, John 27
Havel, Vaclav 190
Hawatmeh, Naif 236
Hawaz, Adam al- 140
Hills, Carla 39
Hitler, Adolph 102
Hopkins, Larry 22
Howe, Geoffrey 172
Hubbard, Carol Brown 89-90, 93, 95, 99, 104, 163, 175, 209, 216-217, 240, 247, 253-254, 361
Hubbard, Carroll 89-91, 93, 95, 99, 104, 107-108,115-116, 130, 209, 229, 238, 247-249, 252-255, 293, 313-319, 324, 326, 361
Hunter, Duncan 21, 88
Hurd, Douglas 125, 207, 244, 334, 355
Hussein, Saddam 125, 207, 265, 335

I

Iacocca, Lee 263, 265, 278
Idris, Muhammad al Mahdi as-Sanusi 52
Idris, Sayyid Muhammed al- 231
Imandi, Marten 197
Irish Republican Army vi, 235-236

J

Jaafar, Khaled 344, 346
Jabril, Shalouf 146
Jefferson, Thomas 143
Jibril, Ahmed 185-186, 190, 195, 198-199, 200, 236, 334, 336, 360
Jones, Jack 4

K

Kahl, P. K. 85
Kelly, Brendan 38-39, 64, 72, 262
Kelly, Jim 105
Kelso, Admiral Frank B. 162
Kemp, Jack 5, 33
Kemp, Joanne 5

Kennedy, John F. 2
Kennedy, Ted 23
Kerry, John 28-31, 67, 71, 80-83, 86, 244
Khaled 107-109, 114-115, 118-119, 173, 176, 179, 181, 183, 209, 212
Khreesat, Marwan 191, 195-198, 360
Kilburn, Peter 171
Kissinger, Henry 145

L

La Belle Discoteque 170, 241
Lambert, Blanche 89
Lautenberg, Frank 5-6, 30
Lawrence, Larry 274
Legwell, Ibraham B. 184
Leiter, David 80
Leland, Jackie 280
Leland, Mickey 279-280
Leonard, Sugar Ray 278
Lewis, Jerry 32-33
Libyan Arab Friendship Society 146
Limbaugh, Rush 77
Lorence, Captain. Paul F. 164-166
Lorence, Dianne 165
Lough, Ted 232
Lowery, Bill 32, 89
Lugar, Richard 33
Lumpert, Ulrich 247, 333

M

MacQuarrie, Jim 11-13, 16
Mancini, Ginny 4
Mancini, Henry 4
Mandela, Nelson 278
Mason, Bob 143
McCain, Cindy 20
McCain, John 20, 22
McFarland, Robert "Bud" v
McMillian, Tom 21
McWerthy, John 170
Meese, Ed 27
Meister et Bollier, LTD., (MEBO) 206, 246-247, 334

Megrahi, Abdel Basset Ali Mohammed al- 125, 129, 183-185, 187, 193, 201-203, 205-206, 209-210, 245-246, 263-264, 269, 284, 301, 310, 331-332, 327, 343, 356-357, 359, 361
Meniar, Abu 230
Michel, Bob 30
Miczkiewicz, Adam 313
Miller, Johnathan 170
Mohtashami, Ali Akbar 186, 195, 197-198, 355-356, 358
Monge, Louis Alberto 35
Motley, Tony 26
Mougrabi, Jamilla 204
Mount, Ferdinand 171
Mubarak, Hosni 150, 152
Mulcahy, Kevin 141
Muntassir, Omar Mustafa 96, 131-133, 225, 296, 325
Murphy, John 64
Musa, Ahmed 140
Myers, Chris 303

N

Nasser, Gamal Abdul 231, 235
National Security Agency (NSA) 153, 178, 198, 248, 251, 296, 356
Newcomb, R. Richard 308
Nidal, Abu 199, 348-349, 355, 360
Nidal Organization 236, 346
Nocera, Brenda 7
Nocera, Gina 7
Nocera, Mickey 7
Noriega, Manuel 182
North, Oliver iv, 34-35, 38, 136, 170, 187, 328, 348
Numeiri, President 152

O

O'Dwyer's Washington Report 63
Office of Foriegn Assets Control (OFAC) 254-255, 262-263, 265, 269, 272, 293-295, 297, 303, 308, 310, 313-314, 316, 323-327
Operation El Dorado Canyon 241
Ortega, Daniel 29, 35
Otten, David 313

P

Q

R

Rogers, Will 22
Rogers, William D. 273
Rogers, William 273
Root, John 200
Rostenkowski, Dan "Rosti" 281
Russ, Jack 275, 277-283

S

Sadat, President Anwar 140, 145, 150
Samoza, Anastasio Garcia 149
Sanbar, David 57
Sanusi Brotherhood 52
Schuller, Dr. Robert 276
Schultz, George iv, 26, 102, 220, 241
Segal, Ellen 3
Service, James E. 149
Seymour, John 22
Shackley, Theodore 141-42
Shah of Iran 57, 147
Sharif, Bassam Abu 56, 58, 60
Sharla 295
Simpson, Alan 25
Simpson, Anne 25
Smith, Bud 105
Simon, Paul 30
Simons, Goeff 100, 139, 240
Snelson, Roy 05
Sol, Billy 105
Sonntag, Has Uurgen 96
Speakes, Larry 102
Steiner, Joshua v
Strauss, Bob 270
Sutherland, Thomas 125, 186, 207
Swire, James 168
Swire, Flora 168
Symms, Steve 22, 25

T

Talb, Abu 199, 204-205, 360
Tambs, Louis 26, 29-32, 34-38
Taylor, Walt 279, 281-282